THE CAMBRIDGE COMPANION TO
BRITISH AND IRISH WOM

This *Companion* provides new ways of readi
women's poetry. Leading international scholars on.. ....g....
writers, drawing out the special function of poetry. They illuminate the poets'
use of language, whether it is concerned with the relationship between verbal
and visual art, experimental poetics, war, landscape, history, cultural identity or
'confessional' lyrics. Collectively, the chapters cover well established and less
familiar poets, from Edith Sitwell and Mina Loy, through Stevie Smith, Sylvia
Plath and Elizabeth Jennings to Anne Stevenson, Eavan Boland and Jo Shapcott.
They also include poets at the forefront of poetry trends, such as Liz Lochhead,
Jackie Kay, Patience Agbabi, Caroline Bergvall, Medbh McGuckian and Carol
Ann Duffy. With a chronology and guide to further reading, this book is aimed
at students and poetry enthusiasts wanting to deepen their knowledge of some
of the finest modern poets.

JANE DOWSON is Reader in Twentieth-Century Literature at De Montfort
University, Leicester.

THE CAMBRIDGE
COMPANION TO

TWENTIETH-CENTURY BRITISH AND IRISH WOMEN'S POETRY

EDITED BY
JANE DOWSON

CAMBRIDGE
UNIVERSITY PRESS

CAMBRIDGE UNIVERSITY PRESS
Cambridge, New York, Melbourne, Madrid, Cape Town, Singapore,
São Paulo, Delhi, Dubai, Tokyo, Mexico City

Cambridge University Press
The Edinburgh Building, Cambridge CB2 8RU, UK

Published in the United States of America by Cambridge University Press, New York

www.cambridge.org
Information on this title: www.cambridge.org/9780521120210

First published 2011

Printed in the United Kingdom at the University Press, Cambridge

A catalogue record for this publication is available from the British Library

Library of Congress Cataloging-in-Publication Data

The Cambridge companion to twentieth-century British and
Irish women's poetry / edited by Jane Dowson.
p. cm. – (Cambridge companions to literature)
Includes bibliographical references and index.
ISBN 978-0-521-19785-4 (Hardback) – ISBN 978-0-521-12021-0 (pbk)
1. English poetry–Women authors–History and criticism. 2. English poetry–Irish
authors–History and criticism. 3. English poetry–20th century–History and criticism.
I. Dowson, Jane, 1955– II. Title. III. Series.
PR605.W6C36 2011
821′.91099287–dc22

2010037665

ISBN 978-0-521-19785-4 Hardback
ISBN 978-0-521-12021-0 Paperback

For
Isabel and Monica

CONTENTS

ILLUSTRATIONS

CONTRIBUTORS

CLAIRE BUCK is Professor of English at Wheaton College in Massachusetts. Her publications include: *H. D. and Freud: Bisexuality and a Feminine Discourse* (1991); *The Bloomsbury Guide to Women's Literature* (1992); and many articles on women's writing. She is currently writing a study of British nationalism, travel writing and the First World War.

BRIAN CARAHER is Chair of English Literature in the School of English at Queen's University Belfast. He has published widely on topics in aesthetics, poetics, theories of literary reading, literary pragmatics, genre theory and cultural politics. He has written on issues in modern and contemporary poetry in *ELH*, *JJQ*, *MLQ*, *The Irish Review*, *Philosophy and Rhetoric*, *Textual Practice*, *Works and Days* and other journals and numerous book collections that include *Intimate Conflicts, Ireland and Transatlantic Poetics*, *Wordsworth's 'Slumber' and the Problematics of Reading*, *Trespassing Tragedy* (forthcoming) and *The Joyce of Reading: Literary Pragmatics and Cultural Politics* (in preparation).

CATRIONA CLUTTERBUCK lectures in the School of English, Drama and Film at University College Dublin, where her research interests centre on contemporary Irish poetry and gender in Irish writing. She has published essays on the Irish poets Derek Mahon, Eavan Boland, Thomas Kinsella, Eiléan Ní Chuilleanáin and Medbh McGuckian as well as on the critical and cultural contexts of Irish poetry. She has further published on the playwrights Lady Gregory, Brian Friel and Anne Devlin, and on the novelist Charles J. Kickham. Work is forthcoming on Vona Groarke.

JANE DOWSON is Reader in Twentieth-Century Literature at De Montfort University, Leicester. Her publications on women's poetry include: *A History of Twentieth-Century British Women's Poetry* (co-authored with Alice Entwistle, Cambridge University Press 2005); *Women, Modernism and British Poetry 1910–39* (2002); and *Women's Poetry of the 1930s* (1996). Her chapter 'Time and Tide and The Bermondsey Book: Interventions in the Public Sphere' is part of *The Critical and Cultural History of Modernist Magazines, Vol. 1: Britain and Ireland 1880–1945*, ed. Peter Brooker and Andrew Thacker (2009). She is working on an electronic archive of Elizabeth Jennings.

ALICE ENTWISTLE is Principal Lecturer in English at the University of Glamorgan. The co-author, with Jane Dowson, of *A History of Twentieth-Century British Women's Poetry* (Cambridge University Press, 2005), she is currently completing several projects exploring the complex relationship between women, poetry and place, including a critical monograph on women's poetry in contemporary Wales, and preparing a single-author study of the bilingual Welsh poet Gwyneth Lewis.

IAN GREGSON is Professor of English at the University of Bangor. His critical books are *Contemporary Poetry and Postmodernism* (1996); *The Male Image: Representations of Masculinity in Postwar Poetry* (1999); *Postmodern Literature* (2004); and *The New Poetry in Wales* (2007). He has published poems and reviews in the *London Review of Books*, the *TLS* and *Poetry Review*, amongst others. His latest book of poems is *How We Met* (2008). *Call Centre Love Song* (2006), a selection of his poems, was shortlisted for the Forward Prize.

LEE MARGARET JENKINS is Senior Lecturer in Modern English at University College Cork. She is the author of *The Language of Caribbean Poetry* (2004), and is the co-editor (with Alex Davis) of *Locations of Literary Modernism* (Cambridge University Press, 2000) and *The Cambridge Companion to Modernist Poetry* (2007). She is currently completing a monograph on D. H. Lawrence and American modernism.

LINDA A. KINNAHAN is Professor of English at Duquesne University in Pittsburgh, Pennsylvania, USA. She has published articles on twentieth-century North American and British poets such as Carol Ann Duffy, Wendy Mulford, Denise Riley and Geraldine Monk, and on North American experimental poetics in the work of Kathleen Fraser, M. Norbese Philip, Erica Hunt and Barbara Guest. Her books include *Poetics of the Feminine: Literary Tradition and Authority in William Carlos Williams, Mina Loy, Denise Levertov, and Kathleen Fraser* (Cambridge University Press, 1994) and *Lyric Interventions: Feminism, Experimental Poetry, and Contemporary Discourse* (2004). Currently, she is completing a study of women Modernist poets and economics, focusing especially on Mina Loy and Marianne Moore.

WILLIAM MAY is Lecturer in English at the University of Southampton. Previously, he was a lecturer in English at St Anne's College, Oxford and tutor at Bath Spa University. He is the author of *Stevie Smith and Authorship* (2010) and *Postwar Literature: 1950–1990* (2010). He is currently working on text-setting and the libretto in contemporary British literature.

MELANIE PETCH teaches at De Montfort University, Leicester, where she completed her Ph.D. on twentieth-century Anglo-American Women Poets. Previously, she has written on Mina Loy, pursuing her interest in the so-called polarity between American experimentalism and British formalism. She has undertaken interviews with Ruth Fainlight and Anne Rouse.

PREFACE

I write this as Carol Ann Duffy makes history as the first woman poet laureate in Britain. Her appointment to a controversial post ignites conversations about the role of poetry in public life and the significance of a poet's sex and sexuality in relation to literary conventions and creativity. The essays in this *Companion* absorb yet see beyond the 'identity politics' that occupied criticism in the second half of the previous century. They dynamically interpret poetry with a more mobile and holistic vision of gender and art. None of the chapters are confined to a single author: instead, they make connections across historical moments, literary movements and nationalities. We take both familiar and innovative concepts to look at how women participate in such narratives as war, Irish history, postcolonialism or the 'post-pastoral'; we approach the diverse range of writers covered here in ways that illuminate the gender-specific aspects of, say, 'Anglo-American', 'confessional', ekphrastic or experimental poetry, yet also revise and expand these categories. Thus, we set up paradigms for reading streams of poetry that ran through the last century and spill over into the present.

This volume is foremost a companion to *poetry* and will accompany readers in their engagement with known and unfamiliar poets. It is also a companion to *The Cambridge History of Twentieth-Century Women's Poetry*, (Dowson and Entwistle, 2005) which can be consulted for a complementary list of published works by the century's hundred-plus important poets, a linear account of poets in their contexts and essays on major poets and trends. Here, as there, we respond to a consensus of poets, editors and scholars as voiced by the Irish-born Colette Bryce (b. 1970): 'While publishing has opened up, criticism has not, and the work of some of our best women poets continues to be neglected or ignored in the current critical climate'.[1]

Note

[1] Colette Bryce, *Modern Women Poets*, ed. Deryn Rees-Jones (Tarset: Bloodaxe, 2005), p. 402.

ACKNOWLEDGEMENTS

This book was completed with the invaluable help of a Small Research Grant from the British Academy, along with teaching relief granted by De Montfort University. I thank all contributors for the privilege and enjoyment of working with them. Sadly, due to illness Vicki Bertram had to withdraw from the project but her generous spirit and influence are here invisibly and visibly through our citations of her work. The Contemporary Women's Writing Network has been a serious yet good-humoured fellowship of like minds. My heartfelt gratitude goes to my special companions through the time of writing, Ruth, Maria, Gerry, Jan and the Still Waters group. Andy Mousley has been the best office companion and patiently given feedback on chapter drafts. Many thanks to Pete Gilbert for the index and to Damir Arsenijevic for his enthusiasm and reminding me to say it how it is. Tim Jana furnished me with food and taught me to live a day at a time; the book is dedicated to his daughters, who represent the future generation of readers.

Every effort has been made to clear rights on poetry extracts. Permission has been granted as follows:

Patience Agbabi: for extracts from *Bloodshot Monochrome* (2008) and *Transformatrix* (2000), by permission of Canongate Books.

Caroline Bergvall: for extracts from *Goan Atom* (Krupskaya, 2001) and from 'Les jets de la poupée', published in the *Oxford Anthology of Twentieth-Century British & Irish Poetry* (Oxford University Press, 2001).

Eavan Boland: for 'At the Glass Factory in Cavan Town', 'The Black-Lace Fan My Mother Gave Me', 'Watching Old Movies When They Were New', 'Formal Feeling', 'The Dolls Museum in Dublin', 'Love' 'The Muse Mother', 'Anorexic', 'The War Horse', 'The Achill Woman', 'Beautiful Speech', 'Bright-Cut Irish Silver', 'The Glass King', 'Degas's Laundresses', 'Anna Liffey' and 'Home', copyright © 2005, 1990, 1982, from *New Collected Poems* by Eavan Boland, by permission of W. W. Norton & Company, Inc. and Carcanet Press Ltd; for the extract from *Object*

Lessons: The Life of the Woman and the Poet in our Time (1995), by permission of Carcanet Press Ltd.

Moya Cannon: for extracts from 'West' and 'Scríob', from *Carrying the Songs* (2007), by permission of Carcanet Press Ltd.

Gillian Clarke: for extract from 'Letter from a Far Country', from *Collected Poems* (1997), by permission of Carcanet Press Ltd.

Anne Cluysenaar: for 'Landfall', from *Timeslips: New and Selected Poems* (1997), by permission of Carcanet Press Ltd.

Imtiaz Dharker: for 'Outline', 'Battle-line' and 'Minority', from *Postcards from god* (1997); 'Honour Killing', 'They'll Say, "She must be from another country" ', 'Stitched' and 'Front Door' from *I Speak for the Devil* (2001); 'Still', 'Rickshaw Rider' and 'Halfway', from *The Terrorist at My Table* (2006), all by permission of Bloodaxe Books.

Carol Ann Duffy: for 'Standing Female Nude', copyright © 1985, 2005, from *New Collected Poems* (1984–2004), by permission of Pan Macmillan; for 'Away and See' and 'Prayer', from *Mean Time* (1993) and 'Warming Her Pearls' from *Selling Manhattan* (1987), by permission of Anvil Press.

Ruth Fainlight: for extracts from Ruth Fainlight, *New and Collected Poems* (2010), by permission of Bloodaxe Books.

Kerry Hardie: lines from 'We Change the Map', from *A Furious Place* (1996) by kind permission of the author and The Gallery Press, Loughcrew, Oldcastle, County Meath, Ireland. www.gallerypress.com.

Rita Ann Higgins: for 'Donna Laura', from *Throw in the Vowels: New & Selected Poems* (2005), by permission of Bloodaxe Books.

Selima Hill: for 'Gloria', from *Selected Poems* (2008), by permission of Bloodaxe Books.

Kathleen Jamie: for 'The Well at the Broch of Gurness', from *Jizzen* (1999) and 'Reliquary', from *The Tree House* (2004), by kind permission of the author and Picador.

Elizabeth Jennings: for extracts from 'The Instruments', 'After a Time', 'Family Affairs', 'The Interrogator', 'To a Friend with Religious Vocation', 'About These Things' and 'Sequence from Hospital', from *New Collected Poems*, published by Carcanet Press Ltd (2002), by permission of Bruce Hunter for David Higham Associates; David Higham Associates and Georgetown University Library for permission to quote from the Elizabeth Jennings Papers; British Library, Department of Manuscripts, London, for extracts from letters by Philip Larkin and Vita Sackville-West in Elizabeth Jennings Papers MSS 52599.

Jackie Kay: for 'Old Tongue' and 'In my Country', from *Darling: New & Selected Poems* (2007), by permission of Bloodaxe Books.

Liz Lochhead: for 'Furies', 'Object' and 'Notes on the Inadequacy of a Sketch', copyright © 1984, from *Dreaming Frankenstein & Collected Poems*; 'Warpaint and Womenflesh', copyright © 2005, from *The Colour of Black & White 1984–2003*, all by permission of Birlinn Ltd.

Mina Loy: by kind permission of Roger Conover and the Estate of Mina Loy for 'Anglo-Mongrels and the Rose', 'Notes on Childhood' and 'America a Miracle' from *The Last Lunar Baedecker* (1982), and for 'The Effectual Marriage' and 'Virgins Plus Curtains Minus Dots' from *The Lost Lunar Baedecker* (1996).

Medbh McGuckian: by kind permission of the author and to Gallery Press, Loughcrew, Oldcastle, County Meath, Ireland, for 'Pulsus Paradoxus' from *Shelmalier* (1998) and 'Drawing Ballerinas' from *Drawing Ballerinas* (2001).

Wendy Mulford: for 'How Do You Live', from *Late Spring Next Year: Poems, 1979–1985* (Bristol: Loxwood Stoneleigh, 1987); extracts from 'Alltud' (*Scintilla* 11, 2007), and from *The East Anglia Sequence* (Paul Green/Spectacular Diseases, 1998), repr. *And Suddenly, Supposing: Selected Poems* (Etruscan Press, 2002).

Maggie O'Sullivan: for extracts from *In the House of the Shaman* (1993), by permission of Reality Street.

Eiléan Ní Chuilleanáin: for 'Site of Ambush', from *Site of Ambush* (1975); 'The Rose Geranium' 5, 11, 13 and 'Cork' 3, 8, 11, from *The Rose Geranium* (1981); 'History' and 'Pygmalion's Image', from *The Magdalen Sermon* (1989); 'Gloss/Clós/Glas', from *The Girl Who Married the Reindeer* (2001), by permission of the Gallery Press; 'Daniel Grosse' and 'The Real Thing', from *The Brazen Serpent* (1995), by kind permission of Wake Forest University Press.

Sylvia Plath: for extracts from 'Zoo Keeper's Wife' and 'Fever 103', by permission of Faber & Faber.

Frances Presley: for 'Minehead', from *Paravane: New and Selected Poems 1996–2003* (2004), by permission of Salt, and *Myne: New and Selected Poems and Prose 1976–2005* (2006), by permission of Shearsman.

Denise Riley: for extracts from *Dry Air* (1985), by permission of Virago Press.

Lynette Roberts: 'Rainshiver', copyright © 2008, from *Diaries, Letters and Recollections*, by permission of Angharad Rhys and Carcanet Press Ltd.

Anne Rouse: for 'England Nil' and 'The Passage', from *The Upshot: New & Selected Poems* (2008), by permission of the author and Bloodaxe Books.

Eva Salzman: for 'Ending Up in Kent', from *Double Crossing: New & Selected Poems* (2004), by permission of Bloodaxe Books.

Zoë Skoulding: for 'Preselis with Brussels Street Map', from *Remains of a Future City* (2008), by kind permission and copyright of the author and Seren Books.

Stevie Smith: for 'Not Waving but Drowning', and 'Si peu séduisante', plus illustrations, copyright © 1978, from *Collected Poems*, by permission of the estate of James MacGibbon and New Directions.

Anne Stevenson: for 'Green Mountain, Black Mountain', 'In Middle England', 'England', 'Travelling Behind Glass', 'The Women', 'Night Thoughts and False Confessions' and 'Skills' (first published in *Poetry Wales* 27.1 [1991], reproduced here by kind permission of the author) from *Poems 1955–2005* (2005), by permission of Bloodaxe Books.

CHRONOLOGY

YEAR	HISTORICAL EVENTS	CULTURAL/LITERARY EVENTS
1901	Death of Queen Victoria.	Rudyard Kipling, *Kim*.
1903	Marie Curie wins Nobel Prize.	George Bernard Shaw, *Man and Superman*.
	Founding of the Women's Social and Political Union by Emmeline Pankhurst.	
1904		Anton Chekhov, *The Cherry Orchard*.
1905	Founding of Sinn Fein, Irish nationalist party.	
1907		Cubist exhibition in Paris.
		J. M. Synge, *Playboy of the Western World*.
1908	Herbert Asquith becomes Liberal Prime Minister.	Gertrude Stein, *Three Lives*.
	Women Writers Suffrage League founded by Cicely Hamilton and Bessie Hatton.	
1909		Ezra Pound, *Personae*.
		Poetry Review founded.
		Cicely Hamilton, *Marriage as a Trade*.
1910	Death of Edward VII.	Post-impressionist exhibition in London.
	General election: Liberals returned.	E. M. Forster, *Howard's End*.
	Suffragette march in Hyde Park.	
1911	Coronation of George V.	*The Freewoman: a weekly feminist review*, ed. Dora Marsden (November); runs until October 1912.

YEAR	HISTORICAL EVENTS	CULTURAL/LITERARY EVENTS
1912	Sinking of the *Titanic*.	Carl Jung (1875–1961), *The Theory of Psychoanalysis*.
		Poetry Society formed; Lady Margaret Sackville made first President.
1913	Royal Commission on Divorce.	Sigmund Freud (1856–1939), *Interpretation of Dreams* (1900) translated into English.
	Suffragette demonstrations in London.	
	'Cat and Mouse' Act to deal with suffragettes' self-starvation.	D. H. Lawrence, *Sons and Lovers*. *The New Freewoman* founded, ed. Dora Marsden.
1914	First World War starts.	James Joyce, *Dubliners*.
		Blast magazine founded.
		The Egoist (formerly *The New Freewoman*), ed. Harriet Shaw Weaver, assisted by Richard Aldington and Dora Marsden; runs until 1918.
		May Sinclair, *Feminist Manifesto*.
1916		Carl Jung, *Psychology of the Unconscious*.
		James Joyce, *A Portrait of the Artist as a Young Man*.
1917	Russian Revolution starts.	T. S. Eliot, *Prufrock and Other Observations*.
1918	First World War ends.	
	Women over thirty get the vote.	
	Countess Marckiewicz elected to Parliament.	
1919	Sex Disqualification Removal Act – all professions open to women except the church.	*The Egoist* becomes Egoist Press, London.
		Inauguration of *Vogue* magazine in Britain.
	Nancy Astor is first woman MP to take her seat in the House of Commons.	
1920	American women achieve the vote.	*Time and Tide* (1920–76) started by Lady Margaret Rhondda.
		D. H. Lawrence, *Women in Love*.
		Katherine Mansfield, *Bliss and Other Stories*.

YEAR	HISTORICAL EVENTS	CULTURAL/LITERARY EVENTS
1921	Mary Stopes opens first birth control clinic in London.	Charlie Chaplin, *The Kid* (film).
1922	Founding of the British Broadcasting Company (BBC).	T. S. Eliot, *The Waste Land*.
		James Joyce, *Ulysses*.
		Virginia Woolf, *Jacob's Room*.
		Criterion magazine founded by T. S. Eliot.
		Good Housekeeping magazine launched.
1923	BBC launches *Woman's Hour*.	Carl Jung, *Psychological Types*.
1924	Workers' Birth Control Group.	E. M. Forster, *A Passage to India*.
		First Surrealist manifesto.
1925	Adolf Hitler, *Mein Kampf*.	Virginia Woolf, *Mrs Dalloway*.
		Gertrude Stein, *The Making of Americans*.
		Scott Fitzgerald, *The Great Gatsby*.
1926	General Strike.	Ernest Hemingway, *The Sun Also Rises*.
1927		Virginia Woolf, *To The Lighthouse*.
		Close-Up magazine founded by Winifred Bryher.
1928	Women over twenty-one get the vote.	W. B. Yeats, *The Tower*.
		D. H. Lawrence, *Lady Chatterley's Lover*.
		Ray Strachey, *The Cause*.
		Nancy Cunard starts The Hours Press, Paris (1928–31).
1929	General election (52.7 per cent electorate female).	Virginia Woolf, *A Room of One's Own*.
		Second Surrealist manifesto.
	Collapse of the New York stock market.	Museum of Modern Art, New York, opened.
1930	W. H. Auden, *Poems*.	Freud, *Civilisation and its Discontents*.
1932		Aldous Huxley, *Brave New World*.
1936	Spanish Civil War starts. Death of George V.	Penguin Books launched.
	Coronation of George VI.	Ray Strachey, *Our Freedom and Its Results*.
1937	The Matrimonial Causes Act.	*Woman* magazine launched.
1938	Inheritance Act.	

YEAR	HISTORICAL EVENTS	CULTURAL/LITERARY EVENTS
1939	Second World War starts.	James Joyce, *Finnegan's Wake*.
1942	Beveridge Report published.	
1944	Education Act.	*Outposts* magazine launched.
1945	Bombing of Hiroshima; Second World War ends.	
	Introduction of Family Allowance, state payment to mothers.	
	BBC launches Home Service and Light Programmes.	
1946	Royal Commission on Equality recommends equal pay for women teachers and civil servants.	Vita Sackville-West's 'The Garden' wins Heinemann Prize.
1947	India and Pakistan granted independence.	
	Princess Elizabeth marries Lt. Philip Mountbatten.	
1948	National Health Service established. SS Empire *Windrush* arrives at Tilbury Docks, bringing the first generation of Jamaicans (nearly 500) to London.	
	John Newsom report, *The Education of Girls*.	
1951	Festival of Britain, May–September.	National Poetry Competition flops.
1952	Death of George VI; accession of Elizabeth II.	
1953	Coronation of Elizabeth II. Kinsey report, *Sexual Behaviour in the Human Female*.	
1954	Rationing ends.	
1955	National Council of Women, conference on single women.	Ruth Pitter awarded The Queen's Medal for Poetry. Elizabeth Jennings wins Somerset Maugham Award.
1956	The Morton Commission, *Report on Marriage and Divorce*.	Outposts Press evolves from magazine. Elizabeth Jennings appears in Robert Conquest's Movement anthology *New Lines*.
1957		Claudia Jones founds *The West Indian Gazette*.

YEAR	HISTORICAL EVENTS	CULTURAL/LITERARY EVENTS
1958	First Aldermaston march. Notting Hill race riots. National Council of Women, conference on working mothers.	
1959	Obscene Publications Act.	Michael Horovitz founds *New Departures*. Frances Cornford awarded The Queen's Medal for Poetry.
1960		R. D. Laing, *The Divided Self*. Jenny Joseph wins Eric Gregory Award.
1961	Contraceptive pill introduced in UK.	Penguin Books cleared of obscenity in *Lady Chatterley* trial. Simone de Beauvoir, *The Second Sex*, published in Britain.
1962	Marilyn Monroe dies. National Housewives Register founded.	Doris Lessing, *The Golden Notebook*.
1963	Profumo scandal breaks.	Stevie Smith, 'Poet of the Year', Stratford upon Avon Festival. Sylvia Plath dies. Betty Friedan, *The Feminine Mystique*.
1965	Mary Quant opens Bazaar.	Approximately 7,000 people attend Albert Hall poetry reading featuring over forty poets.
1966		Juliet Mitchell, 'The longest revolution', in *New Left Review*.
1967	Abortion Law Reform. Family Planning Act.	Writers' Workshop formed.
1968	Martin Luther King assassinated. Enoch Powell's 'rivers of blood' speech. Anti-Vietnam war demonstrations.	Northern Poetry Library founded. Kathleen Raine fails to get Oxford Chair of Poetry.
1969	First landing on the moon. Divorce Reform Act.	Enitharmon Press founded. Poetry Society's Poetry Gala, Royal Festival Hall. Stevie Smith awarded The Queen's Medal for Poetry. *Shrew* magazine launched. Kate Millett, *Sexual Politics*. Sheila Rowbotham, *Women's Liberation and the New Politics*.

YEAR	HISTORICAL EVENTS	CULTURAL/LITERARY EVENTS
1970	First Conference of Women's Liberation Movement, Ruskin College, Oxford (February).	Germaine Greer, *The Female Eunuch*.
	Equal Pay Act.	Kathleen Raine wins Cholmondeley Award.
1971	First International Women's Day (March); women march in London and Liverpool.	Stevie Smith dies.
		Phoebe Hesketh elected Fellow, Royal Society of Literature.
		The Arvon Foundation Centre founded.
1972	First Women's Refuge set up in Chiswick, London.	*Spare Rib* launched.
		PN Review launched.
		Wendy Mulford founds Street Editions.
		Kathleen Raine receives W. H. Smith Literary Award.
		Molly Holden wins Cholmondeley Award.
		Liz Lochhead wins Scottish Arts Council Award.
		Jenny Joseph wins Cholmondeley Award.
		Penelope Shuttle wins Eric Gregory Award.
1975	Sex Discrimination Act. Equal Opportunities Commission set up.	Virago Press launched.
	National Abortion Campaign launched.	International Cambridge Poetry Festival inaugurated.
	Employment Protection Act introduces statutory maternity rights.	
1976	Domestic Violence Act.	Onlywomen Press founded.
	First Rape Crisis centre opens in North London.	Gillian Clarke edits *Anglo-Welsh Review*.
		Fleur Adcock wins Cholmondeley Award.
	Mairead Maguire founds Northern Ireland Peace People and is awarded the Nobel Prize.	

YEAR	HISTORICAL EVENTS	CULTURAL/LITERARY EVENTS
1977		Elaine Showalter, *A Literature of their Own: British Women Novelists from Brontë to Lessing.*
1978	Hite report on female sexuality.	The Women's Press launched.
	Organisation of Women of Asian and African Descent (OWAAD) formed.	Anne Stevenson elected Fellow of the Royal Society of Literature.
1979	Margaret Thatcher becomes first woman Prime Minister.	Medbh McGuckian wins The National Poetry Competition.
	Lowest number of women MPs (nineteen) returned in twenty years.	Pamela Gillilan wins Cheltenham Literature Festival/*Sunday Telegraph* poetry competition.
		Anne Stevenson co-founds The Poetry Bookshop, Hay on Wye.
		Sandra M. Gilbert and Susan Gubar, *The Madwoman in the Attic: The Woman Writer and the Nineteenth-Century Imagination.*
		Denise Levertov elected to American Academy of Arts and Letters.
		Elaine Feinstein made Fellow of Royal Society of Literature.
		Medbh McGuckian wins Eric Gregory Award.
		Dale Spender, *Man Made Language.*
1981	Charles, Prince of Wales, marries Lady Diana Spencer.	
	Brixton riots.	
1982	First Greenham Common peace camp.	April: evening of international poetry at the First International Fair of Radical Black and Third World Books.
	Channel Four television launched.	
1983		Grace Nichols' *i is a long-memoried woman* wins Commonwealth Poetry Prize.
		Carol Ann Duffy wins National Poetry Competition.
		Medbh McGuckian wins Alice Hunt Bartlett Award.
1984	Miners' strike prompts formation of Women against Pit Closures.	Patricia Oxley edits the new *Acumen* poetry magazine.
		Alison Fell wins Alice Hunt Bartlett Award.

YEAR	HISTORICAL EVENTS	CULTURAL/LITERARY EVENTS
1985		*Women's Review* launched.
		Denise Levertov receives Shelley Memorial Award from Poetry Society of America.
		Jo Shapcott wins The National Poetry Competition (joint award).
1986		Carole Satyamurti wins The National Poetry Competition.
		Jenny Joseph wins James Tait Memorial Prize.
		Helen Dunmore wins Alice Hunt Bartlett Prize.
		Poems on the Underground.
1987		Elizabeth Jennings wins W. H. Smith Literary Award.
		Wendy Cope wins Cholmondeley Award.
		U. A. Fanthorpe elected Fellow, Royal Society of Literature.
1988	Berlin Wall comes down (November).	The Poetry Library moves to the South Bank.
	Siân Edwards first woman conductor at Royal Opera House, Covent Garden.	Carol Ann Duffy wins Somerset Maugham Prize.
		Selima Hill wins Arvon/Observer International Poetry Competition.
		Gwyneth Lewis wins Gregory Award.
1989		Carol Ann Duffy wins Dylan Thomas Award.
		E. J. Scovell wins Cholmondeley Award.
1990	Nelson Mandela released from imprisonment on Rabbins Island.	Nicky Rice wins The National Poetry Competition.
	Mary Robinson elected President of Ireland.	Elaine Feinstein wins Cholmondeley Award.
	Poll Tax riots (March); Mrs Thatcher resigns (November).	Helen Dunmore wins first prize in Cardiff International Poetry Competition.
	Tracy Edwards captains first all-women crew to complete Whitbread Round the World Yacht Race.	

YEAR	HISTORICAL EVENTS	CULTURAL/LITERARY EVENTS
1991	Helen Sharman first Briton in space.	Judith Wright awarded The Queen's Medal for Poetry.
		Jo Shapcott's 'Phrase Book' is joint winner of The National Poetry Competition.
		Jackie Kay's *The Adoption Papers* wins a Scottish Arts Council Book Award, Saltire First Book Award.
1992	Ordination of women priests in the Church of England.	Forward Poetry Prize set up. Jackie Kay wins the Forward Prize for best single poem.
	Betty Boothroyd becomes first female Speaker of the House of Commons.	Kathleen Raine awarded The Queen's Medal for Poetry.
		Elizabeth Jennings receives CBE.
1993		Carol Ann Duffy wins Whitbread Poetry Prize.
1994		First National Poetry Day.
		'New Generation' Poets launched.
		Ruth Fainlight wins Cholmondeley Award.
		Alice Oswald wins Gregory Award.
1995		Carol Ann Duffy awarded OBE.
		Wendy Cope wins American Academy of Letters Award.
		Kathleen Jamie wins Somerset Maugham Award.
1996	Prince and Princess of Wales divorce.	Orange Prize for Women's Fiction launched.
		Ruth Padel wins The National Poetry Competition.
		Fleur Adcock awarded OBE.
1997	General election: Labour elected. Tony Blair becomes Prime Minister; 120 women MPs ('Blair's Babes') win seats. Death of Diana, Princess of Wales.	Jenny Joseph's 'When I Am Old I Shall Wear Purple' chosen as the Nation's Favourite Poem on National Poetry Day.
1998	Devolution in Scotland and Wales. High numbers of women elected to Welsh National Assembly and Scottish Parliament.	Poetry on the Buses.

YEAR	HISTORICAL EVENTS	CULTURAL/LITERARY EVENTS
1999	Devolution in Northern Ireland.	Carol Ann Duffy made Fellow of Royal Society of Literature and nominated for Laureateship.
	Minimum wage introduced.	Oxford University Press closes its poetry list.
2000		Kathleen Raine awarded CBE.

I

JANE DOWSON

Introduction

> The best women's poetry may be still unrecognised if, as I suspect, we have not
> yet understood how to read it.
>
> (Germaine Greer, 2001)[1]

During the last two decades of the twentieth century, three inter-dependent questions evolved: who are the women poets? What is the persona of the woman poet? What is the aesthetic, that is, the distinctive 'voice', of women's poetry? In this Introduction, I briefly summarise where these concepts have taken scholars, critics and readers; I then attend to Greer's above challenge that Alice Entwistle and I cited in the Afterword to *A History of Twentieth-Century British Women's Poetry* (2005) and that stimulates this volume: how do we talk meaningfully about poetry by women? In other words, how do we find a vocabulary that can distinguish and evaluate, that frames illuminating connections between poets and that neither ignores gender not reduces a poem to merely a gendered artefact? How do we conserve the century's canons of poets, not simply by a roll-call of names but by identifiable practices that do not just *keep* pace with but also *set* the pace for critical and literary studies? The approaches that follow pertain to the selected poets in each chapter and are transferable to their predecessors, contemporaries and successors across national boundaries.

Since around 1980, revisionary scholarship and publishing have unearthed the forgotten, reread the neglected and reclassified the misrepresented writers of previous centuries. There is now a firm sense of a line of women poets stretching from Sappho to the end of the nineteenth century.[2] With lists of over one hundred female British and Irish poets, the emerging narratives of the twentieth century are beginning to crystallise through poetry collections and critical overviews. Fleur Adcock's *The Faber Book of 20th Century Women's Poetry* (1987) whet readers' appetites for the British and American writers she introduced, and has been followed by Deryn Rees-Jones' extensive and refreshing selection in *Modern Women Poets* (2005). As listed under 'Selected Reading' at the end of this *Companion*, other anthologies have a broader or narrower timespan ('Contemporary', 'New', 'the 1930s' or 'War'), or are confined by sexual/ biological identity (such as lesbian or motherhood) or nationality (Indian,

African, Scottish, Welsh, Irish, black) and women have been well represented in the anthologies of the century that were published around the
millennium.

One consensus finds the distinctive 'voice' inextricably wrought from
the cultural ideologies of gender with which the poet negotiated. Thus, as
in *Contemporary Scottish Women Writers*, edited by Christianson and
Lumsden (2000), or DeCaires Narain's *Contemporary Caribbean Women's
Poetry* (2001), the aesthetic is primarily conceived through a writer's specifically female experience of her national/racial identity. The other branch
of criticism foregrounds writers' circumventions of the devaluing epithets
'poetess' at the start and 'woman poet' at the end of the century. As
I concluded in *Women, Modernism and British Poetry: Resisting Femininity*
(1992), 'the cohering aesthetic is in women's problematic relationship with
both male and female traditions'.[3] The necessary cultural empowerment
and imaginative liberation achieved by claiming ground both in and out of
male-dominant traditions inform the essays in Vicki Bertram's influential
Kicking Daffodils: Twentieth-Century Women Poets (1997) that scrutinize
poets' reconfigurations of literary conventions. In *A History of Twentieth-
Century British Women's Poetry*, we mine the best practices that are often
discernible by a gender-conscious avoidance of the 'personal', namely
androgyny, modernist impersonality, disruptive lyrics and the ventriloquising of social voices. We also draw attention to where poets write boldly in
politically creative ways, such as public commentary, linguistically innovative consciousness-raising or combining science with myth. The woman
poet's imperative to shrug off cultural idealisations of femininity is taken
up by Rees-Jones in *Consorting with Angels* (2005). With reference to
Virginia Woolf's famous injunction to 'kill the Angel in the house' and
Judith Butler's treatise on gender as a performance of difference,[4] Rees-
Jones showcases how women poets, from Edith Sitwell to Jo Shapcott, mask
or meddle with reductive essentialising assumptions about the poet as
subject, through such performative strategies as the dramatic monologue,
multivocality, surrealism and intertextuality. In *Poetry off the Page:
Twentieth-century British Women Poets in Performance* (2004), Laura
Severin traces theatrical devices that unsettle a page/stage divide and that
contiguously deconstruct gender prescriptions, by pairing Charlotte
Mew with Anna Wickham, Sitwell with Stevie Smith, and Liz Lochhead
with Jackie Kay. In *Gendering Poetry: Contemporary Women and Men
Poets* (2004) Bertram's interrogation of masculinity alongside femininity
and men along with women poets signals what Susan Stanford Friedman
coins as the shift from 'binarist ways of thinking' to a unifying

'geopolitics of identity' that allows for differences to be multivalent, global and contextually specific.[5]

As the millennium recedes, we view the previous century with increasing distance and clarity, through the lenses of accelerating globalisation, the collapsing distinction between private and public spheres and the confused terminology of 'post everything'. With the twenty-first century's drive for both innovation and recycling, the labels post-feminism, postcolonisalism, postmodernism and post-nationalism are neither dispensed with nor simply preserved as fixed entities, moments or movements. We maintain their usefulness for rebranding concepts in order to destabilise binary polarities of gender, culture and race. The following chapters were written in a zone where the materiality of libraries, hardcopy books, desks, chairs and computers merge with the virtual reality of the World Wide Web. Not surprisingly, they exhibit contemporary discourses about borderlands that maintain and cross boundaries. Thus we revive or hyphenate existing categories and propose new ones, such as 'interculturalism', 'mid-Atlantic imagination', 'new confessionalism' or 'post-pastoral'.

Recognising that contextual signification is crucial to poets' literary practice and reception, the chapters are loosely arranged in order of the century's major poetic categories: Modernism, the world wars, the Movement and multiculturalism. We show that women poets are not 'also-ran' to these dominant trends but participants who establish and pioneers who change literary terrains. Within the chapters, however, we link political impulses and stylistic features across strict historical periods in order to consolidate alternative models of poetic practice that run through the decades. Similarly, while respecting the delineations of national identity (most obviously British and Irish), the contributors foreground poets' self-conscious textual activities that extend and sometimes unsettle critical orthodoxies. Collectively, the chapters converse about lyric, narrative and dramatic representations in terms that frequently centre female poetic expression yet dislodge binary conceptions of male and female creativity. Friedman charts this 'both/and' dialogue of differences as 'beyond gender', meaning beyond 'fundamentalist identity politics and absolutist poststructuralist theories as they pose essentialist notions of identity on the one hand and refuse all cultural traffic with identity on the other'.[6] The frames of interpretation that follow correspondingly set up discursive spaces that overlay and dissolve such oppositional binaries as the verbal and visual, seriousness and play, nature and culture, war and peace, the local and global.

Whereas in *Kicking Daffodils* critics notice how women use their position outside the tradition to kick at the male prerogative in a metaphor that indicates restriction, anger, playfulness and freedom, the emphasis in these chapters is on women's flexible strategies that weave the established with the radical. They frequently write about the tradition as if it is theirs to manoeuvre. William May moves towards paradigms of women's ekphrastic poetry that not only deal with the painterly tradition of men objectifying and fixing their female subjects but also with the poets who control the artistic practice itself, as illustrated in Alexander Pope's 'Epistle to a Lady' or Shelley's 'On the Medusa of Leonardo Da Vinci'. Stevie Smith, Lynette Roberts and Liz Lochhead, all artists as well as poets, boldly manipulate and tease the similarities and differences between 'this sketch' and 'a simile'. In Alice Entwistle's discussion of 'Post-pastoral perspectives', poets as various as Anne Stevenson, Gillian Clarke and Eavan Boland evoke and bypass the conventions of pastoral and anti-pastoral in ways that also disrupt the binary opposition of a feminised nature and a plundering masculine culture. Poets across the British Isles, such as Kerry Hardie, Moya Cannon, Alice Oswald, Kathleen Jamie and Zoë Skoulding, respond to the political devolution of the United Kingdom. The boundaries between landscape and culture are supplanted by what Terry Gifford calls a more holistic 'vision of the natural world that includes the human'.[7]

Friedman's 'geopolitics of identity' accounts for the multicultural, international and transnational configurations of race and gender that Lee M. Jenkins explores. Whereas postcolonial theories, along the continuum between 'writing back' and transnationalism, have embedded race-based critical approaches, 'interculturalism' opens up a border zone where, as Gloria Anzaldúa suggests, everyone lives.[8] We find Imtiaz Dharker, Patience Agbabi, Jackie Kay and contemporary Irish poets engaging with differences within and connections across cultures; collectively, they indicate that feelings of displacement are a shared condition. Agbabi's sonnet about meeting with Wordsworth on the London Eye exemplifies their skilful manipulations of literary traditions that explode monolithic notions of canonical heritage. As demonstrated here, poets who are born or settled in Britain and Ireland are included in our canon of writers.

Extending Homi Bhabha's yearning for a 'third space of enunciation',[9] Anglo-American women poets also traverse rigid demarcations of nationality and the attendant polarities of formal traditionalism and experimentalism. In their 'mid-Atlantic imagination' poets who migrated between Britain and the United States harmonised the preoccupying disjunctions of being somewhere and nowhere; such a psychological liminality can describe the itinerant lives of poets and readers through and beyond the century. Combining the feminist poststructuralism of Julia Kristeva with the Marxist philosophy and sociology of Henri Lefebvre, Melanie Petch examines how the poem is an imaginative sphere with a contingent materiality that fosters community; thus it offers the potential to appropriate and change the social spaces in which writers and readers find themselves. In chapter 5, 'Towards a new confessionalism', connections between Sylvia Plath and Elizabeth Jennings bridge American enthusiasm and British disdain regarding the 'confessional'. As Isobel Armstrong observes in *The Radical Aesthetic*, psychoanalysis had become the 'primary discourse of emotions this [the twentieth] century' and is the obvious discourse for the poets' reworkings of mental illness.[10] I prefer Jung's insistence on reading symbols as signs of a *poetic* consciousness to Freudian assumptions about the authors' psychological neuroses. Moving from the benchmark of 'authenticity' presumed and demanded by social practices of confession, I stress how the poetic act self-consciously marks and compensates for what cannot be fully spoken.

When it comes to history, women are agents against reductive orthodoxies: they intervene in the record-making that has too easily been biased by male and/or nationalist agendas. In an invigorating rebuttal of imperial narratives about the two world wars as mere punctuation marks in twentieth-century British history, Claire Buck favours Paul Virilio's theory that the threat of violence infiltrates the consciousness of daily life at all times. With an instructive overview of publications and their critical reception, she details how women's poems present the integration and interaction of peace and war, of the domestic space and war zones. Starting with Edith Sitwell's *The Song of the Cold* (1948) about atomic bombing and Sylvia Townsend Warner's *Opus 7* (1931) (modelled on George Crabbe's anti-pastoral), she assembles a huge number of poets who include Denise Levertov, Heather Buck, Smith, Plath, Nancy Cunard, Ada Jackson, Roberts, Sheila Wingfield, H.D. and Mina Loy. In common, they often recast the elegy and other conventional forms to make personal experience a public matter. Tackling the Irish history wars, Catriona Clutterbuck argues that women face how history is mediated; furthermore, they are instrumental in hinging the crude and inflammatory polarisations between revisionism and counter-revisionism. Her probing readings of Eavan Boland and Eiléan Ní Chuilleanáin can apply to the many other poets they represent who 'challenge[s] the categorisation of women's history and national history as automatically at odds'.

The emanating power and pleasure of poetic language keep the reader and critic alert to what poetry can offer that other artistic forms do not. The French feminists' theory of 'écriture féminine', the semiotic ruptures of symbolic language, is problematic for essentialising female writing but enlightens the innate function of poetic expression:

> It is impossible to *define* a feminine [poetic] practice of writing, and this is an impossibility that will remain, for this practice can never be theorized, enclosed, coded – which doesn't mean that it doesn't exist. But it will always surpass the discourse that regulates the phallocentric system.[11]

As indicated in my parenthesis, we could substitute 'feminine' with 'poetic'. Thus it makes sense to suppose that in writing poetry women especially address and transgress available means of expression. So we look for shifting pronouns, customised metaphors and defamiliarisng syntax that configure not one 'voice' but the self-reflexive processes of speaking. In chapter 2, 'Post/Modernist rhythms and voices', Ian Gregson foregrounds sound effects that 'evoke a self-consciously problematic sense of a speaking voice' and disrupt routine patterns of meaning, with reference to Kristeva's emphasis on the interplay between semiotic rhythms within language that approximate to pre-linguistic sound effects: 'Indifferent to language, enigmatic and feminine, this space underlying the written is rhythmic, unfettered, irreducible to its intelligible verbal translation, it is musical, anterior to judgement.'[12] The feminine self-parodying of Sitwell and Smith, manifest in deceptive ingenuousness and confrontational satire, mocks masculine assumptions about its own rational authority and prepares the ground for the frolicking carnivalesque ironies of Jo Shapcott and Selima Hill at the end of the century. Read thus, the poets link to the caricatural methods of painters such as Hogarth and writers from Dryden to Dickens; they also dialogue with each other as identifiably postmodern practices. With a glance at earlier models of experimentalism, by Warner, Mew or Laura Riding, Linda A. Kinnahan celebrates the feminist politics of language innovation in the 1970s, arguing for women's influence on all British experimental poetry in that period and after. Wendy Mulford's deconstructive lyrics, explicitly influenced by the theories of Lacan, Cixous, Irigaray, Derrida and Foucault, were accompanied by Veronica Forrest-Thomson and Denise Riley and then followed by Caroline Bergvall.

Several chapters step into the twenty-first century where the zeitgeist and poetic birth pangs at the end of the twentieth are more visible. Brian Caraher finishes the *Companion* with an account of how Carol Ann Duffy and Medbh McGuckian rupture the poetic line, meaning literally the metres, metaphors and idioms of poetic orthodoxies as well as the genealogy of poetic traditions. These poets' literary revisions and transgressions, such as Duffy's appropriations of Shakespeare's dramatic verse or McGuckian's regendering of war's 'front line', refresh received poetic expression to comment on the states of contemporary Britain and Ireland and set up new linguistic moulds for posterity to recast.

As Caraher's detailed readings demonstrate, one prevalent poetic device that women favour is the conversational construction and examination of dialogue. Dialogue, mostly internal, avoids the fixed lyric subject, negotiates between private and public spaces and allows for a sense of self-in-relation through what Mikhail Bakhtin calls 'hidden dialogicality': 'The second speaker is present invisibly, his [sic] words are not there, but deep traces left by these words have a determining influence on all the present and visible words of the first speaker.'[13] Two or more voices reinforce, counter or expose social and personal power relations, as Duffy, renowned for her 'thrown voices', provocatively constructs in 'The Dummy', where a stooge answers back to his/her ventriloquist: 'Just teach me / the right words.'[14]

All the chapters remind us that every poem is arguably in dialogue with literary tradition and implicitly with the reader. Duffy is also an exponent of the way in which poetry semiotically carves a distinct world of its own – love is 'not there, except in a poem' – yet poetry also urges us to let it transform how we live: 'Away and see the things that words give a name to.'[15] Such maintenance of the distinction yet interaction between life and art is emblematic of this *Companion's* approach to poetry that does not deny differences – whether stylistic, cultural or historical – but finds meeting points, crossings and crossovers that launch new evaluative ways to talk about them.

Notes

1 Germaine Greer, 'To the reader', in *101 Poems by 101 Women* (London: Faber, 2001), p. ix.

2 See Robyn Boland (ed.), *Eliza's Babes: Four Centuries of Women's Poetry in English, c. 1500–1900* (Tarset: Bloodaxe, 2005) or R.E. Pritchard (ed.), *Poetry By English Women* (Manchester: Carcanet, 1990).

3 Jane Dowson, *Women, Modernism and British Poetry 1910–39: Resisting Femininity* (Farnham: Ashgate, 2002), p. viii.

4 Virginia Woolf, 'Professions for women', in *The Death of the Moth and Other Essays* (London: Harcourt Inc., 1942) delivered as a lecture in 1931; Judith Butler, *Gender Trouble: Feminism and the Subversion of Identity* (1990; London: Routledge, 1999).

5 Susan Stanford Friedman, *Mappings: Feminism and the Cultural Geographies of Encounter* (Princeton: Princeton University Press, 1998), p. 4.

6 *Ibid.*

7 Terry Gifford, *Pastoral* (London: Routledge, 1999), p. 147.

8 Gloria Anzaldúa, *Borderlands/La Frontera: The New Mestiza* (1987; San Francisco: Aunt Lute Books, 1999).

9 Homi Bhabha, *The Location of Culture* (New York: Routledge, 1994), p. 37.

10 Isobel Armstrong, *The Radical Aesthetic* (Oxford and Malden, MA: Blackwell, 2000), p. 18.

11 Hélène Cixous, 'The laugh of the Medusa', trans. Keith Cohen and Paula Cohen, *Signs* 1. 4 (1976), 875–93.

12 Julia Kristeva, *Revolution in Poetic Language*, trans. Margaret Waller (New York: Columbia University Press, 1984), p. 26.

13 Mikhail Bakhtin (1963), in Pam Morris (ed.), *The Bakhtin Reader: Selected Writings of Bakhtin, Medvedev, Voloshinov* (London: Edward Arnold, 1994), p. 108. For a full exposition, see Ian Gregson, *Poetry and Postmodernism: Dialogue and Estrangement* (Basingstoke: Macmillan, 1996).

14 Carol Ann Duffy, 'The Dummy', in *Selected Poems* (Harmondsworth: Penguin, 1994), p. 36.

15 Carol Ann Duffy, 'Love Poem', in *Rapture* (London: Picador, 2005), p. 59; 'Away and See', in *Mean Time* (London: Anvil Press Poetry, 1993), p. 23. For discussion of Duffy's line between the expression and deconstruction of meaning see Stan Smith, 'The things that words give a name to: the "New Generation" poets and the politics of the hyperreal', *Critical Survey* 8. 3 (1996), 306–22.

2

IAN GREGSON

Post/Modernist rhythms and voices: Edith Sitwell and Stevie Smith to Jo Shapcott and Selima Hill

There is a strand of twentieth-century women's poetry that foregrounds sounds and rhythms and uses them to evoke a self-consciously problematic sense of a speaking voice. Michael Schmidt emphasises the structural importance of rhythm for both Edith Sitwell (1887–1964) and Stevie Smith (1902–71),[1] and quotes Sitwell as saying that rhythm is 'one of the principal translators between dream and reality', and that the *Facade* poems are 'patterns of sound'.[2] He says that the 'most striking characteristic' of Stevie Smith 's work 'is the rhythm, a speech rhythm slipping naturally into metre and out again, a rhythm so strong that it overrides considerations of syntax and punctuation and – in releasing language from its formal structures – finds new forms, new tones'.[3] Sitwell helped to initiate a female tradition in which poetic sound and rhythm are privileged and so wielded as to disrupt routine patterns of meaning. Smith continued in this vein and extended a caricatural tendency already present in Sitwell but pushed further, in combination with Smith's discordant music and a deceptive ingenuousness, to achieve a confrontational satire which at times is self-consciously childish. The experimental heightening of poetic sound, in these earlier writers, combined with their use of the playful yet angry and even contemptuous imagery of caricature, has influenced more recent poets in the creation of an identifiably feminine postmodernism. The silliness and shrillness of the music of Sitwell and Smith – which turns feminine self-parody into satire of masculine assumptions of its own rational authority, and derisive questioning of masculine dismissiveness towards what it regards as feminine inchoateness – prepares the way for the dancing and demented cows of Jo Shapcott (b. 1953) and Selima Hill (b. 1945), the uproarious sing-song of their flaky carnival.

The best way to achieve a more general understanding of this strand of women's poetry is by reference to Julia Kristeva's distinction between the 'symbolic' and the 'semiotic' and her emphasis on the importance of the latter in poetic language, which is thereby infiltrated by the pre-linguistic.

She illustrates it, in particular, by reference to avant-garde poets such as Mallarmé and Lautréamont. Her linked idea of the 'chora' 'precedes and underlies figuration and thus specularization, and is analogous only to vocal and kinetic rhythm'. So she refers to the 'semiotic rhythm within language':

> Indifferent to language, enigmatic and feminine, this space underlying the written is rhythmic, unfettered, irreducible to its intelligible verbal translation, it is musical, anterior to judgement.[4]

The semiotic can never exist separately from the symbolic, but only in interaction with it: it can never be fully retrieved, but its traces persist and disrupt the patriarchal and legal order of the symbolic. Some feminists, such as Jacqueline Rose,[5] have complained that the theory is essentialist, but the complaint arises from a false emphasis on the 'priority' of the semiotic when the semiotic and the symbolic must above all be understood as in dialogue with each other.[6] It is this point which also suggests why the semiotic can be usefully applied to modern British poetry. Kristeva's theory already privileges poetry as the key cultural site of the semiotic, but its emphasis on the dialogic further indicates why it is an appropriate theoretical model for explaining a recent tradition which is thoroughly polyphonic and novelised, and whose devices include nursery and nonsense rhymes, deliberately prosaic and bathetically flat-footed rhythms, incongruously mingled registers, *faux-naïve* onomatopoeia and verbal/visual cartoon.

Edith Sitwell: the semiotic and the caricatural tradition

The paradox of the semiotic is that it describes a language that self-consciously evokes the unselfconsciously pre-linguistic, which articulates the inarticulate and the bodily. For this reason it constructs an expression in which signifiers float free from the signified, in which the purely physical nature of the sign is allowed a life of its own. Few poets, in their poetic practice, have made sound effects as prominent as Edith Sitwell. In the opening six lines of 'Hornpipe', for example, which are very short, she rhymes 'come', 'drum', 'dumb' and 'glum', and then in the seventh, which is the first long line, she rhymes internally on 'courses', 'horses' and 'Glaucis'.[7] And few poets, in their accounts of their writing, have focused as extensively upon the free-floating signifier, and especially upon the sound of poetry, as Sitwell, whose 'Some notes on my poetry' gives the impression that rhythm, rhyme and assonance are the most shaping motive forces behind her composition.[8] This obsessiveness leads to her associating linguistic sounds with emotional states, as when she analyses 'The Bat', from *Facade*:

some of the 'a's and the 'u's have neither depth nor body, are flat and death-rotten; yet at times the words in which they occur cast a small menacing shadow because of the 'ck' endings, though frequently these shadows are followed almost immediately by flatter, deader, more shadeless words ending in 't' or in 'd'.[9]

Sitwell's view of language is reminiscent of that propounded by Rimbaud, who is quoted twice in her 'Notes', and whose 'Voyelles' assigns each vowel a colour and then a set of images associated with that colour. Reprising the idea in 'Délires II', he explains it as a kind of verbal alchemy in which the form and movement of consonants could also be evoked, and which would lead, in the future, to a poetic language that could thoroughly translate all the senses. In this respect Rimbaud resembles the avant-garde poets who are focused upon by Kristeva. His 'alchemical' project wants to transmogrify the base matter of letters into imaginative gold and is shared by Sitwell, who keeps referring to her texts as a body in which the senses interpenetrate each other, and aspires to an expression which is transformative and synaesthetic. In 'Aubade' she repeatedly refers to the light making an inarticulate noise,[10] and in her 'Notes' explains that the line in which the 'cold dawn light lies whining' was suggested to her by 'the shivering movement' of such light as being like 'a kind of high animal whining or whimpering, a half-frightened and subservient urge to something outside our consciousness'.[11] Synaesthetic imagery, in which a visual object is described as uttering a sound, is associated for Sitwell with a pre-conscious, pre-linguistic striving towards language and understanding: 'Sometimes the poems speak of an unawakened consciousness fumbling toward a higher state, and sometimes of a purely animal consciousness – the beginning of all earthly things.'[12]

Sitwell's attempt to evolve a poetic which enacts the emergence of informed vision out of a primordial semiotic, to evoke 'the cry of that waiting, watching world', shows the strain, in her early work, of its difficulty, and it is not surprising that many readers have been alienated.[13] Blake Morrison describes Sitwell as 'appallingly repetitive' and notes that the word 'creaks' occurs 'six times in the first forty-six lines of her *Selected Poems*, in images which are inappropriate or meaningless or which lose whatever force they have had through dilution'.[14] As Sitwell develops, however, her poems grow more subtle and complex as they become less preoccupied with semiotic purity and increasingly place the semiotic and the symbolic in dialogue with each other. In her 'Notes' she has a habit of describing her texts as bodies, and then insisting that those bodies are dead, as in the death-rottenness in her prose passage about 'The Bat' quoted above. The answer to this apparent contradictoriness lies, as Deryn Rees-Jones points out, in the Kristevan relationship 'between the maternal body and language', but it also indicates that Sitwell's mature poems indict a deathliness in the symbolic, which she exposes by her adoption of satirical modes in which the liveliness of the semiotic clashes with the rottenness of the symbolic.[15] The preoccupation with loss which lies behind that clash is one which Sitwell shares with all the other Modernist poets; like them, she writes poems which constantly verge upon an elegiac mode whose objects of mourning are unspecific – except that they contain a mostly unnamed relationship to the First World War, as recent criticism such as Vincent Sherry's *The Great War and the Language of Modernism* has demonstrated.[16] Sitwell's habit of associating poetic dissonance with death and rottenness is bound to make most poetry readers think of Wilfred Owen, whom she admired, and whose pararhymes continue to reverberate in English verse in the 1920s and after, in poems such as W. H. Auden 's *Paid On Both Sides*, where their authors want to mourn an early twentieth-century sense of devastated pastoral.

Edith Sitwell's best poems are a satirical response to that sense of loss, and *Facade* is her greatest achievement because it is in that sequence that the satirical mode is most successfully sustained. Debora Van Durme has recently characterised *Facade* as 'alienating' and linked it therefore with the search of other early twentieth-century performers for 'dehumanized, machine or puppet-like gestural and vocal expressions' with which to '*épater le bourgeois*'. She quotes Sitwell using imagery of this kind when the poet praises the way in which music hall dissects hypocrisy and 'strips off our flesh and shows us, marionettes that we are, clothed in our primal lust': this is imagery which is a stock motif of the caricatural tradition, which, as I show later in relation to Stevie Smith, is repeatedly referred to in the strand of women's poetry I am describing in this chapter. The title of *Facade* indicates that it is meant to emulate music hall in stripping away the deceptive surfaces of 'Royalty, gentry, religion, art and mores', and its childlike, primitive semiotic energy is directed against the deathlike, mechanistic oppressiveness of those symbolic structures.[17] More obviously than the Modernism of Sitwell's major contemporaries such as T. S. Eliot, Ezra Pound and Gertrude Stein (who was the most crucial influence on her), Sitwell's Modernism is a horrified, frustrated Romanticism which wants poetry to be organic and natural, but finds that the twentieth century imposes upon all art its own mechanistic constructedness, reflected in *Facade* by reducing the humanity of its reciter by withdrawing them behind a curtain and having them speak in level tones through a kind of megaphone, called a sengerphone.

The frustration of Sitwell's Romanticism is enacted at length in 'The Sleeping Beauty', in its depiction of a childhood stifled by a thoroughly conventional upbringing, represented, as Jane Dowson has pointed out, 'in the recurring image of her stuffed parrot in a cage'.[18] The transformation of the living and natural into the dead and mechanical (in the parrot's associations with meaningless repetition) perfectly represents the transformation of the innocent spontaneity of Romantic childhood into the childish aggression of her caricatural Modernism. This is evident in 'The Sleeping Beauty' in its use of the child's point of view as a satirical device which is scathing about the deadening narrow-mindedness of adult authority. A similar trajectory is followed in 'Colonel Fantock', where the children at first walk 'like shy gazelles / Among the music of the thin flower-bells', but are then condemned to an education conducted by the military buffoon of the poem's title, who lies about military victories and is anti-heroically 'blown by the cold wind', exercising authority only over unfortunate children as 'the Napoleon of the schoolroom'.[19] Sitwell's caricatural sensibility is also exercised in her prose work *The English Eccentrics* (1933), whose gallery includes Captain Thicknesses, who bequeaths his severed right hand to his son, and Lord Rokeby, who spends most of his time in his bath and has a knee-length beard. Its most convincing expression, though, is in *Facade*, where fictions like Captain Fracasse are joined by historical characters like Tennyson and Queen Victoria.

The humanity of the characters in *Facade* is reduced by poetic effects which clamour so loudly that the personages are overwhelmed by language and thereby revealed as subject to its symbolic systems. This linguistic belittling already caricatures them, but they are further reduced to cartoons by being defined by merely surface characteristics and being compared to objects and animals and machines. In 'The Bat', the 'mountebank doctor' is compared both to a duck and a bat, but further removed from even animal life because both animals are mere representations, the bat wearing a 'furred cloak' and the duck being both a decoy and reduced to its characteristic 'quack' and then to dust.[20] The bat is also self-consciously a satirical device that treats the world with carnivalesque subversion by turning it upside down – which is literal in bats, but is more widely representative of a poetic in which the symbolic is challenged by the semiotic, the language of authority by the rhythms and noises of nursery and counting rhymes in which 'semi-nonsensical chains of words' are linked 'on the basis of sound and rhythm rather than sense'.[21]

Stevie Smith: the semiotic and the *faux-naïve*

Stevie Smith's interest in the semiotic is evident in what Romana Huk calls her 'many repetitions and song-like riffs', which Huk thinks may have been influenced by Edith Sitwell, 'whose readings Smith was known to attend'.[22] It is also evident in her fascination with noise, with onomatopoeia, with hearts that 'go tumptytum', a little bird that sings 'Pee-wee', horses that go 'Jingle-jog', a river that says 'Hi yih, yippity-yap', a cat that says 'Spit. Spat.', birds of a wood 'piping screaming croaking clacking', and the 'bicker' of a stream, a cock that cries 'cock-a-doooo', the 'swoosh' of an angel's wings as heard by a speaking cat that says 'Ha ha ha ha, ho'.[23] These noises most often childishly represent the cries of animals: they are uttered on the threshold of language, not shaped into the contours of the symbolic. Linda Anderson is making a connected point when she refers to Smith's performances of her poems suggesting 'pre-oedipal drives uncontained by language'. She is accounting for an effect described by Norman Bryson, who attended a reading by Smith in 1965 and found it unnervingly excessive, so that 'the meaning of the words was set aside in the performance': Anderson believes that Smith meant the performance 'to exceed the text, to open up a gap between the words and their orality'.[24] When she links these points to 'pre-oedipal drives' she is very close – although she does not make it explicit – to indicating the role of the Kristevan semiotic in Smith's poems.

In her interviews Smith stressed the importance for her of the music of her poems. She told Peter Orr that her sense of rhythm was 'very, very strong', and that she regarded her poems as 'sound vehicles' which she often organised around well-known tunes in order to ensure 'that other people will get the right rhythm'.[25] In her later interview with Jonathan Williams she referred to the influence of *Hymns Ancient and Modern* as 'tunes I often sing to' and of nursery rhymes like 'Boys and Girls Come Out to Play' and 'Oranges and Lemons'.[26] Smith's critics have linked her rhythms to her *faux-naïveté*. Where Ian Hamilton refers patronisingly to the 'little-girl-lost air to Smith's verse persona' and to her blasphemies as 'a shade infantile',[27] Christopher Ricks agrees with Michael Schmidt that the tendency of her critics to portray her as naive 'reveals the success with which she projected the mock-innocence of her public image'. Ricks shows how her use of 'the stone of bathos falling through the waters of pathos' is deliberately childish, and achieved through discordant metre and rhyme whose conspicuousness waves its arms about but is actually about drowning, about death.[28]

'A Father for a Fool' is meant to be read 'To the tune "Boys and Girls Come out to Play"' and so establishes nursery-rhyme expectations which from the outset cause problems in reader-response, because the reader is required to remember the tune and so focus on the poem's sound. Those problems are compounded, not just because the nursery rhyme has survived in alternative versions, but because the poem veers sharply away from any rhythm that a nursery rhyme could have as early as the third line, which, although it rhymes with the first two, extends to thirteen syllables whose lack of regular metre is exaggerated by aggressively prosaic content – 'What does it feel like to have a father for a fool?' The flat-footed lack of music in that line makes it read like an aside in a stanza which is otherwise quite regular, but whose content is also confrontationally at odds with the nursery-rhyme tune, so that its effect is like the favourite satirical device of children of substituting mundane or scurrilous words for the official text of a hymn or Christmas carol ('As shepherds washed their socks. . .'). These discordances all sharpen the reader's discomfort; most uncomfortable of all, however, is that the poem's mostly jingling music contrasts so starkly with its dismissively cruel authorial attitude. Because of the form, this cruelty sounds like one child bullying another, taunting him that his father has lost his money and blamed fate, 'And shot himself through the head too late'. The greatest shock, however, is that it is Smith herself who is that bully, and she increases the feeling of cruelty by shifting, in the second stanza, to the son's bewildered free indirect thought – as he tries to understand his changed circumstances and misses their seriousness, hoping there will still be shrimps for tea – and then, in the third stanza, returning to her own voice, to gloat that the boy's mother is also 'stone cold dead of a broken heart, the fool'.[29]

The focus on death by Smith's critics is not surprising, given how much she dwells on the subject, but it distracts from an equally important feature of her work which has received far too little attention – its satirical attitude. Terry Eagleton states flatly that her poems are 'about disintegration and death', and as a result he finds her forms, with their reference to nursery rhyme, inappropriate, and the poems ultimately slight. Eagleton is unusual in feeling that she contrives her bathos in order 'to be honest to the facts at the cost of the form – to show how formal predictability is devastated by sheer truth'.[30] While this appears to argue against the dominance of formal effects in Smith's poems, it confirms the key point, which is that their distinctiveness arises from the unique quality of the interaction between form and content, and that Smith is very unusual in the extent to which she places the two in an explicit dialogue. It is out of the self-consciousness of that interaction that Smith produces her tellingly off-key voice, whose impact at readings has been most vividly evoked by Seamus Heaney. His sensitivity to its 'pitching between querulousness and keening' is especially acute because this sound is coloured by class and regional intonations which are thoroughly exotic to his ears. He describes the 'longueurs and acerbities, the nuanced understatements and tactical intonations of educated middle-class English speech' and imagines (bizarrely) how wrong her poems would sound if declaimed in Ian Paisley's North Antrim accent.[31]

For Heaney, the specificities of Smith's voice are finally limiting, and his strictures are similar to Eagleton's – that the style is insufficient to the gravity of the subject matter. His sense that they lack the required largeness of 'orchestration', however, results from his failure to understand that Smith's voice is not a single instrument but multiple, that it acquires plurality through her use of dramatic monologue and parody. Part of the reason he misses this is that he takes the middle-class English speech in Smith's poems to be her own speech, when in fact she retained part at least of her Hull accent, grew up in 'relative austerity', worked as an adult as a secretary and 'critiqued suburbia's snobberies and contradictions from her liminal perspective even as they worked to shape her, a child of the same world'.[32] An understanding of that perspective is necessary if Smith's political anger is to be understood; the animus and feminist resentment that drives poems like 'A Father for a Fool' will be missed if the reader assumes that Smith speaks as an insider in the aristocratic world it evokes, for the poem makes its impact by parodying an upper-class idiom and undermining it with the jauntiness of a nursery rhyme whose origins are in the working-class experience of a poverty-stricken childhood. What Heaney takes to be Smith's endorsement of a ruling-class idiom is actually part of her lampooning of it.

The dismissiveness of Heaney's comment that Smith allows 'the spirit of A. A. Milne' to vie successfully with 'the spirit of Emily Dickinson' backfires because it inadvertently pinpoints how Smith's poems use such bathetic 'vying' to make their satirical impact. It represents for Heaney a 'retreat from resonance' because he most wants to hear the single voice of masculine authority, but his comparison of Smith's poems to 'the clerihew and the caricature' radically underestimates the political potential of such self-consciously reductive modes of expression.[33] Caricature needs to be taken seriously as a satirical device which belongs to an ancient tradition including Hogarth and Gillray in the visual arts, and Dryden, Pope, Swift and Dickens in literature. As I have argued elsewhere, it is a constituent feature of postmodern literature: its impact on novelistic characterisation has been to draw attention away from the subjective interior, which preoccupied Modernist literature, and to flatten characters in a process of ontological reduction in which they are rendered static and mechanical.[34] In postmodern authors as diverse as Joseph Heller, Philip Roth, Joyce Carol Oates, Ralph Ellison, Salman Rushdie and Angela Carter, the human is depicted as reduced to the status of an object, an animal or a machine, or the human body as dismembered to represent the fragmentation of the human spirit.

It is to the 'magic realism' of Angela Carter and Salman Rushdie that Smith's work can be most fruitfully compared; her use of nursery rhyme and other simple forms amounts, like their references to fairy tale, to a form of *faux-naïveté* which disrupts realism and satirically conflates the ingenuous and the sophisticated. This is an art where childishness and cruelty meet, as they do in caricature, which, as Ernst Kris says, 'is not only an historical phenomenon, it concerns a specific process and this process is repeatable and describable, for here we are in the field of psychology'.[35] Kris and E. H. Gombrich, especially in collaboration with each other, have been best at describing this process, drawing upon Freudian concepts to examine the detail of the mechanisms at work. They focus upon the origins of caricature in infantile life, and the wish to regain childhood freedoms which adults are required to renounce:

> Civilisation has taught us to renounce cruelty and aggression which once ran riot in atrocious reality and magical practices. There was a time in all our lives when we enjoyed being rude and naughty, but education has succeeded – or should have succeeded – in turning this joy into abhorrence. We do not let ourselves relapse into that state again, and if ever such impulses break loose under the influence of passion, we feel embarrassed and ashamed. In caricature, however, these forces find a well-guarded playground of their own. The caricaturist knows how to give them scope without allowing them to get out of control. His artistic mastery is, as it were, an assurance that all we enjoy is but a game. In this sphere, the sphere of artistic freedom, we are allowed to indulge our impulses free from fear. Willingly we may yield to the caricaturist's temptation to us to share his aggressive impulses, to see the world with him, distorted.[36]

A key effect of caricature arises from the contrast between its often crude and aggressively energetic materials, whose childlike content is exploited for its simplistic vividness, and the way in which they are mastered by a thoroughly knowing and mature technique. There is a stark contrast between caricatural childishness and classic realist maturity, which suggests a defamiliarising angle on postmodernist 'play', indicating (as with other aspects of the caricatural) a much older provenance for those strategies in postmodernist texts which have subversive fun with the aesthetic norms which are dictated by traditionally sanctioned cultural hegemonies. Here, too, these postmodernist writers can be seen to be drawing upon key aspects of the caricatural tradition in order to rebel against earnestly imposed, or unthinkingly followed, authoritarian values.

Smith's interest in caricature as a visual art is evident from her repeated references in her novel *Over the Frontier* (1938) to the German artist and political satirist Georg Grosz, but also from her own practice in the drawings she made to accompany many of her poems. These were dismissed by her earliest critics, even by admirers like Philip Larkin, who thought 'they have an amateurishness reminiscent of Lear, Waugh and Thurber without much compensating felicity'.[37] More recent critics have appreciated their relevance, Romana Huk pointing out that 'felicity' is beside the point, that their impact is to detract from the 'definitive authority' of the words, and to 'deliver us into the pitiable space of women's objectified status'. Linda Anderson finds a connection between the drawings and Smith's excessive performances because both evade linguistic signification and suggest 'pre-oedipal drives uncontained by language'.[38] Anderson's point is therefore very helpful in hinting at Smith's role in the strand of women's poetry which I am describing: both Smith's focus on poetic sound and her use of 'doodles' disrupt the structural stabilities of the symbolic by interpolating self-consciously inarticulate, and even chaotic, eruptions of the unreconstructed semiotic. The first impression made by the drawing that accompanies 'A Father for a Fool' is of the multiplication of the lines, some straight, some curved, some squiggly, but numerous out of all proportion to the require-ments of representation, in the visual equivalent of excessive noise in music or poetry. The effect is to suggest the frightening disorientation of the 'Little Master', who is a tiny figure looking on and further diminished by the manic hatching, but also to bewilder the stabilities of social hierarchy with hints of the looming presence of turbulent, unstructured forces.

Caricature relies on confrontational crudity, and upon anger and fear as primitive human responses, and it refuses to sympathise with its victims: in drawing upon these resources Smith makes herself vulnerable, like other caricaturists, to charges of narrow-mindedness, and she does seem guilty at times of homophobia and anti-Semitism. She is at her most blatantly cari-catural in short poems like 'Beware the Man' – which warns against the meanness of small-mouthed males and is accompanied by a drawing of a smug man and a disgruntled woman[39] – and 'This Englishwoman', which defines a national stereotype of female refinement involving extreme thin-ness and is supplemented by a drawing of a gaunt woman using an umbrella to shield her from the sun.[40] More substantially, however, Smith's cartoon-ing of the 'objectified status' of women anticipates the caricatural gender politics of female novelists like Joyce Carol Oates – when the American novelist compares female characters like Nada, in *Expensive People*, and Marilyn Monroe, in *Blonde*, to animals and dolls – and Angela Carter when she depicts the adolescent girls in *The Bloody Chamber* as objects of use. Smith is less focused on gender than those writers of the generation after her, and less of an explicit feminist: the objects of her satire tend to wield class, as well as gender, power. 'Sir Rat', in 'Infelice', is an aristocratic politician who treats his mistress, the speaker of the poem, with a cold indifference which she manages to interpret as ardour. His name is a cartoon insult and he is carefully deprived of any individuality, defined by stock references to his life of wealth and power, which evoke an inhuman fixity (his face is twice said to resemble sand) and contrast with the mistress, who is energetic but powerless. Her doting hyper-activity is indicated by her repeated use of present participles whose conspicuousness is heightened by being placed at the end of lines. It is that repeated '-ing' sound which again interpolates traces of the semiotic, especially in the refrain-like 'my heart is singing': the woman's responses to Sir Rat are bodily (she even wants to mother him) and profoundly at odds with the social structures – his gentleman's club and his constituency – which represent the man's world. These signifiers of Sir Rat's power locate him thoroughly in the symbolic, but their caricatural treatment undermines their smug claims to adult sophistication and implies that they are cruder instruments of privilege than they like to claim. However, while the satire of patriarchal power is obvious, Smith is unambiguous about the deludedness of her speaker, who is regarded ruefully rather than sympathetically.[41]

Jo Shapcott and Selima Hill: cartooning the feminine

The animals in Smith's poems are caricaturally half-human; she makes no attempt to evoke a 'real' animal, like poets with ecological concerns such as Ted Hughes and Mary Oliver. She forms a link, in this respect, to contemporary poets like Selima Hill and Jo Shapcott, who 'often transcend the limits of human interaction, especially the confines of a recognisable dialogue of genders, through the personae of vegetables, animals or cartoon characters'.[42] The effects of rhythm and sound in postmodernist women's poetry are very different from those in Sitwell and Smith, because women now – with the exception of comic poets like Wendy Cope – rarely use rhyme, unlike many of the male poets, such as Simon Armitage, Don Paterson and Sean O'Brien. They also opt, almost invariably, for free verse; nonetheless, their rhythms and sounds are still very prominent and have a defamiliarising impact especially when combined with the ingenuous speaking voice they use calculatedly and subversively. Michael Schmidt's reference to *Facade* as full of 'verbal innocence and novelty' and Sitwell's characterising of it as 'the poetry of childhood overtaken by the technician', could also be used to describe the work of Hill and Shapcott, however different it sounds from that of their Modernist predecessor.[43] Such disingenuousness works like an 'innocent eye' whose vision can be explained by reference to the theorising of 'estrangement' by Viktor Shklovsky,[44] but it also in this case amounts to an exaggeration of a conventionally feminine persona – Jo Shapcott's 'Mad Cow' poems[45] can be discussed in these terms, and also Selima Hill when she says 'The Tibetans have 85 words for states of consciousness. / The dozy cow I want to be has none.'[46]

The poems in this strand of women's writing can be regarded as a strategically overstated gender performance, which deconstructs gender assumptions by drawing attention to them through caricaturally vivid simplification. They represent a distinctive achievement which deploys its own language to undermine dominant discourses. Shapcott's 'Robert and Elizabeth' sequence explores the dialogue between masculine and feminine writing – its Roberts are Browning and Lowell, its Elizabeths are Barrett and Hardwick, but they are also generalised as representatives of their genders. So when Robert watches Elizabeth knitting he is bored because he cannot 'get at' its rhythm. Its language is alien to him: he wants to call Elizabeth a series of reductively definitive metonymic names ('string-winder' etc.); he is not attuned to signs in which the play of differences is as important as their reconciling in a symbolic system, he is bewildered by 'a jumper made of space, division and relations'. The further point implied by the epigraph from Gregory Bateson is that biology is also incomprehensible to Robert because the limits of his masculine vision mean that he will be bewildered by DNA, which resembles the linguistic jumper in being all about 'relations' and not about 'end components'.[47]

Shapcott's animal poems take a similar view of biology: they are premised upon the gender stereotype which associates women – by contrast with male rationality – with the irrational and the bodily; which associates the masculine with culture and the feminine with nature. Their caricatural mode invents human/animal hybrids who speak and think in a language in which the symbolic is constantly threatened and disrupted by the semiotic: the holes in the brain of her mad cow are 'wonderful' because they allow ideas and voices to enter 'at top speed'. Shapcott uses the phrase 'mad cow' as other caricatured groups have used the words 'nigger' and 'queer', and wielded them for their own political purposes. The attribution to women of too much biology is fired back at patriarchy and used to satirise its oppressive rigidities, its brains which are so 'compressed' that they are confined and closed, and therefore compelled to control and exclude the natural. By distancing herself from those rigidities, the mad cow is in touch with both the lower and the higher reaches of the human; her mind is shrinking to the size of 'a baby animal's brain' but she aspires to be an angel and climbs towards that status before falling back into 'the world of horn and hoof'.[48] That postmodernist marking of ontological boundaries leads to an expanded sense of what it is to be human when it incorporates (or fully remembers) what it is like to be a baby animal and led by the body. Shapcott uses her characteristically head-over-heels free verse to enact the mad cow's staggers, with her legs splaying in all directions, and a spiralling syntax which implies that the language itself is out of control, and in 'Mad

Cow Dance' uses onomatopoeia ('Swish', 'bam', 'thwack', 'splats') repeatedly in a way that recalls Stevie Smith. The savage primitivism of the mad cow's 'brilliant' dance suggests *The Rite of Spring*, but the mad cow's massiveness, her stomping and banging, introduce a carnivalesque incongruity which typifies the whole sequence and Shapcott's cartoon vision in general. Contrasting the cow's short bulk with the Statue of Liberty may be declaring fat to be a feminist issue when she is being photographed for *Vogue*. But that joke is really being used to make a much more substantial political point in which the contrast is between the cow's joyous physicality and the statue's rigid uprightness which requires 'four gigantic steel supports', so that she is a representation of a woman that in fact is more like a phallic symbol.[49]

Selima Hill shares much in common with Jo Shapcott: both use a free verse with a tendency to run away with itself, and both have the shape-shifting preoccupation of the 'chameleon poet' with projecting the self into non-human forms, and especially with imagining the subjective lives of animals in order to explore the boundaries of human sense and thought. Hill differs from Shapcott because for her the semiotic intervenes most insistently through the disruptive, but also exhilarating, impact of desire. Her sequence 'Portrait of my Lover as a Horse' morphs the hapless male into a series of animals (beetle, butterfly, chicken, cockroach, crocodile and so on, alphabetically) but also a series of objects (bar of soap, cardigan, dress, fall of snow, upmarket snack).[50] In 'Don't Let's Talk About Being in Love', that state, however much it is denied, produces an exquisite discomfort that shapes its own grotesquely sexualised phenomenology which obsesses about womb-like enclosedness (blunted pouches, a dome of glass, dripping tunnels) and phallic pointiness (fingers, beaks). The speaker's dream of her lover's bedroom crammed with ducks climaxes in an irruption of the semiotic, of desire in language, which leads to a collapse into mere noise, as she is

> startled awake by the sound of creaking glass
> as if the whole affair's about to collapse
> and water come pouring in with a rush of fishes
> going *slurpetty-slurpetty-slurp* with their low-slung mouths.[51]

Those lines, which are so characteristic of the feminine postmodernism that has evolved amongst British poets, can be much more thoroughly understood in the context of the tradition I have been defining, in which the problems of articulating the bodily and the inarticulate are solved by invoking the semiotic and the caricatural. Shapcott and Hill look different when defined in this context, but so, too, do Sitwell and Smith, who can be seen from this retrospect as anticipating much of what has happened in postmodernist poetry.

Notes

1 Michael Schmidt, *An Introduction to Fifty Modern British Poets* (London: Pan Books, 1979), pp. 112–13.

2 Edith Sitwell, *Collected Poems* (London: Duckworth Overlook, 2006), p. 112.

3 Schmidt, *An Introduction*, p. 203.

4 Julia Kristeva, *Revolution in Poetic Language*, trans. Margaret Waller (New York: Columbia University Press, 1984), p. 26.

5 Jacqueline Rose, 'Julia Kristeva – take two', in Kelly Oliver (ed.), *Ethics, Politics, and Difference in Julia Kristeva's Writing* (London: Routledge, 1993), pp. 41–61.

6 See Marilyn Edelstein, 'Toward a feminist postmodern politique' in Oliver, *Ethics*, where she discusses Kristeva in relation to the Bakhtinian dialogic, pp. 200ff.

7 Sitwell, *Collected Poems*, p. 155.

8 Edith Sitwell, 'Some notes on my poetry', *ibid.*, pp. xv–xlvi.

9 *Ibid.*, p. xx.

10 Sitwell, *Collected Poems*, p. 16.

11 Sitwell, 'Some notes', p. xxxii.

12 *Ibid.*, p. xxxiii.

13 *Ibid.*, p. xxxi.

14 Blake Morrison, 'Queen Edith: on Edith Sitwell', *Encounter* 57.5 (1981), 93.

15 Deryn Rees-Jones, *Consorting with Angels: Essays on Modern Women Poets* (Tarset: Bloodaxe, 2005), p. 47.

16 Vincent Sherry, *The Great War and the Language of Modernism* (Oxford: Oxford University Press, 2003).

17 Debora Van Durme, 'Edith Sitwell's carnivalesque song: the hybrid music of *Facade*', *Mosaic: A Journal for the Interdisciplinary Study of Literature* 41.2 (2008), 93–110; 100, 103.

18 Sitwell, *Collected Poems*, pp. 51–109; Jane Dowson and Alice Entwistle, *A History of Twentieth-Century British Women's Poetry* (Cambridge: Cambridge University Press, 2005), p. 64.

19 Sitwell, *Collected Poems*, pp. 174–7.

20 *Ibid.*, p. 118.

21 Van Durme, 'Edith Sitwell's carnivalesque song', p. 98.

22 Romana Huk, *Stevie Smith: Between the Lines* (Basingstoke: Palgrave, 2005), p. 49.

23 Stevie Smith, *Collected Poems* (London: Allen Lane, 1975), pp. 65, 110, 112, 238, 288, 311, 536, 564.

24 Linda Anderson, 'Gender, feminism, poetry: Stevie Smith, Sylvia Plath, Jo Shapcott', in Neil Corcoran (ed.), *The Cambridge Companion to Twentieth-Century English Poetry* (Cambridge: Cambridge University Press, 2007), p. 179.

25 Peter Orr, 'Stevie Smith', in Sanford Sternlight (ed.), *In Search of Stevie Smith* (New York: Syracuse University Press, 1991), p. 32.

26 Jonathan Williams, 'Much further out than you thought', in Sternlight (ed.), *In Search*, pp. 40, 42.

27 Ian Hamilton, *Against Oblivion: Some Lives of the Twentieth-Century Poets* (London: Penguin, 2003), p. 139.

28 Christopher Ricks, 'Stevie Smith: the art of sinking in poetry', in Sternlight (ed.), *In Search*, pp. 200, 208.

29 Smith, *Collected Poems*, p. 112.
30 Terry Eagleton, 'New poetry', in Sternlight (ed.), *In Search*, p. 83.
31 Seamus Heaney, 'A memorable voice', in Sternlight (ed.), *In Search*, p. 212.
32 Huk, *Stevie Smith*, p. 36.
33 Heaney, 'A memorable voice', p. 213. See my chapter on Heaney in Ian Gregson, *The Male Image: Representations of Masculinity in Postwar Poetry* (Basingstoke: Macmillan, 1999).
34 Ian Gregson, *Character and Satire in Postwar Fiction* (London: Continuum, 2006).
35 E. H. Gombrich and E. Kris, *Caricature* (Harmondsworth: Penguin, 1940), p. 26.
36 *Ibid.*
37 Philip Larkin, 'Frivolous and vulnerable', in Sternlight (ed.), *In Search*, p. 77.
38 Huk, *Stevie Smith*, pp. 20, 238; Anderson, 'Gender, feminism, poetry,' p. 179.
39 Smith, *Collected Poems*, p. 83.
40 *Ibid.*, p. 68.
41 *Ibid.*, p. 107.
42 Dowson and Entwistle, *A History of Twentieth-Century British Women's Poetry*, p. 192.
43 Schmidt, *An Introduction*, p. 113; Sitwell, 'Some notes', p. xvii.
44 Shklovsky first set out his ideas about estrangement in 'Art as technique', published in his collection of essays, *Theory of Prose* (1925; Champaign, IL: Dalkey Archive Press, 1990).
45 Jo Shapcott, *Her Book: Poems 1988–1998* (London: Faber, 2000), pp. 69ff.
46 Selima Hill, *Gloria: Selected Poems* (Tarset: Bloodaxe, 2008), p. 112.
47 Shapcott, *Her Book*, p. 31.
48 *Ibid.*, pp. 69, 71, 72.
49 *Ibid.*, pp. 73, 109, 69.
50 Hill, *Gloria*, pp. 230–62.
51 *Ibid.*, p. 93.

3

CLAIRE BUCK

Reframing women's war poetry

In her 1975 poem 'The War Horse' (1975), Irish poet Eavan Boland (b. 1944) turns the destructive incursions of a traveller's horse blundering through a suburban garden near Dublin into a meditation on war in late twentieth-century Ireland. The horse brings 'rumour of war' into the seemingly safe world of the suburb. 'No great harm is done. / Only a leaf of our laurel hedge is torn – / Of distant interest like a maimed limb', yet the poet's home is momentarily reframed by a violence both historical and contemporary as '[t]hat rose he smashed frays / Ribboned across our hedge, recalling days / Of burned countryside. . .'.[1] Twenty years later Boland condemned her own poem for being 'public' rather than 'political'. As a public poem, Boland argued that it had acquired an unearned force, since its 'private emblems. . .almost immediately took on a communal reference against a background of communal suffering'.[2] Notably, Boland describes her poem not as a 'war poem' or even as about 'war', but as a poem about 'an intrusion of nature – the horse – menacing the decorous reductions of nature which were the gardens. And of the failure of language to describe such violence and resist it.'[3] Yet Boland puts the word 'war' in its title, and uses the poem to name the collection in which it appears. Her marked ambivalence about the act of writing a war poem tells us much about the position of the woman poet writing about war in the twentieth century. The poem, with Boland's reflection, points to ways in which women's poetry about war can expose the erasures and distortions produced by the category of war poetry itself, as well as make visible the role of war poetry as support for a specifically British history of the twentieth century organised around the First and Second World Wars.

Gender is central to Boland's searching analysis of her failure to recognise 'that I myself was a politic within the Irish poem'.[4] Retrospectively, she recognises that the poem's connections between power and order require an investigation of her own position as young woman, suburban dweller and poet in late twentieth-century Ireland. The urgency of Boland's demand on her own poem arises from the fact that gender is invisible within yet structural to 'The War Horse': invisible because gender is nowhere explicit and structural because the poet speaks from a domestic space, the suburban garden, into which the horse intrudes. War remains elsewhere, a rumour, its maimed limbs and corpses present only through the flowers that register war's violent impact on the body: 'why should we care / If a rose, a hedge, a crocus are uprooted / Like corpses, remote, crushed, mutilated?'[5] The similes emphasise the incommensurability of the domestic and war experiences, playing on the sheer impossibility of equating crocus and corpse. Boland comes tantalisingly close to revealing how the nation at war requires *and* threatens the presumed distinction between these gendered spaces. The poem's concluding link between the distant 'troubles' of early 1970s Ulster and the longer history of British colonial violence raises the question of which nation. However, without an exploration of women's relationship to both Irish and English nations, and recognition of the permeability of those national boundaries, the poem cannot question the assumptions about gender and war in which it remains caught. Instead, in 'The War Horse', Boland joins a poetic tradition in which women must write about war's violence from within the home.

We have only to turn to the recent *Oxford Handbook of British and Irish Poetry* (2007), which assigns no more than 100 of 754 pages to women's poetry, to see how persistently women poets are marginalised and erased from the history of war poetry.[6] Of thirty-seven chapters only two are exclusively devoted to women's poetry and no woman poet is the main subject of a chapter. The critical conservatism of this apparently comprehensive handbook should be astonishing in the face of the volume of feminist scholarship since the 1980s devoted to a reconsideration of gender and war. Feminists such as Sarah Ruddick in *Maternal Thinking: Towards a Politics of Peace* (1989) and Helen M. Cooper *et al.* in *Arms and the Woman* (1989) point in turn to earlier theorists such as Olive Schreiner, Virginia Woolf, Sylvia Pankhurst, Naomi Mitchison and Helena Swanwick.[7] Feminist literary critics have also changed our understanding of women's war writing, through retrieval work such as Catherine Reilly's and Anne Powell's extraordinary efforts to make available women poets from both the First and Second World Wars, and in the ways that Claire Tylee's *The Great War and Women's Consciousness* (1990), Margaret R. Higonnet's *Between the Lines* (1989), Sandra Gilbert and Susan Gubar's *No Man's Land* (1987), Janet Montefiore's *Men, Women, and the Flood of History* (1996), Phyllis Lassner's *British Women Writers of World War II* (1998), among many other works, challenge the assumption that war writing is primarily the expression of male combatant experience.[8]

This substantial body of feminist criticism makes clear that women's writing about war enlarges our understanding of war by representing the specificity of women's experience. Perhaps more important still, these critics have demonstrated war's role in the production and reproduction of gendered subjects for the nation, whether as men or women. New questions emerge about the adequacy of traditional interpretive and evaluative strategies: how have our ideas, feminist or otherwise, about the proper subjects and genres of war writing prevented us recognising important interventions by women? How has the dominance of Modernist aesthetics in the twentieth century skewed our understanding of much war poetry by women? These important questions remain, however, part of a specialist field of feminist scholarship unless we can link them to a larger re-theorisation of war in British twentieth-century historical and literary studies. Boland's struggle to write a woman's war poem about the outbreak of 'troubles' in Northern Ireland in the late 1960s from the safety of a Dublin suburb in the newly decolonised Irish republic suggests one possible approach, if we understand 'The War Horse ' as an effort to engage with what the cultural theorist Paul Virilio has called 'the military's infiltration into the movements of daily life', as opposed to 'real war', the time in which war is executed.[9] From the perspective of the colonial or postcolonial writer, conventional British spatial and period classifications of twentieth-century war – the First World War and the Second World War – operate as convenient national fictions organised around the disavowal of Britain's imperial history. Although technically outside the scope of this chapter, Boland's Irish 'troubles' with war poetry thus challenge both the apparent obviousness of when and where wars happen and an overly simple historical narrative of Britain's war writing in the twentieth century. This chapter refuses, therefore, a chronological account of women's war poetry that would reproduce such national fictions. Instead, poems conventionally treated under the headings of pre-war, inter-war and post-war are discussed in the same section, from the perspective, expressed in Virilio's term 'pure war', that peace is a time in which war is always operative as a potential threat of violence used by the state against citizens and non-citizens alike. A second section discusses under one heading poems from the two World Wars.[10]

Pure war: the time of potential war

Throughout the twentieth century, the First and Second World Wars have been essential to the imagining of a consensual community of the British nation. Stories of traumatic wounding, in for example the 'lost generation' of the 1914–18 war, and national endurance, as in the London Blitz, stand against the complicated and jarring history of Britain's political and economic decline as an empire and world power. Erased or retold as stories of national survival are: the history of Britain's violent efforts, throughout the century, to repress decolonisation movements in Ireland, India, the West Indies and Africa; its internal response to fascism through-out the thirties and in the context of post-Second World War immigration; its struggle with the economic results of that decolonisation; and the later century resistance to devolution for Scotland and Wales.[11] Despite import-ant scholarship by contemporary historians and literary critics on these marginalised histories, the treatment of the First and Second World Wars as both discrete periods and breaks between times of peace allows Britain to refuse a more complex understanding of state violence as a part of its history, internally and externally. This section looks therefore at two works that, like Boland's 'The War Horse', fall outside the conventional periods of war, existing within the liminal categories of the inter-war and post-war. Sylvia Townsend Warner in *Opus 7* (1931) and Edith Sitwell in *The Song of the Cold* (1948) both confront war's persistence in periods of peace and each evades national historical time, one through a focus on the intensely local and insignificant life of a rural woman, the other through apocalyptic myth-making.[12]

Opus 7, modelled after the eighteenth-century poet George Crabbe, is a long narrative poem about Rebecca Ransom, an impoverished drunken wreck with green fingers, who discovers that she can sell the flowers in her cottage garden to buy gin. The poem is regularly cited for the short but powerful sections that anathematise the class and imperial politics behind the First World War, so that the poem has entered the minor canon of women's war poetry. In a strikingly effective passage dominated by images of grotesque physical appetite, Warner compares the war to a 'grandees' feast', in which 'Europe feasted well: / bodies were munched in thousands, vintage blood / so blithely flowed that even the dull mud / grew greedy, and ate men'. Rebecca is one of war's victims, 'Her kin all dead. . .unpensioned, unallowanced, unsupplied', while agricultural jobs go to the land girls who 'run in breeches at [the farmer's] beck and call'. Rebecca's 'sweet flowers', seemingly impractical for one who is starving, initially represent her resist-ance to the war's gross calculations of money and lives. The war is impli-cated in Rebecca's discovery that she can turn flowers into money, since an Australian soldier introduces the idea of 'commerce' to Rebecca by asking to buy wallflowers from her cottage garden. This Anzac, embittered by the war and passionate in his rejection of colonial affiliation, further defines Warner's political interpretation of the war by tying together colonialism and capitalism: he turns his back on an England that had already nearly a century earlier transported his great-grandfather for 'firing ricks', probably as a protest against the impoverishment of agricultural labourers as a consequence of enclosure and the increasing mechanisation of agricultural work.[13]

The direct effects of the war on Rebecca's life are only one way in which Warner puts war at the heart of the poem. War seeps into the poem's imagery quite apart from any direct reference to the First World War. Rebecca views her garden 'as strategist surveys / the dedicated field of victory'. Her annuals are 'summer soldiers' and 'sixpenny squadrons', which in the face of winter's 'iron' are 'mauled and dispersed. . .their fatness to a dismal jelly turned'.[14] Warner thus weaves war into the fabric from which the poem is made. War never entirely disappears from view in the peacetime setting for Rebecca's life, but becomes a perspective on that life, as its violence and its organising systems intrude into the everyday events of the narrative.

Opus 7 does even more than name the persistence of war beyond the time of its waging. Rebecca's 'commerce' mirrors the laissez-faire capitalism to which Warner attributes the war. Driven by her desire for gin, Rebecca turns out to be a capable businesswoman, whose thoughts 'braid / themselves into an order, vivify / into a scheme, blossom, a policy'. Rebecca's commerce bears the hallmarks of capitalist enterprise, most especially in the transformation of wasteful flowers into profitable commodities, yet Warner makes excess and waste central to her poem. Gin is Rebecca's sole motivation, 'drinking flowers, Rebecca drank content', and Warner celebrates her drinking as a vivid, sensual riot in which Bacchus' leopards 'with their thick tails buffet you, and thresh / sharp waves of joy along your drowsy flesh'. Even her drunken 'frolic death', one stormy night in the village churchyard, sums up Warner's doubling of capitalist logic in Rebecca's reckless extravagance. She undermines capitalist calculations of value by turning profit into waste, pouring gin on to a new grave and attempting to out-drink God. Furthermore, Warner asks the reader to understand poetry in terms of Rebecca's perverse economics, declaring herself 'sister-soul to my slut heroine, / she to her dram enslaved, and I to mine', putting *Opus 7* on the side of waste and excess. If it belongs in the canon of women's war poetry, as much as 'Journey to Barcelona', 'Waiting at Cerbere' and 'Benicasim', Warner's accomplished poems about the Spanish Civil War, it is because *Opus 7* asks us to consider the relationships among gender, class, economics and war in a poem about the life of a poor rural woman in peacetime.[15]

Although best remembered for 'Still Falls the Rain', a poem about the London Blitz published during the Second World War, Edith Sitwell, like Warner, arguably wrote her most important poetry about war in peacetime.[16] *The Song of the Cold*, published in 1948, begins with 'Three Poems of the Atomic Age', a sequence about the dropping of atomic bombs on Hiroshima and Nagasaki in August 1945. 'Three Poems' has been interpreted in the context of Sitwell's subsequent conversion to Roman Catholicism as preoccupied with good and evil. Like 'Still Falls the Rain', 'Three Poems' uses a religious discourse of wounds and suffering in which Cain, Dives and Lazarus, together with the crucified Christ, become central figures in Sitwell's conception of the atomic bomb having ushered in a new age. However, these poems, according to Mark Morrisson, powerfully complicate 'our sense of the interaction between public and scientific cultures in the immediate post World War II era'.[17] The poem's wide-ranging citation of scientific texts dating back through nineteenth-century natural scientists, such as Haeckel, Lyell and Oken, to the seventeenth-century Burnet and sixteenth-century Paracelsus, asks the critic to meld science into a religious interpretation. Read thus, 'Three Poems' becomes a call to atomic physics to learn from earlier scientific discourses that integrate the inorganic and the organic (including the human) together. Alchemy, for example, represented in the poem through Paracelsus' integration of medicine, chemistry and cosmology, functions as an alternative paradigm rather than anachronistic metaphor. The poem's complicated ethical and intellectual engagement with science provides a substantial analysis of the paradigms underpinning science's relationship to the military-industrial complex of the twentieth century.

Sitwell's nuclear poetry paved the way for a generation of poets who grew up during and immediately after the Second World War, such as Denise Levertov, whose effort to articulate a vision of engaged anti-war poetry during the Cold War and Vietnam eras in the United States was shaped by her early experience in wartime Britain. For other poets who remained in Britain, the Cold War entailed direct engagement with Europe's role in US foreign policy, in, for example, Heather Buck's sequence 'Provençal House: 1966–1980', which weaves together events from the Second World War, Prague 1968 and the building of nuclear missile bases in the 1970s.[18] Women's 1980s anti-war protests at Greenham Common and other US airbases in Britain generated poetry in which gender and peace were intimately related, in, for example, the work of Zoe Fairbairns, Alison Fell, Pat Arrowsmith and the Irish poet Alana O'Kelly.[19]

Linking Sitwell's nuclear war poetry and Warner's localised rural anti-pastoral through their questioning of British investments in an absolute distinction between times of war and peace, allows us to see how other women's poems explore war's centrality to the organisation of national and transnational culture. Stevie Smith, for example, is recognised for her treatment of psychic and political frontiers in her thirties fiction rather than in her comic grotesque poems.[20] Yet both explore the psychic roots of political cruelty. If we resist the lure of war as historical event, then poems such as 'Bye Baby Brother', 'The Failed Spirit' and 'The Leader' take their place in Smith's continuing exploration of the individual's implication in political violence through his or her unacknowledged sadism.[21] The insistence on the unacknowledged and frequently unwelcome psychic dimensions of political events that marks Smith also fuels Sylvia Plath's highly controversial use of Holocaust imagery in poems such as 'Mary's Song' and 'Getting There', as well as her much more famous 'Daddy' and 'Lady Lazarus'.[22] Less well known is the work of Karen Gershon, Lotte Kramer and Gerda Mayer, who all came to Britain as Kinder-transportees. To write about the Holocaust, these poets have had to revise the dominant English history in which their traumatic displacement figures as 'a heroic tale of rescue and escape, rather than of irretrievable loss'.[23]

Two World Wars

The First and Second World Wars were by no means the only wars Britain fought in the twentieth century. As key components of national mythology, they are, however, central to the ways in which British women poets write about war. Moreover, as is now well recognised, British women played a central role as symbols of the nation for which their men fought. Despite women's extensive participation as war workers and as poets during both wars, their national obligation to represent the domestic heart of the nation in Britain's management of the contradictions of its war policy ensures their marginalisation in and erasure from the historical record. This has been most marked in the arena of poetry. Women contributed in significant numbers to the poetry of both wars. A quarter of the more than 2,000 poets publishing during the 1914–18 war were women, outnumbering soldier poets, who make up a fifth of the total.[24] Their poems were published in national and local newspapers, magazines and anthologies, and even printed in troop newspapers like the *Blighty*. Women poets were similarly productive during World War Two, with Catherine Reilly gathering together the work of eighty-seven poets in *Chaos of the Night: Women's Poetry and Verse of the Second World War* (1984) while Anne Powell's *Shadows of War: British Women's Poetry of the Second World War* (1999) includes 132 poets. Most of these women were publishing at the time with 'a great many' bringing out 'at least one book of poetry between 1940 and 1950'.[25] Despite their productivity, women have been significantly under-represented in general anthologies of war poetry, relegated instead to collections of women's war poetry. Literary criticism likewise consigns women's poetry from both wars to a special category, exempting critics from considering its relevance in general essays and books, despite the excellent work done on women's poetry of war by critics such as Jane Dowson, Gill Plain, Piette, Simon Featherstone, Janet Montefiore and many others.[26]

Arguments as to why women poets are marginalised in the history of the two wars are various, even within the broader framework of women's exclusion from the category of war writing itself. Women's poetry of the First World War is often seen as bad writing, complicit with pro-war patriotism, celebrating male heroism as women mourned the soldiers' slaughter, and trapped in the forms, diction and values of late Victorian and Edwardian England. Women's poetry of the Second World War, although seen as stronger, is submerged within the wider view that the poets of that war fell short compared to the tragic generation of soldier poets such as Wilfred Owen and Siegfried Sassoon. Women's war poetry in the twentieth century is in fact fatally entangled with the emergence of the iconic figure of the soldier poet who protests the wholesale slaughter of the First World War trenches. This poetic figure of angry disillusion, father to Modernist irony, is far from a complete representation of the complex formation of First World War poetry. Soldier poets, a small subset of poets writing about the war, wrote out of patriotism as much as protest. Moreover, the categories of pro- and anti-war poetry in this period are less useful than first appears because almost all poets share the rhetoric of sacrificial death, whatever their political perspective.[27] The grieving and angry soldier poet's immunity to historical accuracy testifies to his role in the national imagination, allowing the nation to elide its own external and internal violence. Sacred and pure figure of Englishness, the soldier poet sacrifices himself for the nation, even as he grieves and protests the deaths of his fellow soldiers. Women could not of course speak from this position with authenticity. Worse still, the metonymic chain of woman, home and home front turns the woman poet into the soldier poet's antithesis, in for example Owen's initial dedication of 'Dulce et Decorum Est' to 'a certain poetess', Jessie Pope, now best remembered for her jingoistic lines, 'Who's for the trench – / Are you, my laddie?'[28] Thus poetry replays in historically specific ways, throughout the century, the problem of women's ideological work for the British nation at war and the subsequent turning of the nation at war into a support for a mythologised national history.

These ideological entanglements make it tempting for feminists to point to explicitly anti-war and pacifist poetry to counter the belief that women's poetry was overwhelmingly naive and patriotic. Women were certainly active in pacifist and anti-war work through both wars, and then made poetry part of that work. The outbreak of war in 1914 proved famously divisive for the pre-war suffrage movement, with pro-war suffragists like Emmeline and Christabel Pankhurst arguing that women's contribution to the war effort could lead to the vote, as well as expand women's roles through new forms of war work. In 'Drafts', Nora Bomford demanded, 'why should men face the dark while women stay / To live and laugh and meet the sun each day'.[29] At the same time, British women contributed to international feminist anti-war work, attending The Hague Women's International Peace Conference in 1915 in the face of systematic government obstruction.[30] S. Gertrude Ford, whose 1928 poem 'The Tenth Armistice Day ' asks England to 'Give them a better monument and fitter; / Build their memorial in the League of Nations!', published an anti-war collection in 1917, *A Fight to a Finish*. The title poem pits 'War-lords', 'profiteers' and 'Armament-kings' against the silenced voices of 'the dying among the dead', 'the poor in the starveling years', 'the wounded, the maimed and blind' and 'the women'. Ford's pithy economic and political verse directly echoes the anti-war speeches of suffragists such as Sylvia Pankhurst and Helena Swanwick who argued against the war on grounds of both gender and class.[31]

Other poets, such as the prominent Scottish activist in peace organisations, Margaret Sackville (1881–1963), challenge the language used to justify war, often with a specific interest in the role of gender. Sackville's 'A Memory' confronts the reader with the public invisibility of civilian deaths:

> There was no sound at all, no crying in the village,
>   Nothing you would count as sound, that is, after the shells,
> Only behind a wall the low sobbing of women. . .

The 'two corpses. . .unburied in the street' and 'a bayoneted woman [who] stares in the market-place' could be of any nationality.[32] Nancy Cunard, who became an important journalist and commentator during the Spanish Civil War, uses macabre parody in 'Zeppelins' to invoke a link between Christian rhetoric and war propaganda. Let loose by their war enthusiasm, Death 'in his surplice' follows as 'the mad crowds ran madly up and down' caught in the air raid.[33] Valentine Ackland's 'War in Progress', her verse commentary on the Second World War, likewise explores the war's nationalistic and capitalistic dynamics, satirising the eugenic maternalism of wartime Britain: 'Drain-deep below the slums another birth / Sets angels singing – the other noise you hear / May be the warning, may be the All-Clear.' Ackland's critique still recognises the need to defeat fascism in her conclusion that her poetry could not survive a German victory: 'Stalingrad did not fall. This poem perhaps / Would have finished if that had ended.'[34] A reliance on labels such as pro- and anti-war, as Phyllis Lassner warns, 'prevents us from noticing the nuanced questions women writers asked of their own politics and participation'.[35] Lassner's advice can help us explore the significance of other women poets of the period, such as Ada Jackson, Lynette Roberts and Sheila Wingfield, who have slipped from view, despite their contemporary significance.[36]

Jackson's extraordinary long poem *Behold the Jew*, which won the Greenwood Prize in 1943 and was published in *Poetry Review*, exemplifies the political challenges that fascism presented poets. Already well known as the winner of the National Poetry Prize in 1933 for her collection *The Widow and Other Poems* (1933) and for the detailed, matter of fact evocations of fascist violence in *World in Labour* (1942), Jackson turns her hand to the modern ode in *Behold the Jew*.[37] Over about 720 lines that mix panegyric, elegy and political commentary, and personal narrative, she invokes the historic achievements of Jewish musicians, writers and scientists. These exceptional figures are matched with stories of individual Jews who have been a part of her life, ranging from Mr Isaacs the local tailor to Anna the young woman who, despite their differences of religion, culture and national origin, 'was my mirror. . .equal inches, equal years; / the same long hands and little ears'.[38] These personal stories are clearly meant to turn the Jew from alien other to a normal and valuable member of English society. Whilst Jackson cannot succeed in the face of the powerful traditions of anti-Semitic representation that insinuates itself into her poem, her mixture of personal story in the public medium of the ode is daring. The poem's public demand for the reader to recognise his or her complicity in Nazi genocide – 'While you read they die' – is underwritten by the poem's use of Anna's melodramatic and horrific death following a tram accident to reframe the narrator's private guilt, 'and if indeed it should be I / and not *my image* who must die' [my italics], with the genocidal political implications of that identification.[39]

The war poems of writers such as Ford, Sackville, Cunard, Ackland and Jackson confront recognisable issues of public concern, such as civilian deaths, genocide, the arms industry and propaganda. Poets whose approach to war is more elliptical have frequently been overlooked as war poets especially where they fall between national borders, as is the case with H.D. and Mina Loy. Although an American, H.D. lived her entire adult life in Europe and spent both wars in London. Much of H.D.'s later poetry, in particular *Trilogy* (1944–6) and *Helen in Egypt* (1952), directly addresses questions of militarism and gender through a combination of contemporary details, 'rails gone (for guns)', spiritual vision and myth, most especially in her extended exploration of the stories surrounding Helen of Troy. It is only comparatively recently that the engagement with war in her earlier Imagist poems has been recognised.[40] The classical settings and references for the poems in *Sea Garden* (1916) seem to distance the war, but the relationship between violence and the male body threads through the text.

Mina Loy's wartime work, written before her emigration to the United States, is similarly not easily recognisable as First World War poetry, yet, as Simon Featherstone persuasively argues, her 1917 'Songs to Joannes' powerfully explores the 'ways in which human intimacy was invaded by the forces and the language of a new kind of violence in Europe'.[41] For example, heterosexual desires and war are engaged in the 'irresolvable' ambiguity that Loy creates by dropping the phrase 'humid carnage' into a scene of intense sexual pleasure.[42] Featherstone proposes a poetics of ambiguity and indirection, represented by writers such as Loy, Gertrude Stein and E. J. Scovell, as the basis for reconfiguring the category of war poetry itself. However, as he privileges 'indirection' over direct commentary in his revision of the category of female war poetry, the larger body of women's First and Second World War poetry is effectively re-marginalised, as part of a feminist cultural history rather than mainstream literary history.

By far the majority of women poets during both wars wrote elegies for dead soldiers. To the consternation of later critics, women poets repeatedly situate themselves in a feminised and domestic role, thus continuing the popular nineteenth-century tradition of the patriotic sentimental elegy, represented most famously by Felicia Hemans.[43] Even Vera Brittain, who worked as a VAD throughout the war, devotes almost all of her *Poems of a VAD* to mourning her fiancé, brother and other close male friends who died in the war, writing little about her own and other women's work despite the title's implied promise.[44] However, the assumption that these twentieth-century elegies are private, and therefore typically feminine expressions of grief, has misrepresented the way in which women engage this poetic tradition. Rather than a disposable addendum, women's elegy is a fundamental part of the history of British poetry. These elegies produce and reproduce ideas about women in a time of war, as well as managing contradictions between women's war work outside the home and their proper domestic femininity. More fundamentally, women's war elegy stages the feminine and domestic space of the home as the heart of the nation, rather than as a private space, making female poetic mourning an important ideological component for the nation at war. Women's mourning converts the soldier's violent actions on behalf of the state into pure and sacred sacrifice by the private individual for the nation, as he is received back into the home/heart of the nation.[45] As Tricia Lootens' ground-breaking work on nineteenth-century women's poetry shows us, the woman's elegy, understood in its patriotic as well as domestic dimension, plays an important role in investing the British soldier with national meaning.[46] The category of war poetry, as it emerges out of the First World War wedded to the soldier poet, thus depends on the necessarily unacknowledged ideological grief work of the sentimental elegy.

Since war poetry requires the domestic elegy, it is not surprising to find women poets struggling with the elegy. Illustrative here is one of Scovell's most anthologised war poems, 'An Elegy'. Scovell strives to write an elegy to '[fit] this time and nation' in the tradition of the national domestic: 'The quiet days before the snow, / The child's feet on the yellowing grass – / How can I make a rite of these / To mourn the pang I do not know. . .'[47] Scovell's strengths as a war poet rely on showing 'that the domestic and the local' are not 'comforting escapes . . . but . . . necessary parts of the wider experience of that catastrophe'.[48] In 'An Elegy', the maternal domestic operates as a separate privatised and individualised sphere from which she could construct a mourning ritual that really might purify the nation: 'Take as my rite this winter tune: / The child's walk in the darkening afternoon.'[49] Scovell's problem is not, as Featherstone has suggested, the explicit articulation of questions about war, but her uncharacteristic failure to question the nature of the relationship between domestic and national. But, to recognise this problem we have to understand that the domestic space from which the woman speaks with authority is never private or individual.

There are plenty of examples of poems where the national work is explicit, in for example Marjorie Wilson's 1919 elegy addressed to her three-year-old son at bedtime on the subject of his dead father. The husband's death is recalled as a sacrifice that 'win[s] that heritage of peace' for his son and the 'quiet fields' of a pastoral England.[50] Even the most seemingly private elegies do national work. In 'Easter Monday', Eleanor Farjeon locates her poem about Edward Thomas' death in wartime domestic routine. Grief is registered through the intimacy of their correspondence, using details from Thomas' last letter about a gift of apples and an Easter egg. But of course the poem links the domestic to a Christian pastoral of promised resurrection, albeit painfully ambivalent, as the morning ritual of sowing 'our earliest seeds' is set against the evening news of Thomas' death. As death breaks the intimacy of their correspondence, 'There are three letters that you will not get', Farjeon translates its privacies into a public elegy in which the sacred and natural dimensions of the domestic do national work.[51]

Elegy became increasingly fraught, however, as government propaganda, which explicitly named a national effort and a home-front, co-opted the domestic. Home could no longer function as the pure and sacred site to which men return, whether as demobilised soldiers, corpses or ghosts. Instead it became a site of war. Even so, many women's war elegies conform to this tradition of the national domestic, in for example poems by Constance Scott, Marie Stopes and Molly Holden responding to naval defeats, or in elegies for RAF pilots, the new national heroes, such as Patricia Ledward's 'In Memoriam' and Wrenne Jarman's 'In Memoriam: Richard Hillary RAFVR'.[52] We also see the national elegy reworked for regional purposes, as in the case of the Welsh poet Brenda Chamberlain, who begins her elegy 'For Alun' with words from the poet Alun Lewis' last letter promising to walk with her on the Welsh hills, 'in flesh or ghost'. This promise allows Chamberlain in a seemingly private expression of grief to bring Lewis home – in spirit if not body – from the 'orange grove' and 'blood hibiscus' of India, where lies the 'earth-resting body / of Alun, son of the grey Valleys'. The poem cleanses Lewis of 'war's dirt' through the poet's 'tidal tears' and his 'homing spirit smiles through mountain rain'. While she does not invoke a rhetoric of sacrifice, Chamberlain certainly nationalises the death of the 'dreaming poet, / Lover and soldier'.[53] She uses elegy to create emotional and potentially political links between the distant grave in colonial India and the home country – links strikingly similar to those made in Hemans' 'England's Dead', even if Chamberlain's hills are Welsh, not English.[54]

The scale and effects of the Blitz on civilian Britain, ranging from direct experience of war deaths to the mass evacuation of children out of the larger cities, made the domestic a new resource for women's poetry and for the elegy during the Second World War. Many Second World War women poets, such as Pamela Holmes, Naomi Mitchison, Scovell, Stopes, Joy W. Trindle and Dorothy Wellesley, wrote poems for the civilian dead, some of which make the elegy the basis for questioning and even resisting the gendered national work demanded of the feminine domestic. Mitchison, for example, takes on the traditional voice of the mother to mourn two very different deaths, of her own baby daughter, Clemency Ealasaid, who died the day after her birth on 4 July 1940, and of a young Scottish poet, Jim McKinven, whose death in a Glasgow air raid becomes the occasion for a specifically Scottish history of war deaths.[55] Mitchison is much better known as a novelist and memoirist whose *The Moral Basis of Politics* (1938) locates her as a socialist and feminist commentator to rival Woolf in *Three Guineas* (1939).[56] Much of her poetry remains uncollected so that a handful of war poems anthologised in *Shadows* and *Chaos of the Night* may be her best-known works as a poet.

The reach of 'Clemency Ealasaid ' is most fully visible if the poem is read at the intersection of the female elegy with Mitchison's poetic and political commitments to socialism in the thirties. Mitchison sets against the public events of the war the insignificant death of her daughter, 'a small weight' buried at sea, within sight of her house, in Carradale Bay. This strategy of putting the newborn baby in the scales against the 'Harvest of dead babies, disease, hatred' and 'The tortured in the concentration camps' would seem doomed. Yet, Mitchison manages to explore and make complex the relationship of feeling to political events. In the second verse, the speaker uses the political rhetoric of socialism to castigate herself for this private grief: 'Thinking of these things, wrongly, archaically, personally, / I must retract, I must say to myself / She was not yet human, not individual, cannot be lonely. . .' This rational logic is set against the resistance of her maternal and domestic grief, but also cultural bogey men such as the Norwegian 'Boyg in the Dovrefelt', who 'Still remains above half-starved, half-beaten Norway, / And will remain'.[57] Projections of sentiment, Mitchison tells us, return in the figures of history.

Mitchison does not, however, rest content with her rejection of a rational political discourse of the left. Her initial evocation of the intimate details that speak to her of the dead child, 'the woolly coats and the vests' and 'the old cot with the new green blankets', as well as the memory of the 'new dark soft head, the faint breathing, the warmth and love', represent a nationalised domestic. But, as she reaches out to the idea of a Europe in ruins, the politics of economics and war complicate the potential identification through the maternal so central to female elegy. Motherhood suggests self-interest as well as empathy, 'clutching out for lives on the spread bargain counter', as Mitchison yearns to keep her other children safe. Her reference to those in concentration camps, 'Who thought themselves safe' but 'have been betrayed to the vultures', questions the illusion of safety conjured through domestic imagery. Emotion is both essential and subject to political vicissitudes. The maternal, which also frames military and civilian war deaths in the poem, whether the dead 'sailors at Oran' or the babies dying of cold and hunger in 'France, Belgium, Holland, Denmark, Norway, Poland', can lead to hatred as much as understanding: 'If my baby had been starved by England, would I ever forgive? / Roll up the map of Europe.' In long Auden-influenced lines, Mitchison shifts between intellectual scrutiny and the rocking rhythms associated with the baby, its sea-grave, and the 'strong current' of time and history in which everything 'Will be forgotten, with other evil things, will be interpreted, / Will be forgiven at last'.[58] Mitchison powerfully dramatises what her poem demands: in order to rescue emotion from the marginal and privatised domestic, without giving in to the violent rationalisations of reason, the entanglements of feeling and reason require scrutiny.

Conclusion

Between 2006 and 2008 ten well-known poets and critics, including Sandra Gilbert, Eavan Boland, Gail Holst-Warhaft, Marilyn Hacker and Alicia Ostriker, participated in the Poetry Foundation's online forum, responding to the question: 'Can poetry console a grieving public?'[59] The essays reflect on whether or how poetry might play a role in giving voice to a grief that is in some way communal and collective, whether arising from genocide, war, the events of 9/11 or AIDS. Threading through these reflections, regardless of the writer's position on the question, is a persistent anxiety about the way poetry can be co-opted and contaminated if it takes on a public role. The danger is not the same for each writer: for some, poetry's contact with commercial media makes mourning conventional and sentimental. Others, like Jahan Ramazani, fear the power of governments and commercial media to 'rationalize death by countenancing the rebirth of the dead in nature, divinity, the nation, or even poetry itself'.[60] These are important concerns, but they presume that poetic elegy should give some kind of authentic and pure form to grief, whether in Hacker's words to 'preserve a "personhood", that is apart from the public sphere', or to 'finger the communal wounds of grief without closing them up' in order to resist death's rationalisation.[61] Mitchison, in her elegy for Clemency, knew better. These twenty-first-century writers rely on a division between public and private spheres, which lends both poetry and emotion an imaginary authenticity through association with the private. Mitchison dismantles this fiction as the condition of writing poetry about war. The study of British women poets who struggled to give poetic expression to war in the twentieth century is not an optional annexe to the history of war writing. It allows us to comprehend and disrupt relationships between poetry and war, which are foundational for British national history.

Notes

1 Eavan Boland, *Collected Poems* (Manchester: Carcanet Press, 1995), p. 28.
2 Eavan Boland, *Object Lessons: The Life of the Woman and the Poet in Our Time* (Manchester: Carcanet Press, 1995), p. 177.
3 *Ibid.*, p. 176.
4 *Ibid.*, p. 179.
5 Boland, *Collected Poems*, p. 28.

6 Tim Kendall (ed.), *The Oxford Handbook of British and Irish War Poetry* (Oxford: Oxford University Press, 2007).

7 Sarah Ruddick, *Maternal Thinking: Towards a Politics of Peace* (Boston: Beacon Press, 1989); Helena M. Cooper, Adrienne Auslander Munich and Susan Merrill Squier (eds.), *Arms and the Woman* (Chapel Hill: University of North Carolina Press, 1989); Olive Schreiner, *Women and Labour* (1911; London: Virago, 1978); Virginia Woolf, *Three Guineas* (London: Hogarth Press, 1938); Sylvia Pankhurst, *The Home Front* (London: Hutchinson, 1932); Naomi Mitchison, *The Moral Basis of Politics* (London: Constable and Co., 1938); Helena Swanwick, *The War in its Effect on Women: and Women and War*, ed. Blanche Wiesen Cook (New York: Garland Press, 1971).

8 Catherine Reilly (ed.), *Scars upon My Heart: Women's Poetry and Verse of the First World War* (London: Virago, 1981); Catherine Reilly (ed.), *Chaos of the Night: Women's Poetry and Verse of the Second World War* (London: Virago, 1984); Anne Powell (ed.), *Shadows of War: British Women's Poetry of the Second World War* (Stroud: Sutton Publishing, 1999).

9 Steve Redhead (ed.), *The Paul Virilio Reader* (New York: Columbia University Press, 2004), p. 55.

10 *Ibid.*, p. 47.

11 For a good account see Eric Hobsbawm, *The Age of Extremes: A History of the World, 1914–1991* (New York: Pantheon Books, 1990).

12 Sylvia Townsend Warner, *Collected Poems* (Manchester: Carcanet, 1982), pp. 195–230; Edith Sitwell, *The Song of the Cold* (New York: Vanguard, 1948), pp. 11–21.

13 Warner, *Collected Poems*, pp. 198, 199, 200.

14 *Ibid.*, pp. 204, 201.

15 *Ibid.*, pp. 201, 217, 205, 35–7.

16 Reilly (ed.), *Chaos of the Night*, pp. 114–15.

17 Mark Morrisson, 'Edith Sitwell's atomic bomb poems: alchemy and scientific reintegration', *Modernism/Modernity*, 9.4 (2002), 605–33; 605.

18 Heather Buck, *The Sign of the Water Bearer* (London: Anvil Press, 1987), pp. 18–23.

19 For an excellent discussion of these poets see Adam Piette, 'Pointing to east and west: British Cold War poetry', in Kendall (ed.), *Oxford Handbook*, pp. 646–8.

20 Janet Montefiore, *Men and Women Writers of the 1930s: The Dangerous Flood of History* (London: Routledge, 1996), pp. 68–70, 129–32.

21 Stevie Smith, *Collected Poems* (New York: New Directions, 1983), pp. 144, 218, 289.

22 Sylvia Plath, *Collected Poems* (London: Faber, 1981), pp. 257, 247, 244; *Ariel* (London: Faber, 1965), pp. 54–6.

23 Claire M. Tylee, 'British Holocaust poetry: songs of experience', in Kendall (ed.), *Oxford Handbook*, p. 607.

24 Catherine Reilly, *English Poetry of the First World War: A Bibliography* (London: George Prior, 1978); Reilly (ed.), *Scars upon My Heart*, p. xxxiv.

25 Powell (ed.), *Shadows of War*, p. xx.

26 Simon Featherstone, 'Women's poetry of the First and Second World Wars', in Kendall (ed.), *Oxford Handbook*, pp. 445–60; Stacy Gillis, ' "Many Sisters to Many Brothers": the women poets of the First World War', in Kendall (ed.),

Oxford Handbook, pp. 100–13. See also Joan Montgomery Byles, *War, Women and Poetry, 1914–1945* (Newark: University of Delaware Press, 1995); Dorothy Goldman (ed.), *Women and World War 1: The Written Response* (Basingstoke: Macmillan, 1993); Gill Plain, '"Great Expectations": rehabilitating the recalcitrant war poets', *Feminist Review* 51 (Autumn 1995), 41–65; Nosheen Kahn, *Women's Poetry of the First World War* (London: Harvester, 1988).

27 Elizabeth Marsland, *The Nation's Cause: French, English and German Poetry of the First World War* (London: Routledge, 1991), p. 157.

28 Reilly (ed.), *Scars upon My Heart*, p. 88.

29 *Ibid.*, p. 12.

30 Byles, *War, Women and Poetry*, pp. 17–32.

31 Reilly (ed.), *Scars upon My Heart*, p. 38.

32 Margaret Sackville, *Pageant of War* (London: Simpkin, Marshall, Hamilton, Kent & Co., 1916), p. 3; Reilly (ed.), *Scars upon My Heart*, p. 95.

33 Reilly (ed.), *Scars upon My Heart*, p. 26.

34 Powell (ed.), *Shadows of War*, p. 75.

35 Phyllis Lassner, *British Women Writers of World War II: Backgrounds of Their Own* (London: St Martin's Press, 1998), p. 8.

36 For fuller discussion of these poets see Jane Dowson and Alice Entwistle, *A History of Twentieth-Century British Women's Poetry* (Cambridge: Cambridge University Press, 2005), pp. 43–57.

37 *Ibid.*, pp. 25, 50.

38 Ada Jackson, *Behold the Jew* (New York: Macmillan, 1944), p. 16.

39 *Ibid.*, p. 18.

40 H.D., *Trilogy* (Manchester: Carcanet, 1973), p. 3. See Gary Burnett, 'A poetics out of war: H.D.'s responses to the First World War', *Agenda* 25.3–4 (Autumn–Winter 1987–8), 54–63; Claire Buck, '"This Other Eden": homoeroticism and the Great War in the early poetry of H.D. and Radclyffe Hall', in Ann Ardis and Leslie W. Lewis (eds.), *Women's Experience of Modernity* (Baltimore: Johns Hopkins University Press, 2003), pp. 63–80.

41 Featherstone, 'Women's Poetry', p. 450.

42 Mina Loy, 'Songs to Joannes', in *The Lost Lunar Baedeker*, ed. Roger L. Conover (Manchester: Carcanet, 1997), p. 53.

43 See Tricia Lootens, 'Hemans and home: Victorianism, feminine "Internal Enemies", and the domestication of national identity', *PMLA* 109.2 (March 1994), 238–53.

44 Vera Brittain, *Poems of a VAD* (London: Macdonald, 1918).

45 Lootens, 'Hemans and home', p. 242.

46 *Ibid.*, and Tricia Lootens 'Victorian poetry and patriotism,' in Joseph Bristow (ed.), *The Cambridge Companion to Victorian Poetry* (Cambridge: Cambridge University Press, 2000), pp. 255–79.

47 Powell (ed.), *Shadows of War*, p. 194.

48 Featherstone, 'Women's poetry', p. 460.

49 Powell (ed.), *Shadows of War*, p. 194.

50 Reilly (ed.), *Scars upon My Heart*, p. 130.

51 *Ibid.*, p. 36.

52 Powell (ed.), *Shadows of War*, pp. 129, 142, 149, 139, 201.

53 *Ibid.*, p. 255.

54 Felicia Hemans, *Siege of Valencia* (New York: Garland, 1978), pp. 308–10.
55 Powell (ed.), *Shadows of War*, pp. 62–5, 102–3.
56 Lassner, *Women Writers*, p. 71.
57 Powell (ed.), *Shadows of War*, p. 63.
58 *Ibid.*, pp. 62, 64, 63.
59 Available, www.poetryfoundation.org/journal/article.html?id=178622
60 Available, www.poetryfoundation.org/journal/article.html?id=178621
61 Available, www.poetryfoundation.org/journal/article.html?id=178619

4

WILLIAM MAY

Verbal and visual art in twentieth-century British women's poetry

This sketch / became a simile. . .
(Liz Lochhead)[1]

In the eponymous poem in Carol Ann Duffy's 1985 collection *Standing Female Nude*, the female subject describes herself being painted. She imagines her future as an art object to be discussed and analysed in museums, and comments wryly on the gap between her world of Parisian prostitution and the bourgeois perspective of the man who paints her. The last withering put-down – 'It does not look like me'[2] – signals a failure of representation; a school of painting often associated with heightened realism is rewritten as a process of appropriation and disfigurement. The poem both resists and underlines what, for many, is a truism of Western portrait painting. As John Berger has argued in *Ways of Seeing*:

> According to usage and conventions which are at last being questioned but have by no means been overcome – *men act* and *women appear*. Men look at women. Women watch themselves being looked at . . . and are always depicted in a different way to men – because the 'ideal' spectator is always assumed to be male and the image of the women is designed to flatter him.[3]

Berger's thesis suggests that the way we read Titian's *Venus of Urbino* (1538) or Vermeer's *The Milkmaid* (c.1658) is less a subjective or contextual response than a product of highly codified social and sexual dynamics. The notion of a female portrait embodies how women have been, and continue to be, viewed and objectified by a male society. Berger's argument has a particular relevance for ekphrastic poetry, verse which makes verbal portraits from visual ones. Although rarely identified as such, this poetic tradition is as gender-specific as its painterly counterpart. This chapter, drawing on visual theory, will explore how twentieth-century British female poets as diverse as Stevie Smith (1902–71), Lynette Roberts (1909–95) and Liz Lochhead (1947–) have reshaped the ekphrastic genre for their own ends.

Traditional poems of the ekphrastic genre set up a tension between looking and reading, the male of act of reading further objectifying the female verbally represented on the page. Alexander Pope's 'Epistle to a Lady' (1743) is in part a poem taking sides in the competitive battle between visual and verbal art, but one that seems ambivalent as to whether its target is women or the male depiction of them:

> How many pictures of one Nymph we view,
> All how unlike each other, all how true!
>
>   . . .
>
> Let then the Fair one beautifully cry,
> In Magdalen's loose hair and lifted eye,
> Or drest in smiles of sweet Cecilia shine,
> With simp'ring Angels, Palms, and Harps divine;
> Whether the Charmer sinner it, or saint it,
> If Folly grows romantic, I must paint it.
>
> Come then, the colours and the ground prepare!
> Dip in the Rainbow, trick her off in Air,
> Chuse a firm Cloud, before it fall, and in it
> Catch, e'er she change, the Cynthia of this minute.   (lines 5–6, 11–20)[4]

Here, the poem's speaker suggests both a compulsive need to objectify and represent ('I must paint it') and also distances himself from the efficacy of a static visual portrait ('how unlike each other'). Paintings and femininity make an unsteady match both because of the limitation of the art form and the apparent capriciousness of the female character. In a poem written in tribute to Pope's friend Martha Blount, the only way he can praise her is by denigrating the host of female archetypes decorating the gallery walls. Here Pope enacts a process of double-objectification, identifying the paintings as inert canvases yet simultaneously reifying their status as iconic images of womanhood. As the extract above suggests, the male ekphrastic poet assumes a male audience just as the portrait painter does, even if, as in this case, the poem's addressee is female.

The lineage and language of the ekphrastic poem reaffirm the sense of women as objects and men as their conspiratorial audience. In Shelley's 'On the Medusa of Leonardo Da Vinci in the Florentine Gallery' (1819), the poet finds in the tangle of snakes and degradation an

>   ever-shifting mirror
> Of all the beauty and the terror there –
> A woman's countenance, with serpent locks,
> Gazing in death on Heaven from those wet rocks.[5]   (lines 37–40)

Although the painting in question, *The Head of Medusa* (*c*.1600),[6] shows its Gorgon subject looking skywards rather than towards the viewer, the iconology of the Medusa makes the female face into a site of horror. Once again, the surveyed woman is either elevated to become a goddess or debased into the grotesque. Even a poem like Keats' 'Ode on a Grecian Urn' (1819), which addresses an art object, makes its apostrophe to an imagined female addressee: 'Thou still unravish'd bride of quietness'.[7] The inference is that through writing his ekphrastic poem, Keats will deflower this virginal and silent 'bride', making sex (poetry) from death (the urn).

Theories of how the visual and verbal might counteract or interact with each other are as old as poetry or painting itself. From Horace's notion of 'Ut pictura poesis' (what is true of a painting is true of a poem) to more recent attempts to set the two media in opposition, notions of resemblance, equivalence and hierarchy have continued to dominate interdisciplinary methodologies. Yet despite the prevalent notion of the male gaze in cultural studies over the last thirty years, there has been a reluctance to make the battle between the arts into a battle of the sexes. The sense of the ekphrastic process being about male control and re-ownership of the female depicted in the art work – or even about control of the female art work itself in Keats' case – is only hinted at in W.J.T. Mitchell's 1994 *Picture Theory: Essays on Verbal and Visual Representation*. It is a dynamic that seems to make Mitchell wary; whilst he links the 'fear of literary emulation of the visual arts' to the notion of 'castration', he asserts that 'female otherness is an overdetermined feature in a genre that tends to describe an object of visual pleasure and fascination from a masculine perspective, often to an audience understood to be masculine as well'. Overdetermined or even inevitable as it may be in a predominantly male tradition, Mitchell's own description of ekphrasis becomes suggestively and then explicitly gendered before he too, as if giving in to Pope's need to obsessively describe the very paintings he rejects, imagines 'the male poet or reader fondling the mental image of ekphrasis, indulging the pleasures of voyeurism, actual or remembered'.[8] Here the ekphrastic act itself, like the female subject of the art work, becomes objectified, appropriated, pored over. It is set up as a fetishistic and highly self-aware genre. Other studies of ekphrastic poetry, such as James A.W. Hefferman's *Museum of Words: the Poetics of Ekphrasis from Homer to Ashbery*, attempt to set up an alternative to what Hefferman describes as 'the formidable tradition' of male ekphrasis, but do so by focusing on the few female characters in canonical ekphrastic texts who are permitted to tell their own story.[9] In Ovid's *Metamorphoses* Book VI, for example, Philomela's weaving tells of her own rape by Tereus, thereby regaining narrative control of the ekphrastic act of ravishment. Yet if Hefferman identifies a counter-tradition, he situates it within the context of an exclusively male poetic canon. The work of a range of twentieth-century British women poets suggests that, if gender and ekphrasis are overdetermined partners, unpicking the assumptions of that union is equally necessary and inevitable.

The female writer's re-examination of painting's assumptions and expectations is not limited to the twentieth century. In *Villette* (1853), Charlotte Brontë created a heroine, Lucy Snowe, who was able to dismiss the female archetypes in a Flemish gallery as 'insincere, ill-humoured, bloodless, brainless nonentities'[10] and Elizabeth Barrett Browning in *Aurora Leigh* (1856) was similarly deliberate in setting up a verbal picture that aspired less towards the public gallery than 'a portrait for a friend, / Who keeps it in a drawer' (I, lines 5–6).[11] Yet the interdisciplinary push of Modernist experiment and the new possibilities offered by cinema and photography meant that poets as diverse as Stevie Smith, Lynette Roberts and Liz Lochhead seemed particularly conscious of the visual as a category where they might both draw attention to and escape the label of 'women' writers. The status of all three as artists (Smith accompanied her poems with sketchy illustrations, Roberts painted Primitivist domestic scenes throughout her career and Lochhead studied at the Glasgow School of Art) makes a sustained focus on their work usefully illustrative of wider trends in women's ekphrastic poetry of the period.

Memos on the male tradition: Liz Lochhead

Of the three poets, it is Lochhead who most deliberately engages with and attempts to rewrite the male ekphrastic tradition. Her art training, and her subsequent period as an art teacher both in Glasgow and Bristol, found her continually questioning her own inculcation into a particular Western tradition. Her stubborn resistance to that tradition is captured in the early poem 'Object' from *Memo for Spring* (1972), where the process of female portrait-making is continually refracted. The poem splits into two halves; the first has its subject as she is being painted imagine the difficulties she poses for the artist, whilst the second takes in her own nomadic perspective as an artist's model:

> I, love,
> am capable of being looked at
> from many different angles. This
> is your problem.
> In this cold north light it may
> seem clear enough.
> You pick your point of view
> and stick to it, not veering much –

this
being the only way to make any sense of me
as a formal object. Still
I do not relish it, being
stated so – my edges defined
elsewhere than I'd imagined them
with a crispness I do not possess.
The economy of your line does not spare me
by its hairsbreadth.[12]   (lines 1–17)

The speaking subject makes the problem of representation one facing the artist rather than the sitter – the model's character is 'your problem', an aggressive challenge to the formal certainties of the picture. The poem's opening also sets up a dialogue between sketch and text, always suggesting that the sitter's verbal description might outdo that of the artist. The flat verb of 'state' equates the picture with the legal or the journalistic rather than the poetic; the portrait's 'economy' of line hints it is governed by a constraint that does not trouble the poet being drawn, whose bold free verse expands and contracts to follow the train of her wandering thoughts. Lochhead co-opts the competitive verbal–visual debate into a gendered one, as the distracted and irritable sitter notices 'a woman in an overall' out of the corner of her eye. Here, by inference, is a verbal description without an agenda, not bound to the rigid dictates of canvas and perspective. Rather than re-objectify through the ekphrastic genre, Lochhead unpicks the process, making the act of objectification the subject of the poem. As the poem's speaker notes, the female subject is 'at once / reduced and made more of' via the artist's attempt at exact representation.[13]

Lochhead's identification of the reductions and elevations suffered by women in art runs through much of her poetic output. In her triptych poem series 'The Furies', she once again sets out a double-edged response to a painting, in this instance Pieter Brueghel's *Dulle Griet* (1562). The narrative vitality of Brueghel's work has made him a popular ekphrastic subject for modern poets from W.H. Auden to William Carlos Williams, but here Lochhead turns away from the storytelling tendencies of the subgenre. The painting depicts Dulle Griet or 'Mad Meg', the figure of Flemish folklore who, according to the proverb, could plunder in front of hell and remain unscathed. With her jumble of pots and pans, she leads a group of female revellers across the canvas, as the jaws of apocalypse loom in the far upper right of the painting. Her obliviousness suggests both obduracy and the superficial: even as judgement day comes, she remains the acquisitive domestic scourge.

The primary response to this figure in Lochhead's poem is academic, and attempts to situate the painting in its historical context:

> Mad Meg on my mantelpiece,
> Dulle Griet by Brueghel, a Flemish masterpiece,
> in anybody's eyes. 'Well worth consideration'
> was how I looked at it. The surrealist tradition
> from Bosch to Magritte is such a Flemish thing![14]   (lines 1–5)

Yet the half-rhyme between 'mantelpiece' and 'masterpiece' suggests a bifurcated response, split with domestic appropriation of the image. There is a similar opposition between the subjective view of the painting (with the inert metaphor of 'how I looked at it') versus the received opinion ('in anybody's eyes'). If the speaker at first puts the painting at the service of a stable Western tradition – the speaker chooses it 'for my History of Art essay' – those opening tensions between the domestic and the academic suggest a fear of true engagement with the work.[15] The poem, like 'Object', instead moves us away from a conditioned response to Mad Meg to a subjective empathy for her:

> Oh that kitchen knife, that helmet, that silent shout,
> I knew Meg from the inside out.
> All she owns in one arm, that lost look in her eyes.
> These days I more than sympathise.[16]   (lines 18–21)

The painting, in the final analysis, elicits more than sympathy, and rather than provide the female viewer with another unflattering archetype as in *Villette*, offers an emotional outlet.[17] The poem itself, rather than performing ekphrastic double-objectification, individualises Mad Meg, unframing her folklore to assess her significance for contemporary women.

As well as reviewing the depiction of women throughout art history, Lochhead's work also grapples with how a contemporary female visual artist might respond to that tradition. In 'Notes on the Inadequacy of a Sketch at Millport Cathedral, March 1970' she puts her own drawing under the critical microscope, the competitive energy of ekphrasis here given a new emphasis by virtue of the poem assessing both itself and its subject as a point of enquiry. Yet the problems of reduction and symbolic formal choices that plagued 'Object' resurface here:

> I selected what seemed to be essentials.
> Here, where wind and rain
> made a scapegoat of a scarecrow, my pen
> took it for an easy symbol. But its plain
> setting down in black and white
> wasn't enough. Nor underlining
> certain subtleties. This sketch became
> a simile at best. It's no metaphor.[18]   (lines 35–42)

The visual offers a failed figurative language, a tentative facsimile rather than a transformative work of mimesis. The metaphoric becomes the mode to which all art aspires. Agency in the poem shifts from the artist to their instrument – 'my pen / took it for an easy symbol' – yet the work remains a curatorial apology. It suggests the verbal as a medium of revision, of allowing us to reconfigure visual approximations. Yet if Lochhead takes the visual to task here, the accusations made of her sketch might be made of the poem, too, whose formless 'notes' give us a verbal counterpoint to the messy and anomalous 'sketch'. The lengthy poem is full of parentheses and broken syntax – the form of the sentence itself apparently as constricting as the rectangular landscape page. Lochhead's admission of this difficulty comes with the poem's final lines:

> From my quick calligraphy of trees
> no real loud rooks catcall the sea's
> cold summersalt.[19]   (lines 52–54)

Whilst we are offered yet another equivocation on her sketch, the final 'summersalt' pun is specifically graphic in nature. Even as Lochhead suggests the limitations of the visual, she works to bring the aesthetic to bear on her own writing. It is a literal summersault then, turning the hierarchical (and, by inference, male) jousting of the visual and verbal into a union offering complementary symbiosis.

These enriching possibilities are restated with defiance in Lochhead's rousing tributes to her contemporary female Scottish artists.[20] 'Warpaint and Woman Flesh' is dedicated to the painter Lys Hansen (1956–), best known for her Guernica-like depictions of the Irish conflict, or her Cubist-influenced portrait paintings such as *The Divided Self* (1985). The latter is a telling work, offering a triptych of female body parts suggesting Picasso's *Les Mademoiselles d'Avignon* (1914), yet with particularly feminist objectives. It is this politicised art that Lochhead celebrates in her poem:

> because the lady can bellylaugh
> because the lady's got guts
> because the lady's not for turning
> because of the good times
> because of the war crimes
> because of the iron maiden
> because of the presidential wink
> because of everything except the kitchen sink
> Lys Hansen must be always painting.   (lines 52–60)[21]

In Lochhead's paean of praise, the history of Western painting necessitates Hansen's work rather than overshadows it, the final imperative – 'Lys

Hansen must be always painting' – offering a corrective to Pope's 'I must paint it'. Rather than paint from an obsessive need to objectify and control, Hansen's imperative stems from political compulsion. In this instance, Lochhead cannot offer the verbal equivalent of Hansen's vivid canvases and does not attempt to, creating her poem as a personal gift rather than gauntlet thrown down in challenge. The painting provokes rather than prevents a response from its female audience.

The leica-memory: Stevie Smith's illustrated poetry

Stevie Smith's poem 'Salon d'Automne', meanwhile, seems to return to Lucy Snowe's Flemish gallery in *Villette*, dismissing an exhibition of nude female painting as 'pedantic and unsympathetic'.[22] Yet the poem's bristling indignance is atypical. If Lochhead sets up a neat paradigm with her sustained and deliberate engagement with the tradition of Western painting, poet, novelist and illustrator Stevie Smith provides a counterpoint that is at once messier and more contrived.[23] Her poem 'Deeply Morbid ' tells of a secretary who is whisked off to a magical land via a Turner painting in the National Gallery. This disorientating combination of death and whimsy is typical of Smith, yet the poem's contest between Joan's monotonous world of type and the ineffable possibilities of a painted sky suggests a further link between the mixed-media subject of the poem and its disjunctive tonal shifts. Smith's insistence on publishing her poems with doodled illustrations throughout her career, even when that meant changing publisher, suggests a tenacious commitment to her own art. Yet if Lochhead's poetry releases female art objects and rewrites them as individuals, Smith feared that her work and public persona itself might become objectified and identified as an easily identifiable type. Through various eccentric interventions in her critical reception, from self-written reviews to off-kilter public performances, she worked hard to make her oeuvre a process rather than a product. Her various engagements with art throughout her career reveal the extent of her anxiety about how she might be read, and, more importantly, how the visual might conceal that same anxiety.

In an early essay, 'Art ' (1937), Smith offers a quixotic description of the National Gallery, prompting her to ask the question 'how do people see pictures?'. In typically bathetic fashion, she goes on to avoid answering, qualifying her interrogative by noting 'it was such a hot afternoon' and 'the question is such a lazy one'.[24] This dismissal belies the importance of this question to her work as well as suggesting her ambivalence about posing it. Galleries, paintings and art critics haunt her three autobiographical novels *Novel on Yellow Paper* (1937), *Over the Frontier* (1938) and *The Holiday*

(1949), where she descants on her 'telescopic', 'leica-memory', often 'not quite in focus', suggesting a writer's mind composed of still images. Elsewhere, she describes herself as 'full of painting and writing'.[25] Early notebooks show meticulous recreations of art works she saw at exhibitions, suggesting the direct influences of etchings by Goya and drawings by George Grosz on her own work. Yet her determination to publish her illustrations with her poems was accompanied with a self-deprecating insistence on their artlessness – she confessed conspiratorially to Peter Orr in 1961 that 'I just sort of sit and draw sometimes' and often told inter-viewers about her practice of accumulating doodles in a box which she would match arbitrarily to poems. Smith's poetry itself is similarly split by a desire to be serious and flippant, suggestive both of artistry and the arbi-trary.[26] Just as her illustrations suggest both the hurried sketch and the influence of Goya and Grosz, her poems allude to classical French, Roman-tic poetry and Augustan satire but with cryptic bathos. Her illustrations and ekphrastic poems provide a starting point for reconsidering their deceptive techniques.

Smith's more traditional ekphrastic poems take sides in the long-running competitive genre of the visual versus the verbal. Her poem 'Brueghel' conjectures on the dialogue spoken by his subjects which 'in a clatter / Of meaningless sound / Without form or matter / Echo around'.[27] Here, unheard words bounce off the frame in tumult without the ordering of a written text. In 'A King in Funeral Procession', the dead sovereign recounts that his cortège has made him a posthumous commodity – 'I am their picture book', he complains.[28] Conversely, in 'Silence ', the dejected poet reflects in an age of 'too many words' that it is 'better to see the grass than write about it', the verbal offering a fixity ill matched with the uncertainties of the period.[29] Smith's uneasy balancing between the forms suggests a mixed-media art that uses the friction between the visual and the verbal as a deliberate point of contest.

This is borne out in her most famous poem, 'Not Waving but Drowning' and its accompanying illustration:

> Nobody heard him, the dead man,
> But still he lay moaning:
> I was much further out than you thought
> And not waving but drowning.
>
> Poor chap, he always loved larking
> And now he's dead
> It must have been too cold for him his heart gave way,
> They said.

Fig. 4.1. Stevie Smith, 'Not Waving but Drowning' (1957). Published in *Stevie Smith, Collected Poems*, ed. James MacGibbon (London: Penguin, 1978).

Oh, no no no, it was too cold always
(Still the dead one lay moaning)
I was much too far out all my life
And not waving but drowning.[30]

Readings of this poem by Seamus Perry, Christopher Ricks, Catherine Civello and Kristin Bluemel all highlight the perplexing mismatch between the poem's male speaker and the female figure depicted in the illustration (Fig. 4.1).[31] In a poem whose effect relies upon the ambiguity of the final stanza, which can be voiced either by the drowning male subject or the poem's narrator, the addition of a third possible referent via the enigmatic girl in the illustration further disorientates the reader's perspective. It stakes a prior claim to the text, never allowing the reader to trace the source of the third stanza. The girl's half-smile suggests she is the reader who has got

Fig. 4.2. Stevie Smith, 'Not Waving but Drowning' (undated draft illustration *c*.1957). From a typed proof of the poem.

there first, and is now quietly amused at our attempts to tie up her presence with the words of the poem. Yet the original illustration for the poem which was used alongside it at proof stage is seemingly a much more straightforward accompaniment to the text (Fig. 4.2). In sharp contrast to the published drawing, it enacts closure on the text, silencing the moaning dead man by adding a final narrative gesture, the poem's speaker dragging the man from the water. Smith's decision to abandon this drawing for the apparently unrelated figure of the smiling girl at publication stage suggests a need to qualify definitive readings of her work, casting her less as the capricious doodler than the wayward curator, delighting in the disjunction of juxtaposing texts and images from rooms at opposite ends of the gallery.

The very process of constructing these destabilising figures seems to be the subject of her poem 'Si peu séduisante', where Smith shifts from English to French and back again to produce a coded description of a young girl:

> *Elle était une petite fille de dix ans,*
> *Si peu séduisante,*
> *Qui entra dans le wagon-restaurant*
> *Pour retrouver ses parents.*

Fig. 4.3. Stevie Smith, 'Si peu séduisante' (undated draft illustration, *c.* 1966). From a typed proof of the poem.

Fig. 4.4. Stevie Smith, 'Si peu séduisante' (1966). Published in Stevie Smith, *Collected Poems*, ed. James MacGibbon (London: Penguin, 1978).

> *Elle portait son* school uniform,
> *Si peu séduisante,*
> And a perfectly frightful little pair of shoes,
> *Mais ses yeux, malgré des lunettes hideuses,*
> *Etaient si pleins de bonté et de franchise*
> *Que tout autre* aspect of this little schoolgirl,
> *Si peu séduisante,*
> Really only made one like her more.[32]

Smith's switching between two languages blurs the poem's apparent aim of giving us a stable meaning or reliable verbal portrait. The speaker's perspective is further modified by the repeated titular phrase, that qualifies her presentation of the *'petite fille de dix ans'*. The intruding English in the poem's conclusion makes it emphatically ambiguous: does the closing 'like' refer to the speaker's affection for the girl described or present the speaking subject as a facsimile of the original? The like and the unlike are further contrasted in the changes made to the poem's illustration at publication stage. The final proofs offer us a visual accompaniment to the poem (Fig. 4.3). The drawing, as in many of her early drafts, emphasises the authenticity of the verbal text – we see the girl wearing a 'perfectly frightful little pair of shoes', dressed in 'school uniform', with her eyes hidden behind *'des lunettes hideuses'*. Yet if Smith's first illustration shared her subject's *'franchise'* (sincerity) in its fidelity to the printed poem, the published drawing shows the girl stretching the lexical possibilities of the text, a figure dressed up by the poem's repeated refrain of *'si peu séduisante'* (Fig. 4.4). Smith consciously erases the visual indications that the drawn girl is the one in the poem, removing her glasses and making her 'frightful little pair of shoes' tantalisingly out of reach. The girl's myopic eyes become our own, as we struggle to tie up what we see with what we read. The safe authority of a portrait, framed by its author and its readers, is undermined by Smith's amendments to her drawing.

Her attempts to be 'liked', that is, to create an engaged and responsive readership, rely on her continued ability to create 'likes' – repeated versions of herself, competing editions of the authentic original. In a very different way from Lochhead, Smith questions the efficacy of visual representation, and uses art to deflect the male gaze of the reading audience.

Lynette Roberts and the graphic image

In contrast to Smith's disorientating mix of art, text, performance poetry and music, the Argentine-Welsh painter and poet Lynette Roberts insisted on separating her various media. Roberts completed illustrations for the

Argentine paper *La Nacion*, studied at the Central School of Arts and Crafts during the 1930s and in 1955–6 set up the Chislehurst Caves art project in Kent, but was reluctant when approached to contribute to the Caseg broadsheets, a series of poetry and woodcut publications for popular distribution, instinctively feeling her verbal art should evoke the visual without recourse to illustration.[33] If her own paintings drew on Primitivist colour schemes and subjects, her poems looked to Imagism for their aesthetic. It is the concatenation of these glacial images that makes her work so distinctive, from the Welsh quilt 'frozen stiff upon the washing line' ('Displaced Persons') to the lake of pools where 'icebergs stand firm on the ground, / And refrain to move for beauty of their image' ('Xaquixaguana'). This latter example is a key phrase for Roberts. Objects practise an enforced stasis; everything commits itself to spiky intractability, from the 'anthracite glitter of death' (*Gods with Stainless Ears: a Heroic Poem*) to the rain that 'freezes our senses' ('Rainshiver'). Whilst rain 'freezes' our senses, however, memory 'widens them' ('The New World') creating a poetry that melts, contracts and expands, asking its readers to put together its shattered crystals into a narrative.[34] Each static image waits for the reader to join it with the subsequent line. Yet if Roberts resisted the possibilities of finding an audience for her work via collaborative media – in opposition to Smith's dogged insistence to do the same – her works rely on visual perception and an optic poetics that goes beyond traditional ekphrasis.

The recent publication of Roberts' wartime diaries illuminate the centrality of the visual to her work, as suggested by an entry from 23 June 1940:

> Yesterday it rained, so I spent most of the time transplanting in the garden. The parsnips, beetroot, leeks, onions, are all thinned out. I experimented with a poem on Rain by using all words which had long thin letters so that even the print of the page would look like thin lines of rain. The poem called 'Rainshiver' looks like it. Rain
>
> Chills the air and stills the billing birds
> To shrill not trill as they should in
> This daffodil spring[35]

Here, her poem 'Rainshiver' aspires to the visual neither through the recreation of a painting nor a series of sense impressions but through the imprint of words on a page. The phonic chiming of the words is secondary to their typographic impression. Roberts brings to mind W.J.T. Mitchell's argument that 'writing, in its physical, graphic form, is an inseparable suturing of the visual and verbal, the "imagetext" incarnate'.[36] Roberts' work, as suggested by the 'transplanting' that inspires it, moves to an organic union of these two competing modes. Her horticultural frame for the poem moves it far from the concrete poetry label her graphic equation might suggest.

Elsewhere, a profusion of colour informs her poetic and textual canvas, from the 'tinting page' of 'Cwmcelyn' to the 'rainbow of books' lining the shelves in 'Ty Gwyn', Roberts' poetic tribute to the cottage where she and her husband Keidrych Rhys lived during the war.[37] In both images, the world of print and publication is shaded into a painted pallet. Colour haunts her writing like a sixth sense, from the description of a rural winter as a 'cupboard of darkness' to the Welsh soils which glisten with a 'green impaled with age'.[38] If Roberts' concern with the visual speaks less of a gendered preoccupation than a painter's training, the primacy of visual media seems key to her taking on the male tradition of the epic poem in *Gods With Stainless Ears: a Heroic Poem* (1951). Her preface to this powerful and still neglected work notes it was written to be filmed, and aimed for a narrative as 'continuous as *newsreel*'.[39] By invoking the generic fluidity of cinema, Roberts recalls Dorothy Richardson and Gertrude Stein, and hints at a twentieth-century female tradition which looks to the silver screen for the promise of liberating viewers and subjects alike from the reductive gaze of spectatorship and its accompanying limitations. Whilst the props of cinema cannot and should not 'solve' the dense complexities of this poem – as Woolf once argued, 'the images of a poet . . . are compact of a thousand suggestions of which the visual is only the most obvious or the uppermost' – the work's interest in apocalypse, the mental breakdown of the creative artist and man's desecration of his natural environment offers it as a pointed comment on post-war Britain.[40] It is through the language of film and documentary that Roberts disrupts and coerces the tradition of the epic, and it is this language that will provide the best tool for exploring its effects. Even as her poetics move closest to the structures of narrative, with the poem's organisation into a five-part argument, it reaches with ever more surety to the visual. As the two lovers that are the poem's subjects face the blankness of nuclear horror, it is the night sky that proves to be the 'braille in a rock of frost', offering the tentative blind reading that can lead us through the poem.[41] Roberts not only draws on a visual aesthetic to inspire and structure her work, but asks for a peculiarly visual response to interpret it.[42]

Women's ekphrastic tradition

These three very different poets and their parallel struggles or set of arguments with the visual might help illuminate a hitherto hidden genre of female ekphrastic writing. U.A. Fanthorpe (1929–2009) wrote a series of poems which balance verbal and visual representation ('Women Ironing', 'Portraits of Tudor Statesmen', '3 poems for Amy Cook (1909–1999)'), but moves beyond conventional ekphrastic concerns in 'Painter and Poet', which compares the two professions in the shrewd light of economics. Her comic market appraisal of the painter suggests that not only his work but his act of composition is captivating, and the dizzying prices fetched by modern painters become symptomatic of a voyeuristic male society, that prefers looking to reading and art to literature. The contemporary poet's cultural value can only be measured by becoming a 'set' text, with Fanthorpe punning on 'set' to suggest a mummified static piece of work.[43] Institutional canonicity has reduced the vibrant poem to a statuesque *objet d'art*; it is lessened by moving into a spatial and temporal world. Fanthorpe's jocular despair here suggests an anxiety about the reception of contemporary poetry, sounding a familiar female concern with audience.

Religious art, meanwhile, is the preoccupation for Elizabeth Jennings (1926–2001), from titular hints in collections such as *A Way of Looking* (1955) and *The Sonnets of Michelangelo* (1961) to her series of poetic tributes to painters as diverse as Caravaggio, Chagall and Goya. Yet her primary fascination with painting seems to centre on the possibilities of impersonality for the artist through the act of creation. 'Paint' and 'restraint' are key rhymes for Jennings, as in 'Visit to an Artist' or 'A Picture', where she praises the artist for his 'bold restraint' in 'guessing the hint and not the climax kills'. Elsewhere, as in 'Michaelangelo's First Pietà', she imagines how 'wordless' communication might bring the painter 'rest', asserts that visual art can make the 'wildest, darkest dream serene' ('Samuel Palmer and Chagall') or acknowledges 'an art of rest, / And sophistication' in Klee's work ('For Paul Klee'). The visual offers 'unity' ('Goya'), 'form' ('Tribute to Turner') and an 'accurate' hand ('Caravaggio'), distinct from the 'nervous hands' that 'leave their own tension' in verbal 'Words of Art'. It appears that the artist, unlike the writer, can see the imperfection in his work as 'he is, in little, a God' ('After a Painting is Finished').[44] There is almost a jealousy in Jennings' dissection of this tranquillity, suggesting that each stanza (or strain) of her verse at once aspires to the condition of art whilst acknowledging the strain of its own composition. The idea of visual restraint for Jennings promises both release and agitating comparison. A similar anxiety haunts the depiction of a painter in 'A Bowl of Apples' by Ruth Fainlight (1931–), ever mindful that it is 'Impossible / to write a poem impersonal / as a still life'.[45]

Eavan Boland (1944–), like Lochhead, uses the ekphrastic genre to question male representations of women. In her poem 'From the Painting *Back from Market* by Chardin' she describes Chardin's vacant peasant woman only to reflect on 'what great art removes / Hazard and death, the future and the past, / This women's secret history and her loves', and in 'Self-Portrait on a Summer Evening' she again identifies Chardin's depictions as 'slighting', a skewed mimetic process of 'light unlearning itself', whilst the female subject is 'glazed over'. A consideration of Renoir prompts prurient images of 'full-skirted girls' depicted 'full / of fantasy' by the male painter's 'anaemic' pencil ('Growing up from Renoir's Drawing *Girlhood*), whilst in 'Degas's Laundresses', the female subjects of the French painter's works are given a haunting, retrospective warning of the reductive process of representation:

> Wait. There behind you.
> A man. There behind you.
> Whatever you do don't turn.
> Why is he watching you?
> Whatever you do don't turn.   (lines 19–23)[46]

Here, Boland returns to the past and finds it wanting, reanimating a dialogue from the frozen image of the working women to cast the male painter-viewer as an intrusive threat.

The sense that female ekphrasis is in dialogue with the history of female representation as much as with painting is suggested finally by Carol Ann Duffy's 'Mrs Icarus', which draws not only on Brueghel's *Landscape with the Fall of Icarus* (c.1558) but also on W.H. Auden's 'Musée des Beaux Arts', arguably the most famous ekphrastic poem of the twentieth century. Half in homage and half in bathetic slight to Auden, whose poem memorialised the tension between the tragic and the quotidian on the brink of war, Duffy imagines Icarus' wife watching in exasperation at the descent of her husband, the 'Grade A pillock'. As a comment on the relationship between the visual and verbal, it lacks the earnest anguish of Jennings, the aesthetic purism of Roberts or the off-kilter inscrutability of Smith. Yet what it shares with these very different writers is the sense that it is working both as part of and against a tradition. Whilst a world-weary Mrs Icarus insists on precedent and antecedent, commenting that she is neither the 'first or the last' woman to be in her position, we might also reflect that Duffy herself is neither the first nor last to write a poem about a painting by Brueghel, nor to reinterpret a canonical male artist from a female perspective.[47] These poets rework the male tradition of Western painting and its connotations of spectatorship from burden to incitement, before taking this legacy and transforming it back into art.

Notes

1 Liz Lochhead, 'Notes on the Inadequacy of a Sketch at Millport Cathedral, March 1970', in *Dreaming Frankenstein & Collected Poems* (Edinburgh: Polygon, 1984), p. 141.

2 Carol Ann Duffy, *New Selected Poems 1984–2004* (London: Picador, 2004), p. 19.

3 John Berger, *Ways of Seeing* (London: Penguin, 1972), p. 45.

4 Alexander Pope, 'Epistle to a Lady', lines 5–6, 11–20, in *Poetical Works* (London: Oxford University Press, 1966), pp. 291–2.

5 Percy Bysshe Shelley, *Collected Poetical Works of Percy Bysshe Shelley*, ed. Thomas Hutchinson (London: Oxford University Press, 1965), p. 583.

6 This painting, now in the collection of the Uffizi Gallery, was misattributed to Da Vinci in the eighteenth century. It has been identified as Flemish, but its authorship remains contested.

7 John Keats, 'Ode on a Grecian Urn', in *Poems* (London: Everyman, 1974), p. 191.

8 W.J.T. Mitchell, *Picture Theory: Essays on Visual and Verbal Communication* (London: University of Chicago Press, 1994), pp. 155, 168.

9 James A.W. Heffernan, *Museum of Words: the Poetics of Ekphrasis from Homer to Ashbery* (London: University of Chicago, 1993), p. 46.

10 Charlotte Brontë, *Villette* (Harmondsworth: Penguin, 1979), chapter XIX, p. 278.

11 Elizabeth Barrett Browning, *Aurora Leigh*, ed. Margaret Reynolds (Athens: Ohio University Press, 1992), p. 163.

12 Lochhead, 'Object', in *Dreaming Frankenstein*, pp. 155–6.

13 *Ibid.*, lines 53, 62–3.

14 Lochhead, 'The Furies', *ibid.*, p. 74.

15 *Ibid.*

16 *Ibid.*

17 See also Lochhead's afterword to *Scotland's Favourite Paintings: Beyond the Sun – Poems by Edwin Morgan* (Edinburgh: Luath Press, 2007), which praises Edwin Morgan's ekphrastic poems for taking the paintings 'personally', p. 46.

18 Lochhead, 'Notes on the Inadequacy of a Sketch', p. 141.

19 *Ibid.*

20 Alan Riach has noted that the ekphrastic poem can also be a national genre, and situates Lochhead in a series of Scottish painter poets such as Alasdair Grey and John Byrne, in 'Poetry and painting: sketches for an essay', in *Scotland's Favourite Paintings: Beyond the Sun*, p. 14.

21 Lochhead, *The Colour of Black & White 1984–2003* (Edinburgh: Polygon, 2005), p. 97.

22 Jane Dowson (ed.), *Women's Poetry of the 1930s* (London: Routledge, 1996), p. 144.

23 See Lochhead's collaborations with linocut artists such as Willie Rodgers in her collection *The Colour of Black & White 1984–2003*.

24 Stevie Smith, 'Art', in *London Guyed*, ed. William Kimber (London: Hutchinson, 1938), pp. 153–64; p. 154.

25 Stevie Smith, 'The ironing board of Widow Twanky', *Queen* 219 (20 December 1961), 11; *Over the Frontier* (London: Virago, 1980), p. 242; *Novel on Yellow Paper* (London: Virago, 1980), p. 114; 'Some impediments to Christian commitment', in *Me Again* (London: Virago, 1981), pp. 155–70: 156.

26 'Stevie Smith', in Peter Orr (ed.), *The Poet Speaks* (London: Routledge and Kegan, 1966), pp. 225–31; 229.

27 Stevie Smith, *Collected Poems*, ed. James MacGibbon (Harmondsworth: Penguin, 1978), p. 84.

28 Smith, *Ibid.*, p. 164.

29 Smith, *Me Again*, p. 236.

30 Smith, *Collected Poems*, p. 303.

31 See Seamus Perry, 'Practical criticism: Stevie Smith's "Not Waving but Drowning"', *English Review* (September 1988), 14–15; Christopher Ricks, 'Stevie Smith: the art of sinking in poetry', in *The Force of Poetry* (London: Faber, 1992), pp. 244–55; Catherine A. Civello, *Patterns of Ambivalence: the Fiction and Poetry of Stevie Smith* (Columbia, SC: Camden House, 1997), pp. 72–3; Kristin Bluemel, 'The dangers of eccentricity: Stevie Smith's doodles and poetry', *Mosaic* 31.3 (1998), 111–32.

32 Smith, *Collected Poems*, p. 435. Translation by George May: 'She was only a little ten year-old, so very plain, so very artless, who stumbled into the dining car to find her parents. She was in her school uniform, so very plain, so very artless, and a perfectly frightful little pair of shoes, but behind her pebble glasses, her eyes were so full of good nature and sincerity, that every other aspect of this little schoolgirl, so very plain, so very artless, really only made one like her more.'

33 John Pikoulis, 'Lynette Roberts and Alun Lewis', *Poetry Wales* 19.2 (1983), 9–29; 18: '[Roberts] thought the blending of poems and engravings mistaken'.

34 Lynette Roberts, *Collected Poems*, ed. Patrick McGuinness (Manchester: Carcanet, 2005), pp. 91, 30, 64, 24, 28.

35 Lynette Roberts, *Diaries, Letters and Recollections*, ed. Patrick McGuinness (Manchester: Carcanet, 2008), p. 21.

36 Mitchell, *Picture Theory*, p. 95.

37 Roberts, *Collected Poems*, pp. 34, 89.

38 'Fisherman' and 'Fox', *Village Dialect: Seven Stories*, in *Ibid.*, pp. 104, 94.

39 Preface to *Gods with Stainless Ears* in *Ibid.*, p. 43: 'when I wrote this poem, the scenes and visions ran before me like newsreel . . . this poem was written for filming'. The lovers' ascent to heaven in the poem is described as 'continuous as *newsreel*', p. 68.

40 Virginia Woolf, 'The cinema', in *The Captain's Death Bed and Other Essays* (London: Hogarth Press, 1950), pp. 169–70.

41 Roberts, *Collected Poems*, p. 61.

42 The growing secondary criticism on Roberts is in accord over her visual appeal, from her editor Patrick McGuinness, whose excellent introduction to her work situates her as a 'painterly poet' (Roberts, *Collected Poems*, p. xxxiv), to

Anthony Conran's essay on Roberts, which places her in the Primitivist context of Henri Rosseau, in 'Lynette Roberts', *Frontiers in Anglo-Welsh Poetry* (Cardiff: University of Wales Press, 1997).

43 U.A. Fanthorpe, *Safe As Houses* (Calstock: Peterloo Poets, 1995), p. 54.

44 Elizabeth Jennings, *New Collected Poems* (Manchester: Carcanet, 2001), pp. 45, 71, 132, 75, 297, 176, 175, 67, 177.

45 Ruth Fainlight, *Moon Wheels* (Tarset: Bloodaxe Books, 2006), p. 17.

46 Eavan Boland, *New Collected Poems* (Manchester: Carcanet, 2005), pp. 17, 131, 144, 108.

47 Carol Ann Duffy, *The World's Wife* (London: Picador, 1999), p. 16.

5

JANE DOWSON

Towards a new confessionalism: Elizabeth Jennings and Sylvia Plath

In the current media climate – where columnists discuss their cancer and marital break-ups, memoir-writers explain their incestuous relationships and Springer guests say 'Surprise, honey, I'm a man!'– poetry must at least stop disowning the original confessional movement, and instead celebrate how it made emotional exposure matter, and confronted us with uncomfortable truths. The confessional movement needs to be revalued as an important progression in twentieth-century poetry – one that was not just outpoured emotion, but emotion transformed into art by often ignored technical mastery.[1]

In the article from which the above extract comes, 'Getting Poetry to Confess' (2001), the lyric poet Claire Pollard examines the enduring appeal of public exposure of private suffering and calls for a 'New Confessionalism' that will reclaim poetry's potential readership. Pollard pinpoints the particular inhibitions for women:

It [Confessionalism] has also – via sectioned Anne and suicidal Sylvia – been attached to the image of woman as hysterical harpy: disturbed, hormonal, her own muse before she is an artist . . . To revert to a confessionalist mode now might be to reaffirm the cultural image of the 'Mad Poetess'. After a period of great acclaim following her death, it was a notable fact that in *Poetry Review*'s 1994 'New Generation' issue, none of the women poets cited Plath as an influence.[2]

The association between women's authorship and artless feminine senti-mentality or female neuroses is long-standing and hard to eradicate.[3] In selecting for *The Faber Book of 20th Century Women's Poetry*, Fleur Adcock approves Plath with the disclaimer 'to call [her poems] "confes-sional" is misleading', discards Anne Sexton as 'repellingly self-indulgent' and dissociates herself from ' "primal scream" writing, that is slabs of raw experience untransformed'.[4] If we are to break the negative mould of a literary tradition in which women excel, we need a critical grammar that can rehabilitate the work of Plath alongside Sexton, her other American predecessors and British poets such as Elizabeth Jennings or Pollard and her contemporaries.[5] This chapter will draw out some qualitative features from poems by Jennings and Plath that also dissolve a hardened division between American proclivities and British aloofness towards confessionalism.[6] As Pollard proposes, a more invigorating critical approach will arguably revive poetic *practice*. While the poets' fixation with their fathers, their mental instabilities, suicide attempts and psychiatric treatment lay them open to Freudian readings, Jung's theories of creativity attend to their *poetic* consciousnesses, particularly their ingenious symbolism, shifts between individual and collective voices and the role of art in consoling as well as representing pain.

Due to their self-disclosing manner, both Elizabeth Jennings (1926–2001) and Sylvia Plath (1932–63) have been labelled 'confessional' yet have markedly different life experiences and profiles in literary and popular imaginations. Jennings was born in Boston, Lincolnshire, and educated in Oxford, where she lived for the rest of her life. She had a broken engagement then a relationship with a married man but never married or had children. Plath left America in 1955 for Cambridge University and later lived in Devon with her husband Ted Hughes. Following their separation in 1962, she moved to London and published one volume of poetry before her death. The posthumous *Ariel* (1965) was followed by three further volumes before the *Collected Poems* (1981) and *Selected Poems* (1985). In contrast, Elizabeth Jennings published over twenty poetry collections, a book on poetics and several critical essays; she edited influential anthologies and appears in many others. She was awarded prestigious poetry prizes and in 1992 a CBE. There are two major *Collected Poems* (1986, 2002) and a forthcoming *Collected Works*.[7] Jennings enjoyed high esteem in the decade following her graduation from St Anne's College (1949) and was the only woman poet of the post-war 'Movement',[8] among whom her admirers included Philip Larkin.[9] Her traditional formalism was praised in the 1950s and 1960s but was later considered too cautious.[10] Nevertheless, the sales of *Collected* and *Selected Poems* made her a best-selling poet on the Carcanet list and the 1980s was one of her most commercially successful decades.[11] To date, there are merely a handful of articles and a number of interviews but no full-length critical work or biography. Jennings suffers from poor image material, with most photographs presenting her elderly, otherworldly persona. At the other extreme, Plath's publicity showcases her youthful intelligent beauty and she attracts biographies, critical works, conferences, a film and recently the unabridged journals (2000). Her victim image and expression of female anger have appealed to women readers, with her autobiographical novel *The Bell Jar* (1963) achieving the status of a feminist manifesto. Jennings' shyness about making gender distinctions and notoriously downtrodden appearance in her final years have not. However, the high and continuing sales of her books suggest a poetry that speaks for and to a broad readership.[12]

Both poets had breakdowns and periods of hospitalisation that send the reader to their correspondence and notebooks for clues to their illnesses and that lay their poetry open to reductive interpretations as the expression of psychological crises. The torment of Plath's poetry concerning her father's death and husband's infidelity consolidated her centrality to the post-war American confessional school with whom she had some personal associations; their work was characterised by a direct address to the reader of socially transgressive intimate confidences along with a casual style that defined itself against the impersonality of the High Modernists or the technical formality of the New Critics. However, Plath expressly denounced 'raw' autobiography for being antithetical to literary artistry: 'I *cannot* sympathise with these cries from the heart that are informed by nothing except, you know, a needle or a knife, or whatever it is. I believe one should be able to control and manipulate experiences, even the most terrifying, like madness, like being tortured.'[13] In turn, Jennings battled with the ghosts of a sentimentalised female confessionalism:

> It has become so involved with poets like Anne Sexton. It usually means absorption in some mental . . . I don't think poetry has got anything to do with sickness. I had a breakdown and the poems in this book, *The Mind Has Mountains* (1966), a title from Hopkins, most of them are not about me. They are not like Anne Sexton's. I think Sylvia Plath was a marvellous poet. I do not like 'Lady Lazarus' and 'Daddy'. I think they have gone way over. The term confessional has been associated with me, mental illness and revelation, but I don't think that's interesting.[14]

In 1961, a reviewer stated 'Elizabeth Jennings has steadily closed in to the emotional life of her poetry and sloughed off her rather cold remoteness'[15] and in 1965, 'The Night-Mare' was included in a respectful radio discussion about confessional poetry;[16] but in 1967, a review of her *Collected Poems*, entitled 'Cool Comfort', declared, 'Looked at as a whole, the poetry of Elizabeth Jennings seems full of paradoxes and puzzles. To characterize it, one perhaps might use the word "reserved"; yet it is also often astonishingly, and even embarrassingly, open, as "confessional" as anything one finds in Robert Lowell, Sylvia Plath and Anne Sexton.'[17] Faced with accusations of both 'cold remoteness' and embarrassing openness, Jennings was evidently in conflict: adamant that 'art is not self-expression' and '"confessional poetry" is almost a contradiction in terms'[18] she also stated, 'My own most urgent poetic problem today is to bring into my poetry more personal experience directly and in detail.'[19]

We need a new critical discourse around confessionalism that establishes it as an artistic act with its own genealogy. M.L. Rosenthal famously christened the twentieth-century genre in his review 'Poetry as Confession' (1959): '[Robert] Lowell removes the mask. His speaker is unequivocally himself, and it is hard not to think of *Life Studies* as a series of personal confidences, rather shameful, that one is honor-bound not to reveal.'[20] Whereas Rosenthal wanted the subject to reveal all, a New Confessionalism requires a set of expectations and evaluative criteria that are not about truth to experience. Instead, it needs to stress that poetry allows for the unfathomable, inexplicable and inexpressible. In contrast with the voyeuristic detachment of a television audience, the scientific authority of the psychiatrist or the spiritual infallibility of the priest, the poet draws in the reader as fellow sufferer or confidant/e, along with the distancing element of self-reflection.[21] Poetry both expresses *and explores* our 'deepest scars, secrets, griefs and desires'; its pleasure is not only empathetic identification but also aesthetic resolution or consolation that seem unavailable elsewhere.[22] Specifically female practices seek intimate connection with the reader and may foster a sense of community; they are often inwardly dialogic and evoke renewal alongside despair.

The reader as listener/subject

If the expectation of confession is honest disclosure by the speaker to their audience, poetic confession emphasises the contingency and limitations of the available language to do so. We look for the mutuality of the exchange, where the reader may enjoy the privilege of shared intimacies and the healing of self-awareness, but importantly it also reminds us that we are not being told everything and that everything cannot be told. In 'Tulips', Sylvia Plath addresses us as a hospital patient confiding in a visitor: 'Look how white everything is, how quiet, how snowed in.' She satirises the counsel of the medical professionals and instead shares with the reader her unspoken misery: 'I have given my name and day-clothes up to the nurses / And my history to the anesthetist and my body to surgeons'. The series of questions, images and colour-coding simultaneously reveal and conceal her feelings of alienation and death-in-life: 'The tulips are too red in the first place', 'My patent leather overnight case like a black pillbox'.[23] Her highly individualised symbolism is compelling yet frustrating if we attempt to fully unlock it as the doctor might.

Many a reader can sympathise with Peter Dale's complaint about Plath's 'obscurity' in his review of *Ariel*:

> The best poems in the book are those where her highly private fears, guilts, failures and neuroses are made objective in concrete situations such as in the beekeeping poem, or in the hospital of 'Tulips'. Where this concreteness is lacking, there remain obscure associations on an unexplained theme. In such poems as 'Fever 103°', 'Medusa', 'The Couriers', the reader is lost in a welter of private associations.[24]

We see here how 'neuroses' are brought in and literary merit equated with the poet's success in making her 'private fears' comprehensible. As Carl Jung (1875–1961) asserts in 'On the Relation of Analytical Psychology to Poetry', although art is a psychological activity, questions about the *nature* of art are aesthetic. He condemns the scientific approach of the Freudian school of criticism for reducing the artist to a clinical case and their work to repressed psychic content. Whereas for Freud, dream symbols are clues to a *knowable* unconscious, Jung reads poetic symbols as an 'attempt to express something for which no verbal concept exists'.[25] Interestingly, Plath read Jung's *Symbols of Transformation* in 1959[26] and for Jennings, the shared resonance of a Universal Unconscious that is manifest in archetypes and dreams was a chosen resource: 'Jungian theories do, I think, lend themselves more easily than most other concepts of mind and man to deployment in literary form. His archetypes, animus and anima, shadow side and so on, make lively metaphors when they are handled sensitively and sparingly.'[27]

If, as Jung recommends, psychology provides the language for reading *creative processes* that are partly unconscious, the obscurity of Plath's symbolism is charged with the dynamic of disclosing what has yet to be understood. She certainly aimed to avoid hermetic solipsism: 'I think that personal experience is very important, but certainly it shouldn't be a kind of shut up box and mirror-looking, narcissistic experience.'[28] The many studies of her symbolism explore recurring motifs that pertain to her unique imagination but sometimes overlook their association with literary traditions.[29] For example, her father, a biology professor, specialised in bees, which famously depict her anger and distress; but they are also ancient archetypes of industry. One poem in the brilliantly evocative bee sequence, 'The Bee Meeting', is set in the context of an idyllic English village and opens with a question that draws in the reader as her secluded companion and fellow observer: 'Who are these people at the bridge to meet me?' However, the dense metaphors, such as 'Pillar of white in a blackout of knives', also signify the inexpressibility of her dislocation. In 'The Bee-eper's Daughter' universal symbols of the Fall that resonate with biblical and Milton's epic sources – 'A fruit that's death to taste: dark flesh, dark parings' – interweave with an impossibly private allusiveness: 'Father, bridegroom, in this Easter egg / Under the coronal of sugar roses // The queen bee marries the winter of your year.'[30] Instead of trying to 'translate' such images, we can allow the poetic expression to speak of a condition that cannot readily be verbalised. Plath both mines and personalises literary tradition, classical and biblical metaphors in ways that unsettle conventional assumptions about their validity; as Adam Kirsch observes, 'Plath calls upon many mythologies without really believing in any of them.'[31] Jennings, on the other hand, uses literary and biblical archetypes less critically.

For Jennings, poetry was about communication, between herself and the reader as well as between readers: 'the poem is a way of making love / Which all can share. Poets guide the lips, the hand' ('The Feel of Things'). One wave of her poetry is occupied with the emotional ebbs and flows of seeking close relationships, and the reader is positioned as both listener and universal subject. 'Delay', that launches *New Collected Poems* and concludes 'And love arrived may find us somewhere else', reverberates with readers' experiences of love's bad timing.[32] The connectedness is characteristically enhanced by the pluralised first-person pronouns, 'we'/ 'our'/ 'us'. Some poems are dedicated to individuals but most are not personally specific. We can surmise that several pertain to the relationship with the man she could not marry, the end of which closely preceded her breakdown. Apart from a passing reference to 'B' in her autobiography, this core event is glaringly absent from her personal papers. Tellingly, however, many poems express and explore unfulfilled yearnings:[33]

> A touching, then a glancing off.
> It is your vows that stretch between
> Us like an instrument of love
> Where only echoes intervene.
> Yet these exchanges are enough
> Since strings touched only are most keen.[34]

Whilst presented as personal, the archetypal metaphor of unplayed music universalises the experience of repressed passion. Additionally, the hidden dialogic, where the second-person pronoun invokes an absent addressee, positions the reader as eavesdropper on the most private of revelations. The argument of the poem reaches some kind of acquiescence that is supported by the end rhymes which remind us that this is a poetic, rather than a lived, resolution. Similarly, 'Resolve', that starts, 'I'll keep this heartbreak, let it hurt and tear / My spirit', ends with lyrical consolation: 'But you've cast your spell / And left a magic which I can live by.'³⁵ Like 'The Instruments' and many more, the lyric 'I' converses with a significant 'Other' and thus establishes a subjectivity enacted through dialogue.

In contrast with the facile wisdom of an 'agony aunt' column, Jennings involves the reader in being both spoken to and spoken for. She does not fake solutions, and frequently draws attention to the aesthetic nature of poetic catharsis that she believes is the poet's job: 'We shape, we cut, we steal, we wrap, we are / Makers to order where there wasn't one.'³⁶ The joys and pains of friendship are a Jennings' trademark, and here too the neatness of rhyme jostles with the untidiness of feeling:

> What takes me through the corridors
> Of grief? Was it the touch of love, that leading thread
> Which drew me to glad grief from wrong remorse,
> Wiped off the dust and let me see the dead
> With new care now, new laws?³⁷

The commonplace symbols open up space for every reader's imagination and correspond to Jung's judgement that 'The special significance of a true work of art resides in the fact that it has escaped from the limitations of the personal and has soared beyond the personal concerns of its creator'.³⁸

As we observed with Plath, transcending the merely personal is also effected by dialogue with conventional literary tropes. In Jennings' 'A Sonnet', the containment of the literary form and its associations with a tradition of romantic love produce a self-reflexive dynamic that draws attention to the necessity and failure of linguistic expression when it comes to intense feeling: 'Run home all clichés, let the deep words come / However much they hurt and shock and bruise.'³⁹ The sentiment has several literary echoes, including W.H. Auden's 'Stop All the Clocks', and the flexibility of Jennings' iambic pentameter in achieving colloquial familiarity qualifies as Audenesque 'memorable speech'.⁴⁰ As we have seen, the poem's movement to a resolution is typical of Jennings but also the traditional property of the lyric and of the elegy in particular.

If the poetic confessional implicates social practices that presume the speaker's total revelation and total reception by the listener, we have to question the purpose of using autobiographical material as a benchmark of 'authenticity'. Quite simply, the prose of autobiography best serves as a foil that illuminates the poetry's distinctive diction, form and evocation of what cannot be easily expressed. For example, Jennings records difficulties with her upbringing in her journals and autobiography: 'Sometimes I am ashamed that my life has been comparatively sheltered, I feel guilty that so many things were made easy for me; and yet I was never sheltered from acute unhappiness.

Family rows and inward turmoil were the condition in which I spent my late childhood and the whole of my extended adolescence.'[41] In 'Family Affairs', rhyme and regular form impose an order that both compensates for and skilfully enhances the tension of unfinished business:

> Have we then learnt at last how to untie
> The bond of birth, umbilical long cord,
> So that we live quite unconnected by
> The blood we share? What monstrous kind of sword
> Can sever veins and still we do not die?[42]

The questions are rhetorical and addressed both to the family members implied in the poem and to readers. Likewise, in 'A Game of Chess', 'A Game of Cards', or 'Cousins, Aunts, Uncles', readers are positioned as both audience and subjects in search of themselves in relation to blood relations. Ultimately, the poem is the place for creative harmony that is missing from memory and life experience: 'We want more order than we ever meet / And art keeps driving us most hopefully on.'[43] Martin Booth recognises this largely unappreciated transformative power: 'Taken as a whole, Elizabeth Jennings' poetry is a corpus of peace and one that many should enter in turbulent times . . . From her melancholic and sadly beautiful shell she produces poetry of exceptional lyrical qualities.'[44]

As Jung points out, poetry asks to be judged on aesthetic qualities, not medical or ethical grounds that require truth to experience.[45] Interestingly, in her unpublished autobiography, Jennings wrote then crossed out: 'I realise that Freud would have much to say about many of my revelations but I propose to leave him on one side and let my story speak for itself.'[46] During her time in the Warneford Hospital in Oxford, Jennings' notebooks and correspondence record her troublesome relationship with her Freudian psychiatrist and his diagnoses of her unresolved infantile anxieties and desires. She relieved the humiliations of his patriarchal treatment in amusing limericks and jottings. In her poem 'The Interrogator', however, she empoweringly writes back against the godlike stature of the psychiatrist who is 'always right', 'always has an answer', 'always knows best' and 'can always find words'. She enlists the reader as ally in wishing for the upper hand:

> And if you covered his mouth with your hand,
> Pinned him down to his smooth desk chair,
> You would be doing just what he wishes.
> His silence would prove that he was right.[47]

Thus the poem's fantasy repudiates the politically unequal process of social confession while transforming it into a bonding conspiracy between poet and reader. Glancing back to Plath's 'Tulips', poetry's function here is both a commentary on the medical profession and an alternative that takes the individual from isolation to community.

Similarly, Jennings' 'First Confession' can be read in terms of Freudian therapy where the one who confesses is released from the hold which the unspoken secret has had, but, more creatively, through Jung's emphasis on artistic reconstruction and completion.[48] In adult voice, the poet revisits her seven-year-old self confiding a theft to a priest whose judgemental response contaminated the girl's formerly innocent and carefree (Wordsworthian) condition. While criticising the religious authority figure, she undertakes a poetic confession that transgresses a taboo on questioning the sacred rite; the sacrosanct secrecy of the religious confessional appears unhealthy, while the poem brings self-revelation into a community of readers, and it is here that Jennings finds the release that she did not get from the psychiatrist or priest. Similarly, in 'A Litany of Contrition', the reader is privy to a most intimate disclosure of unspoken jealousy that has constituted 'the terrible depth/ of dark' in the poet as speaker.[49] Here, we find the dialogue that is common in Jennings' confessions: first of all she addresses Nature – the flowers, rain, stars and moon – and finally turns to Christ as her only hope of cure. Again, the poem moves private suffering to a more public domain; although most likely about the jealousy that Jennings felt towards her sister, the absence of specifics and the universalising elemental symbols allow the reader to share the enlightenment of self-knowledge.[50] The process of bringing unconscious drives to consciousness is operative in the languages of poetry, prayer and psychology: in Jung's words, 'One does not become enlightened by imagining figures of light, but by making the darkness conscious.'[51] At the same time, the half lines in 'A Litany of Contrition' typographically signify what eludes full expression; thus the poem contradicts the assumptions of social confidences or psychiatric therapy that purport to get to the bottom of things.

A poetics of despair and healing

> What the poem discovers – and this is its chief function – is order amid chaos, meaning in the middle of confusion, and affirmation at the heart of despair.[52]

Most central to the 'confessional' are the competing impulses to hide and to tell the untellable. As we have seen, poetry both enforces and goes beyond the assumption that talking equals cure. Since the mystery surrounding Plath's intentions on the day of her tragic death, her work has inevitably been read through auto/biography and psychology,[53] and too easily reduced to 'a case study in female neurosis and Freudian guilt'.[54] In 'The problem of biography', Susan Van Dyne addresses the controversy over whether Plath's writing was life-giving or life-taking: 'Her death is understood as a tragic but inevitable byproduct of her poetic method; her suicide is proof that the violent unresolved materials of her unconscious, once courted or confronted as subjects for poetry, couldn't finally be transmuted, ordered and contained by words.'[55] In the often cited 'Stillborn', Plath colludes with the view that writing poems kept her going: she starts, 'These poems do not live: it's a sad diagnosis', and concludes: 'But they are dead, and their mother near dead with distraction, / And they stupidly stare, and do not speak of her.'[56] While the maternal metaphors are harrowing, the poem's existence contradicts the attested writer's block. In the relentlessly bitter and self-absorbed 'Kindness', the whole puzzle of writing to live or living to write typically rests on the symbol: 'The blood jet is poetry, / There is no stopping it.'[57] The image contains the possibility of unstoppable life and unstoppable bleeding to death; although maddening in not giving us a definitive clue to her state of mind on 1 February 1963, ten days before her death, it is a brilliant device of literary ambiguity.

A strong tide of recent criticism insists on the futility of seeking a 'real' Plath and champions her literary processes.[58] For a start, the editorial incisions of her letters and journals, by her mother and husband respectively, have skewed any full or balanced portrait, so that headaches over the relative authenticity of her letters home versus the poems written on the same day are fruitless. As we have seen with Jennings, the correspondence and journals provide a personal context to illuminate the poetic consciousness that connects with the community of readers and community of poets. Plath's letters to her mother in October 1962 appear as genuine articulations of her struggle with poor health, finances and children: 'It was the bloody fever that finished me. I went to the doctor – no medication of course – then to bed at 8 p.m. Yesterday I was much better. . . I guess my predicament is an astounding one, a deserted wife knocked out by flu with two babies and a full-time job!'[59] In contrast, the poems of this period read like discourses of intolerable desperation:

> Darling, all night
> I have been flickering, off, on, off, on.
> The sheets grow heavy as a lecher's kiss.[60]

The sequence of dark images, such as 'aguey tendon', 'hothouse baby in its crib', 'ghastly orchid' or 'devilish leopard', are biting alternatives to more accessible metaphors for feeling near death. In no uncertain terms, this is Plath's unique suffering, but the intertextual echoes give it theatrical proportions that reverberate with sufferings that run through the literary canon. The 'snuffed candle' echoes Macbeth's bleak death-wish and the 'fat Cerberus' takes us to the gates of classical Hades. The first word 'Pure?' summons classical and Dantean myths about purgatorial fire that T.S. Eliot wove into 'The Fire Sermon' section of *The Waste Land*. Plath also becomes a Madonna figure with 'old whore petticoats', attended by cherubims, who finally ascends to a Paradise where, with Plath's brilliant and maddening ambiguity, she either dissolves or is resurrected.[61]

The possibility of rebirth and healing that the poem can imaginatively include are vital ingredients that rescue the female subject from the perpetual status of victim, sufferer or self-destroyer. Kirsch comments on Plath's appropriations of the rite of passage myth and Jacqueline Rose observes that 'the myth of female transcendence becomes one half of one of the most classic and alarming stereotypes of femininity itself'.[62] 'Lady Lazarus', Plath's well-known 'dying is an art' piece, ends with the phoenix rising from the ashes that both maintains and mocks such stereotypes: 'Out of the ash / I rise with my red hair / And I eat men like air.'[63] Thus, the female poetics of despair corresponds to Freudian diagnoses of psychological wounds crying out from a place not easily available to language, but goes beyond his cure of introspective talking to symbols and evocations that bring a cathartic connectedness as long as they are not overly individualised.

The ingredient of a panacea has traditionally marked the confessional lyric from the merely 'raw utterance' and was a conscious mission for Jennings: 'My thoughts with almost tenderness now turn / To making poems, creation's hopefulness.'[64] She asserts that poetry isn't 'therapy'[65] and 'Poets cannot say what they feel or think – poetry says it for them, in its voice, its cadence.'[66] For Jung, the best artists are prompted by such a 'creative autonomous complex'[67] that surpasses their individual memory sources as Jennings explores in 'To A Friend with a Religious Vocation':

> My poems move from feelings not yet known,
> And when a poem is written I can feel
> A flash, a moment's peace.[68]

As here, Jennings frequently arrives at some epiphany. Like Plath's 'Stillborn', the poem's creation compensates for the declaration of stunted inspiration with which it ends:

> It is the dark, the dark that draws me back
> Into a chaos where
> Vocations, visions fail, the will grows slack
> And I am stunned by silence everywhere.[69]

Jennings believes that the best poets always have 'a darkness' but their challenge is to retain the element of inexpressibility that points beyond language and rationality.[70] She made three attempts to take her own life and noted in her journal, 'There are some unhappinesses which can never be transformed into art. They are deep, dark, cold places – utterly infertile. Nothing grows there.'[71] In 'About These Things', Jennings' archetypal symbols of clothes and scars, the former a fabricated and the latter a natural protection, explore the inability to access some parts of the irrational:

> Perhaps I say
> In lucid verse the terrors that confuse
> In conversation. Maybe I am dumb.
> Because if fears were spoken I would lose
>
> The lovely languages I do not choose
> More than the darknesses from which they come.[72]

The typographical gaps elicit unfathomed pain, yet Jennings marvels how her poetry brings solace and healing to readers. This interface between private experience and public audience marks the best confessional from the weak forms that omit the dialectical tension between revelation and concealment.

Largely through symbolism, Jennings' poetry written from and about the Warneford Mental Hospital in Oxford especially succeeds in evoking the unsayable and in merging the personal with the collective: 'A Human cry cuts across a dream. / A wild hand squeezes an open rose'.[73] She is both a subject and an observer here, and the book's title *The Mind Has Mountains* (1966) weaves her collapse with the desolate sonnets of Hopkins, whom she greatly admired. *Recoveries* (1964), the title of her other collection on the period of her breakdown, endorses an imaginative renewal found through poetic transformation and connection rather than as a lived reality: 'The muffled cries, the curtains drawn, / The flowers pale before they fall –'.[74] Typically, the elliptical dash points to the space where words fail. In 'Pain', the first of 'Sequence from Hospital', she resists the over-tidying of her lines that mar some of her later work:

> Bed, ward, window begin
> To lose their solidity. Faces no longer
> Look kind or needed; yet I still fight the stronger
> Terror – oblivion – or the needle thrusts in.[75]

At her best, she warrants the tribute, 'Without ever having been a genuinely confessional poet, Elizabeth Jennings has explored more territory in more depth than most poets writing today.'[76] Note here, the undefined 'genuinely confessional' that suggests the 'truth to experience' assumptions that we are exchanging for a model that emphasises the literary processes.

Unsettling gender archetypes

Although Jung's concept of a 'collective unconscious' sounds unfashionably essentialising, he believed that a writer's treatment of universal archetypes are negotiations with cultural norms: 'Therein is the social significance of art: it is constantly at work educating the spirit of the age, conjuring up the forms in which the age is most lacking.'[77] When it comes to gender, Plath's fierce intellectualism defines her work against the feminine 'anima' and Jennings transcends it by daring a lyric persona that blends and speaks for everyman and everywoman. On a personal level, Jennings recorded dreams of being a boy in search of a mother and father and of a third sex 'nether wholly masculine or feminine, but partaking of both'.[78] This ambivalence of sex and gender is manifest in her all too familiar conflict concerning female authorship: 'There never seems to be many good women poets at any given time.'[79] She did find some literary mothers in Emily Dickinson[80] and Christina Rossetti,[81] appreciated the acquaintance of Edith Sitwell and Lynette Roberts, met Adrienne Rich, Anne Ridler and Kathleen Raine, broadcast a poetry reading with Anne Stevenson (9 September 1977) and was in a Radio 3 transmission, 'Three Women Poets', in 1971.[82] More often, she appropriated the male tradition, such as Wordsworth's *Prelude* in 'A Cliff Walk in North Devon When I was Twelve', without any political challenge to gender norms.[83] We might consider that her constant intertextual allusions to and echoes of male poets (from Shakespeare and Traherne to Hopkins and Auden) constrain her creativity. As we have seen, she sometimes argues with the archetypal doctor or priest but more frequently immerses her ego in the idealised archetypes of holy women such as the Virgin Mary ('The Annunciation', 'Meditation on the Nativity') or St Teresa ('Teresa of Avila').[84]

Whereas Jennings was preoccupied with the approval of male writers and critics and her method is much the same throughout her oeuvre, Plath's discernibly developed. She recorded on 20 January 1959, 'Finished a poem this weekend, "Point Shirley, Revisited," on my grandmother. Oddly powerful and moving to me in spite of the rigid formal structure. Evocative. Not so one-dimensional.' The poem is diligently technical, with an obvious dynamic of assonance and dissonance: 'She is dead / Whose laundry snapped and froze here.'[85] In a journal entry a few weeks later, she wrote her own manifesto for a more refreshing confessionalism:

> My main thing now is to start with real things: real emotions, and leave out the baby gods, the old men of the sea, the thin people, the knights, the moon-mothers, the mad maudlins, the Lorelei, the hermits, and get into me, Ted,

friends, mother and brother and father and family. The real world. Real situations, behind which the great gods play the drama of blood, lust and death.[86]

For Plath, freeing up her creativity was tied to discarding the influence of her husband, who praised her 'artisan-like' technical mastery.[87] She confronts the inheritance of femaleness in 'The Disquieting Muses' and in her journal: 'How odd, men don't interest me at all now, only women and women-talk. It is as if Ted were my representative in the world of men . . . Must try poems. DO NOT SHOW ANY TO TED. I sometimes feel a paralysis come over me: his opinion is so important to me.'[88] Whereas in her early adulatory 'Ode for Ted' she is 'this adam's woman', later, the 'real emotions' of her bitterness are manufactured into exaggerated metaphors of animals that plunder and satirise Hughes' poetic purse:

> You wooed me with the wolf-headed fruit bats
> Hanging from their scorched hooks in the moist
> Fug of the Small Mammal House.[89]

The assonance and dissonance are still here, but we find the free association of Plath's later work that resonates in the auditory imagination. Famously, in 'Daddy', Plath smashes archetypes of the animus: 'If I've killed one man, I've killed two', and reduces masculine symbolic language to 'your gobbledygoo'. 'The Colossus' famously stands both for the men in her life and for the overbearing weight of the male literary tradition: 'Thirty years now I have laboured / To dredge the silt from your throat' – the anagram of 'slit' marking an unsubtle killer instinct that is sharply unfeminine.[90]

Plath's meddling with gender archetypes is a feminist aesthetic that interrogates Jung's maintenance of binary polarities through universalising the animus and anima as gendered opposites. Although Shakespeare's Ariel is the androgynous spirit eventually set free from the mastery of the god-like Prospero, the poems in Plath's *Ariel* overturn the idealisations of the 'anima' as conceived in the male imagination. Most obviously, she ruptures symbolic idealisations of motherhood in 'Metaphors' ('I'm a means, a stage, a cow in calf') and desentimentalises pregnancy in 'Morning Song': 'The Midwife slapped her footsoles', 'All night your moth-breath // flickers among the flat pink roses'. As we have seen in 'Tulips', Plath's floral symbols tend to be unbearably bleak defamiliarisations of archetypal femininity. She thus succeeds in reworking her antagonisms towards her mother to produce a more collective expression of female anger and experience. She also famously speaks for the female race about the injuries from her father and husband, as in 'Burning the

Letters' and 'For a Fatherless Son': 'You will be aware of an absence, presently, / Growing beside you, like a tree'. Like Jennings, we see here how second-person pronouns present the self/other dialogue that often constitutes female subjectivity and that signals to the reader the most intimate of confidences. In Plath's last poem, 'Edge', the chilling third-person narration of a woman's stiffening body beside her two dead children is poignantly personal and yet magnified by the tropes of Greek theatre and Shakespeare's Cleopatra: 'The illusion of a Greek necessity // Flows in the scrolls of her toga.'[91] Sylvia Plath's belief in poetry as a transformative process is a tragic irony that accentuates both the cross-over and the distinction between what is written and what is lived: 'Writing is a religious act: it is an ordering, a reforming, a relearning and reloving of people and the world as they are and as they might be. A shaping.'[92]

Conclusion

So called 'confessional' poetry has a tricky history of critical responses that are muddied by psychology, religion and a conflicted Anglo/American divide. Harnessing Jung's emphasis on the creative processes, critical practice can look for 'technical mastery' in the following ways: the interaction between the text and the reader; poets' shifts between private and communal voices that are tied to an equation between personal and social identities; the evocation of the *un*knowable and *un*said. A specifically female aesthetic might meddle with mythologies of the masculine animus and feminine anima, within a spectrum between the creative androgyny that appealed to Jennings and the explicitly female expressiveness of Plath. As Pollard hopes, such a 'New Confessionalism' will revitalise both critical and poetic practices, recognising continuities with and breaks from the colloquial self-revelatory characteristics of the post-war Americans, and that stretch back to the Romantic, Metaphysical and classical poets. Such a *poetic* confessionalism enables the woman poet to align herself with such predecessors as Keats, Dickinson, Sexton, Lowell or Larkin and now Plath or Jennings without the baggage of 'primal scream'.[93] Into the twenty-first century, Gwyneth Lewis is a luminary whose preoccupation with the relationship between language and the fathoming and articulation of cultural duality, depression and psychotherapy manifests as counter-discursive to professional treatments of confessional talk.[94] She continues the best poetry that self-reflexively retains elements of the unspeakable and the ambiguous nature of experience through skilful metaphoric and metrical versatility.

Notes

I am grateful to Michael Schmidt and to the librarians who assisted me with the papers of Elizabeth Jennings: Stella Halkyard at the John Rylands University Library, University of Manchester and Nicholas Scheetz at the University of Washington, Georgetown, for their enthusiasm, knowledge and expertise; and to the willing staff at the University of Delaware, the SUNY University at Buffalo and the Olin Library, Washington University in St. Louis for their help.

1 Claire Pollard, 'Getting poetry to confess', *Magma* 21 (Autumn 2001), 41–4. www.poetrymagazines.org.uk/magazine/record.asp?id=4935

2 *Ibid.*

3 See, for example, Suzanne Clark, *Sentimental Modernism: Women Writers and the Revolution of the Word* (Bloomington and Indianapolis: Indiana University Press, 1991); Jane Dowson, *Women, Modernism and British Poetry 1910–39: Resisting Femininity* (Aldershot: Ashgate, 2002).

4 Fleur Adcock, *The Faber Book of 20th Century Women's Poetry* (London: Faber & Faber, 1987), pp. 5, 13.

5 For further discussion, see Claire Pollard, 'Anne Sexton, the Cold War and the idea of the housewife', *Critical Quarterly* 48.3 (2006), 1–24; Jo Gill, *Anne Sexton's Confessional Poetics* (Gainsville: University Press of Florida, 2007); Deryn Rees-Jones, *Consorting With Angels: Essays on Modern Women Poets* (Tarset: Bloodaxe, 2005); Alice Entwistle, 'Plath and contemporary British poetry' in Jo Gill (ed.), *The Cambridge Companion to Sylvia Plath* (Cambridge: Cambridge University Press, 2007); and Elizabeth Gregory, 'Confessing the body', in Jo Gill (ed.), *Modern Confessional Writing* (London: Routledge, 2005). Jo Gill has my thanks for her encouragement and feedback on the chapter.

6 In commenting on my final draft, Jo Gill drew my attention to the 'Anglo/ American split in the field . . . that Alvarez addresses in "Beyond all this fiddle" and it has re-emerged countless times'.

7 *Elizabeth Jennings, The Collected Poems*, ed. Emma Mason (Manchester: Carcanet, 2012).

8 See John Press, *Rule and Energy: Trends in British Poetry since the Second World War* (Oxford: Oxford University Press, 1963).

9 Letter from Philip Larkin (4 February 1956), 'The great thing about your poems, if I may say so, is the way in which, as I think of it, you give your words room to breathe as nobody else does . . . It used to be called "ear".' Another admirer at that time was Vita Sackville-West in a letter dated 22 February 1956: 'how much I like your poems'. Elizabeth Jennings Papers, MSS 52599 (London: British Library, Department of Manuscripts).

10 See for example, review of *Lucidities*, *Times Literary Supplement* (TLS) (11 December 1970), or Julian Symons, 'A distilled despair', review of *Moments of Grace* and *Selected Poems*, TLS (1 February 1980).

11 See letter from Michael Schmidt (7 July 1989), about weekly requests for anthology rights: 'and your books continue to sell very well indeed. Statistically speaking, you are now unrivalled as our best-seller. Indeed you must be one of the best-selling poets in England.' (Elizabeth Jennings Papers, University of Manchester: John Rylands Library.)

12 Jennings was one in the top twenty-four best-selling twentieth-century poets in Gary Mckeone and Jane O'Brien (eds.), *A Poetry Survey for the Arts Council of England: Key Findings* (London: Literature Department and Policy Research and Planning Department, Arts Council of England, 1996), p. 29. Her *Selected Poems* (1979) sold over 50,000 copies and her *Collected Poems* (1986) 35,000. See Michael Schmidt, Preface, *New Collected Poems* (Manchester: Carcanet, 2002), p. xx.

13 Sylvia Plath, *The Poet Speaks* (Argo Record Co. No. RG445 Lm, 1962). See the 1967 correspondence between Hughes and Sexton for his distancing of Plath from Lowell and Sexton: *Letters of Ted Hughes*, ed. Christopher Reid (London: Faber, 2007).

14 Interview (26 August 1993) in Appendix to Gerlinde Gremang, *Elizabeth Jennings* (New York: Edwin Mellor Press, 1994), pp. 93–101: 96. See also Jennings' review of *Charlotte Mew and her Friends* by Penelope Fitzgerald: 'until quite recently the term "woman poet" has all too often become an equation for suicide', *Daily Telegraph* (10 November 1982). This stance is unhelpfully reinforced by Germaine Greer in *Slipshod Sibyls: Recognition, Rejection and the Woman Poet* (Harmondsworth: Penguin, 1996).

15 Thomas Blackburn, 'In the fifties', in *The Price of an Eye* (London: Longman, 1961), p. 151.

16 Discussion of confessional poetry by a number of poets and critics, 30 July 1965, BBC3. See M.L. Rosenthal, ch. 3 'Other confessional poets', in *The New Poets: American and British Poetry since World War II* (New York: Oxford University Press, 1967), pp. 79–80.

17 *TLS* (21 September 1967).

18 Elizabeth Jennings, Preface, *Collected Poems* (Manchester: Carcanet, 1987), p. 13.

19 Elizabeth Jennings, 'Contexts', *London Magazine* (February 1962), 51.

20 M. L. Rosenthal, 'Poetry as confession', *The Nation* (19 September 1959). Rpt. in M.L. Rosenthal, *Our Life in Poetry: Selected Essays and Reviews* (New York: Persea Books, 1991), pp. 109–12.

21 Jo Gill offers a Foucauldian way of looking at the relationship between subject, text and reader/confessor in 'Anne Sexton and confessional poetics', *Review of English Studies* 55.3 (2004), 425–45.

22 Pollard, 'Getting poetry to confess', 41–4.

23 Sylvia Plath, *Collected Poems*, ed. Ted Hughes (London: Faber, 1981), pp. 160–2.

24 Peter Dale, ' "O Honey Bees Come Build" ', *Agenda* (Summer 1966), 49–55. Rpt. in Linda W. Wagner (ed.), *Sylvia Plath: The Critical Heritage* (London and New York: Routledge, 1988), pp. 62–8, 67.

25 'On the relation of analytical psychology to poetry' (lecture 1922; England 1923, 1928), in C.G. Jung, *The Spirit of Man, Art and Literature* (London: Routledge, 1984), pp. 65–83; p. 74.

26 For a lengthy discussion of Plath's treatment of archetypes, see Judith Kroll, *Chapters in a Mythology: The Poetry of Sylvia Plath* (New York and London: Harper and Row, 1976).

27 Notes after reading *A Time to Die* by Mark Pegrin, autobiographical account of his cancer experiences in hospitals and extracts from journals describing his talks with two Jungian analysts. Box 10, Notebook D, Elizabeth Jennings Papers, WTU00061 (St Louis: Washington University Library).

28 Plath, *The Poet Speaks*.

29 For example, Kroll, *Chapters in a Mythology*, and Susan Bassnett, *Sylvia Plath: an Introduction to the Poetry* (Basingstoke: Palgrave Macmillan, 2005). Bassnett includes an insightful discussion of the bee references in Plath's journals and poems, pp. 31–3.

30 Plath, *Collected Poems*, pp. 211, 118.

31 Adam Kirsch, *The Wounded Surgeon: Confession and Transformation in Six American Poets* (New York: W.W. Norton & Co., 2005), p. 73. Kirsch makes a fascinating yet critical parallel between confessional poetry and Freudian analysis.

32 Jennings, *New Collected Poems*, pp. 198, 1.

33 See, for example, *Ibid.*, Jennings on emotional conflict: 'Having it Both Ways', p. 300; 'Touch,' p. 301; 'Love's Struggle', p. 324; on heartbreak: 'On its Own', p. 140; 'Shock', p. 83; 'Hurt', p. 91; 'Transformation', p. 93; on loss: 'A New Pain', p. 72; and on regret: 'Endings', p. 160; 'Absence', p. 19; 'The Unfulfilled', p. 54.

34 'The Instruments', in *Ibid.*, p.55.

35 *Ibid.*, p. 216.

36 'Order', in *ibid.*, pp. 298–9.

37 'After a Time: for a Friend Dead Two Years', in *Ibid.*, p. 100.

38 Jung, 'On the relation', p. 71.

39 Jennings, *New Collected Poems*, p. 90.

40 W. H. Auden and John Garrett, Introduction, *The Poet's Tongue* (London: Bell, 1935).

41 Jennings, *Autobiography Vol. 1: The Inward War*. Box 12, Notebook I, Elizabeth Jennings Papers, WTU00061 (St Louis: Washington University Library).

42 Jennings, *New Collected Poems*, p. 35.

43 *Ibid.*, pp. 35–6, 71–2, 271–2; 'Works of Art', in *ibid.*, p. 67.

44 Martin Booth, *British Poetry 1964–84: Driving through the Barricades* (London: Routledge & Kegan Paul, 1985), p. 178.

45 Jung, 'On the relation', p. 71.

46 Jennings, *As I Am: An Early Autobiography*, p. 11. Elizabeth Jennings Papers, Series 2, Box 32, Fold. 1 (Washington DC: Georgetown University Library).

47 Jennings, *Collected Poems*, pp. 73–4.

48 *Ibid.*, p. 250.

49 *Ibid.*, p. 234.

50 See Jennings on her jealousy towards her sister in her unpublished autobiography (see note 42).

51 Carl Jung, 'Alchemical studies', in *The Collected Works of C.J. Jung*, vol. XIII (Princeton: Princeton University Press, 1967), p. 265. www.shadowdance.com/cgjung/cgjung.html

52 Elizabeth Jennings, *Poetry To-day* (London: Longmans, Green and Co., 1961), p. 56.

53 See Susan R. Van Dyne, 'The problem of biography', in Gill (ed.), *The Cambridge Companion to Sylvia Plath*, pp. 3–20.

54 Michiko Kakutani, 'Sylvia Plath', *New York Times* (11 September 2008). http://topics.nytimes.com/top/reference/timestopics/people/p/sylvia_plath/index.html

55 Van Dyne, 'The problem of biography', p. 5.

56 Plath, *Collected Poems*, p. 142.

57 *Ibid.*, pp. 269–70.
58 See, for example, Jacqueline Rose, Preface, *The Haunting of Sylvia Plath* (London: Virago, 1992), pp. xi–xiv.
59 Sylvia Plath, 18 October 1962, *Letters Home*, ed. Aurelia Plath (London: Faber 1975), pp. 470–1.
60 Plath, 'Fever 103°', in *Collected Poems*, pp. 231–2.
61 *Ibid.*
62 Rose, *The Haunting of Sylvia Plath*, p. 161, Kirsch, *The Wounded Surgeon*, p. 74.
63 Plath, *Collected Poems*, pp. 244–7.
64 Jennings, 'Well-Being', in *New Collected Poems*, p. 342.
65 'I DON'T believe in such theories of poetry as therapy at all.' Interview with Jennings, *Acumen* 1 (1985), 8–17: 10–11.
66 Jennings, 'Reflection' 21, Box 8, Notebook C (1957–65), Elizabeth Jennings Papers (St Louis: Washington University Library).
67 Jung, 'On the relation', pp. 75–9.
68 Jennings, *New Collected Poems*, p. 50.
69 *Ibid.*
70 Letter to Michael Schmidt, 20 March 1996: 'I miss a darkness in Seamus' work. The best poets always have it.' Elizabeth Jennings Papers (Manchester University: John Rylands Library).
71 Jennings, 'Reflection' 23, Box 8, Notebook C (1957–65), Elizabeth Jennings Papers, WTUU0061 (St Louis: Washington University Library).
72 Jennings, *New Collected Poems*, pp. 53–4.
73 Jennings, 'Night Garden of the Asylum', in *ibid.*, p. 77.
74 Jennings, 'Hospital', in *ibid.*, pp. 65–6.
75 In *Ibid.*, p. 63.
76 Margaret Byers, 'Cautious vision: recent British poetry by women', in Michael Schmidt and Grevel Lindop (eds.), *British Poetry since 1960* (Manchester: Carcanet, 1972), pp. 74–84; 83.
77 Jung on anima and animus: 'Every man carries within him the eternal image of woman'; '[the woman] too has her inborn image of man'. 'The development of the personality', *Collected Works*, vol. XVII (1970), p. 338. http://psikoloji.fisek. com.tr/jung/animus.htm; Jung, 'On the relation', pp. 80, 82–3.
78 Elizabeth Jennings, 'My dreams during the first 3 weeks of May 1965.' Box 8, Notebook D, Elizabeth Jennings Papers, WTUU0061 (St Louis: Washington University Library).
79 Elizabeth Jennings, *Poetry To-day*, p. 51. She did note the emergence of Jennifer Joseph and Patricia Beer.
80 Elizabeth Jennings, 'Emily Dickinson and the poetry of the inner life', *A Review of English Literature* 3. 2 (April 1962), 78–87.
81 'Like many, perhaps most, women poets, Christina Rossetti seems to lean towards the dark side of life . . . Like other women poets, such as Emily Dickinson and Charlotte Mew, she is always close to the melancholy, the withdrawn, the broken things.' Introduction, *A Choice of Christina Rossetti's Verse*, ed. Jennings (London: Faber, 1970), pp. 9, 10.
82 Producer George Macbeth (22 August 1971).
83 Jennings, *New Collected Poems*, p. 269.
84 *Ibid.*, pp. 31–2, 101, 33–4.

85 *The Journals of Sylvia Plath*, ed. Ted Hughes (New York: Dial Press, 1982), p. 293; see 'Point Shirley Revisited', *Collected Poems*, p. 110.

86 Plath, *Journals*, p. 298.

87 Hughes, Introduction to *Collected Poems*, p. 13.

88 Plath, *Collected Poems*, pp. 74–6; *Journals*, p. 295.

89 Plath, *Collected Poems*, pp. 29–30; 'Zoo Keeper's Wife', in *ibid.*, pp. 154–5.

90 *Ibid.*, pp. 222–4, 29.

91 *Ibid.*, pp. 116, 156–7, 204–5, 205–6, 272–3; see Kroll, *Chapters in a Mythology*, pp. 144–5.

92 Sylvia Plath (12 December 1958), in *The Journals of Sylvia Plath 1950–62*, ed. Karen V. Kukil (London: Faber & Faber, 2000), pp. 436–7. For more analysis of Plath's drafts and revisions see Susan Van Dyne, *Revising a Life: Sylvia Plath's Ariel Poems* (Chapel Hill and London: University of North Carolina Press, 1993).

93 A seminal essay is Laurence Lerner's 'What is confessional poetry?' *Critical Quarterly* 29.2 (1987), 46–66.

94 See Gwyneth Lewis, *Sunbathing in The Rain: A Cheerful Book of Depression* (Tarset: Bloodaxe, 2002) and *Chaotic Angels: Poems in English* (Tarset: Bloodaxe, 2005). These are discussed by Alice Entwistle in '"A Kind of Authentic Lie": authenticity and the lyric sequence in Gwyneth Lewis's English-language poetry', *Life Writing* 6 (1 April 2009), 27–43.

6

MELANIE PETCH

The mid-Atlantic imagination: Mina Loy, Ruth Fainlight, Anne Stevenson, Anne Rouse and Eva Salzman

> Maybe one of the hallmarks in my work is a mid-Atlantic suspension.
> Or Nowheresville.[1]

This chapter aims to give a place to poets who can qualify as both American and British but often get claimed by one side of the divide or fall in between. These poets include British-born Mina Loy (1882–1966) and American-born Ruth Fainlight (1931–), Anne Stevenson (1933–), Anne Rouse (1954–) and Eva Salzman (1961–). Collectively, their publications span nearly the entire century: Loy's output covers the early twentieth century (although she produced work right up until the 1960s); Fainlight and Stevenson – Plath's contemporaries – are post-war poets still publishing today; Rouse and Salzman are late twentieth-century poets whose careers began in the last decade with the arrival of Salzman's *The English Earthquake* in 1992 and Rouse's *Sunset Grill* a year later.[2] The need to define these poets as a national product often leads to the stamping out of their cultural duality. Loy is mostly regarded as American, despite her orthodox upbringing in Victorian England. Stevenson and Fainlight are usually perceived as British, even though they spent their formative years in America. Rouse and Salzman, having both established themselves in Britain for many years, are only ever seen as American. A term that fully captures their affiliation with two cultures is needed. Despite 'Anglo-American' literally meaning a British-born American, it comes closest to reflecting their sense of 'bothness'. Also recognising its potential, Keith Tuma stresses the importance of painting 'some detail into the larger picture of the blind struggles across the hyphen in "Anglo-American" in order to complicate it, without necessarily blotting the picture out'.[3] In keeping it to describe poets who emigrated one way or the other, I use it to define who they are rather than how they write. I prefer 'mid-Atlantic imagination' to describe how they transform their preoccupations with geographical location, journeys and home through the poetic act that is contingent upon yet moves them out of these material experiences of place.

The mid-Atlantic imagination does not have the 'writing back' of colonised cultures but can satirise its own and its adopted lands; it plays with being an insider and outsider, sometimes through female-specific perspectives and symbols, and it meddles with American experimental/British formal polarities.

The perceived polarity between American experimentalism and British formalism is outlined rather crudely by Donald Davie: 'American poetry was allowed to be expansive and exciting; British poetry had to be unexciting and comfortable and "little".'[4] Davie implies that 'unexciting and comfortable' poetry is the kind that conforms to traditional metres and rhythms, the highly crafted, if predictable, type of poetry which is associated with British verse forms; on the other hand, 'expansive and exciting' is considered to be writing that is delivered through free verse, ruptured syntax, distorted lines and line lengths, and the manipulation of typography and space. These deeply embedded views have often perpetuated the labelling of Anglo-American poets as one nationality or another. While it is true that most of them favour free verse, at times they also claim such tight forms as the English sonnet or the villanelle. Moreover, while Fainlight and Stevenson lean towards a genteel, slightly reserved idiom, Loy, Rouse and Salzman are mostly satirical and provocative. The allegiance to their country of birth is sometimes evident in imagery or in the stance of the observer of their adopted lands. More often, we witness the sense of 'suspension' that Salzman articulates in the above interview statement. Rather than finding expressions of cultural alienation as spoken by a colonised minority, we witness 'in-betweenness' as frequently constructed as a superior stance and always a creatively productive condition.

Marxist philosopher and sociologist, Henri Lefebvre,[5] and French feminist and poststructuralist critic, Julia Kristeva,[6] describe how these poets evoke artistic subjectivity as preferable to the socialised self, creating a 'somewhere' out of 'nowheresville'. Lefebvre refers to 'the dominated – and hence passively experienced – space which the imagination seeks to change and appropriate. It overlays physical space, making symbolic use of its objects.'[7] Thus, through the poem, lived experiences that are governed by social constructions can be re-imagined; for Kristeva making 'a game, a space of fantasy and pleasure, out of the abstract and frustrating order of social signs, the words of everyday communication' defines the specifically female artistic act. Furthermore, the woman poet, she claims, represents 'the enigmas of the body, the dreams, secret joys, shames, hatreds of the second sex'.[8] In the poems to be discussed we find women as keen surveyors of place and negotiators of uncharted spaces who explore and express their 'mid-Atlanticism' through such female symbols and perspectives as maternal metaphors, self/other reflections in windows and simultaneous attachment/detachment in relation to the domestic sphere and their geographical environment.

Mina Loy (1882–1966)

Loy is the only British-born poet presented here; significantly she is also the most radical in terms of her candid voice and innovations with poetic form. Despite critics playing up her American influences, Loy's radical poetics were as much tied to her stifling Victorian upbringing in England as they were to her expatriation to Europe and then eventually America in 1916. Her auto-mythological poem *Anglo-Mongrels and the Rose* (1923–5) shows how her memories of England are often intrinsically tied to her mother, perceived as 'Albion / in female form'.[9] Roger Conover, editor of her posthumous collections *The Last Lunar Baedeker* and *The Lost Lunar Baedeker*, makes clear just how dominating her mother's presence was upon Loy during her adolescent years by suggesting that her aptitude for art and poetry, although encouraged by her father, was strictly censured and stifled by her mother.[10] In an autobiographical extract, 'Notes on childhood', Loy writes: 'drawings and poems were the prey of her [mother's] attacks'.[11] For Loy, escaping from England was as much about releasing herself from her mother's grasp to reinvent herself in Europe and America. In Europe, Loy, who was influenced by other radical thinkers and artists such as Mabel Dodge, Filippo Tommaso Marinetti and Gertrude Stein, began conducting her verbal experiments, such as 'Parturition', 'Italian Pictures' and 'Three Moments in Paris' (all published in 1914). Even though these early poems were written while Loy was staying in Florence, it was in America that her poetic reputation was first established. Magazines such as *Camera Work* and *Trend*, under the editorship of Alfred Stieglitz and Carl Van Vechten respectively, were Loy's first receptors across the Atlantic and published her early pieces.

Loy's antipathy towards English conservatism is reflected in the way her poetry has been placed. Virginia Kouidis presents her as *Mina Loy: American Modernist Poet* in the first full-length re-evaluative analysis. Kouidis asserts that Loy's poetry warrants a national label 'because of its contributions to feminist thought and art and to an understanding of the origins, practice, and aims of American poetic modernism'.[12] It took until 1985 for her poetry to be edited and championed by Roger Conover for a British audience although he too conceived that 'Loy never belonged to England.'[13] The title *Anglo-Mongrels* suggests that Loy perceives herself as an English hybrid, preferring to align herself with her Jewish father, whom she calls

'Exodus'. In contrast, Loy expresses her initial awe of America in 'America A Miracle' (*The Last Lunar Baedeker*, 1982) as she finds it 'incomparable / to the tortoise history' of her English ancestry.[14]

Loy's negotiations with national territories are reworked in poems in which she is the observer/outsider who negotiates the thresholds and boundaries of the home. Her energetic 'The Effectual Marriage or the Insipid Narrative of Gina and Miovanni' (*The Last Lunar Baedeker*, 1982/1985) is one of the most satirical domestic poems of the twentieth century. In spatial terms, she maintains and subverts the ideal of distinct yet co-operative gender roles and spheres. The speaker firmly allocates Gina a female space 'among the pots and pans' in the kitchen. Gina is consumed with the idea of submerging herself within her woman's role; she wants, 'To be everything in woman',[15] but Loy's candid idiom and disruptive syntax undercut the viability of her aspirations. Loy's sharply ironic treatment of the home space is again evident in 'Virgins Plus Curtains Minus Dots' (*The Last Lunar Baedeker*, 1982/1985), where the house becomes a holding shell for these women who are only capable of staring into the outside world without the freedom to participate in it. Referring to their passive observations of men who are 'going somewhere', her speaker notes: 'Men's eyes look into things / Our eyes look out.'[16] Her marked typographical spaces visually recreate the desirable female space that Kristeva theorises. By exposing the unrealistic and undesirable binaries of traditional gender roles, Loy diminishes social codes that have elevated the public space of men and re-imagines a space where female authority is achieved through linguistic ingenuity. By articulating her 'mongrel' state in highly innovative syntax, Loy arguably creates a poetic persona that overlays her lived 'outsiderdom'.

Ruth Fainlight (1931–), Anne Stevenson (1933–)

Dana Gioia describes Anne Stevenson as the 'finest American woman poet-critic of her generation now active'. Gioia, who understands the problems of trying to reclaim a poet who has made another country her home, uses the term 'American' ironically because Stevenson 'has been shamefully neglected by her native land'.[17] Stevenson spent her formative years growing up in America before moving to Britain in 1954,[18] and like her contemporary, Ruth Fainlight, is recognised in British anthologies, but, as Gioia admits, 'It is a pleasure to share [Anne Stevenson] with England but not at the expense of excluding her from the American canon where she also belongs.'[19] Fainlight, who also spent her childhood growing up in America and has now lived in England longer than anywhere else, in a recent interview confessed that she is still dogged by unbelonging: 'when I was in

America I was regarded as English, and when I was in England I was regarded as American'.[20] However, Fainlight's reflection on her dual identity has as much relish as anxiety; this self-satisfaction, almost egotism, in evading national typecasts can also be detected in Stevenson and Loy.

Stevenson and Fainlight are equally adamant about sidestepping stereotypes of English or American literary performance. Stevenson does not fit tidily into an American critical landscape, suspecting that 'there isn't really such a thing as free verse. Or if there is, I don't think I've written any.'[21] Notably, 'The Fiction Makers ' (*The Fiction Makers*, 1985) shuns Pound's attempts at 'squeezing the Goddam iamb / out of our verse'.[22] On the other hand, she claims that 'it's good to get away from the straightjacket of overstrict meters'.[23] Above all, she strives for individuality in her poetry and finds liberation in perching just outside national typecasting. Fainlight is equally keen for uniqueness: 'I don't really want to be called an American poet, or an English poet, or a Woman poet, or heaven forbid, a Jewish poet. I am an English Language poet.'[24] Often her poems are conservative and tight in appearance but she can also work poetic form in innovative ways – a tendency that is rarely commented on. Her 1966 *Cages* collection brims with neat-looking poems that are mostly written in free verse with an emphasis on cadence rather than strict metrical schemes. *Burning Wire* (2002) includes such innovative pieces as 'Potatoes', written in three solid stanzas of dense prose, and an epic narrative, 'Sheba and Solomon', is eclectically intertextual.

I am grouping Fainlight and Stevenson together here because they are of the same generation, and because of their identical pattern of migration and their shared diffidence to both native and adoptive lands. Stevenson, a prolific reporter of place, has built up a collection of work that reflects her own geographical journeying around locations in the United Kingdom and America. Emily Grosholz notes that Stevenson's 'home country is uncertain, and the tensions between Here and Elsewhere in her writing remain unresolved'.[25] Her poem 'Green Mountain, Black Mountain' (*A Report from the Border*, 2003) holds together these 'unresolved' tensions and perpetuates Lefebvre's theory that poems can create what is unachievable in material conditions. Stevenson's green mountain connects with the landscape in the National Forest conservation area in Vermont; her black mountain, on the other hand, offers a snapshot of an area in the Brecon Beacons National Park in Wales.[26] The backdrops that symbolise the two continents where she has lived become indistinguishable in the poetic imagination where she may love and loathe both places at once: 'In dread of the black mountain', evokes 'Gratitude for the green mountain'.[27] The subsequent lines are then reversed as she expresses dread for the green mountain and gratitude for the black mountain. The poem becomes a place that contains the contradictory flux of feelings and an alternative space in which to retreat.

The journey is at once a context and metaphor for in-betweenness. A growing area of critical interest, the journey has also become a politicised arena. Caren Kaplan recognises the creative potential of these transitional spaces: 'In the age of telecommunications and transnational cultural production . . . distance does not inevitably lead to exile or war but to new subjectivities that produce new relationships to space as well as time so that distance is not only a safety zone or field of tension but a terrain that houses new subjects of criticism.'[28] Expressing some of the new subjectivities to which Kaplan refers, in the poems I am about to discuss feminine archetypes of self-reflection, namely windows and mirrors, suggest a heightened female awareness. In the journey space poets project their enjoyment at being apart from the thrust of social imperatives: 'It is in the aspiration towards artistic and, in particular, literary creation', writes Kristeva, 'that woman's desire for affirmation now manifests itself.'[29] Stevenson writes compellingly on the subject of female affirmation in 'Travelling Behind Glass' (*Travelling Behind Glass*, 1974). Affirmation is sometimes the mood of the traveller or it can empathetically compensate for a keen sense of loss. Journeying by car is a state of being that is 'safe behind glass'. As the driver absorbs her surroundings, we witness how the window ambiguously marks an almost suffocating boundary between the world outside the car and the one within. This oppressive inside space forces the speaker to confront herself: 'Who is that woman?' she asks, 'sitting . . . / in the shadow-broken mirror / of her window'. At this point the two women become unified in the glass: 'Avoiding her eyes, / I discover her own in my face'.[30] There is a palpable sense of female affiliation as the two women merge, and yet, uncomfortably, their eyes cannot meet.

Fainlight's 'The Journey ' (*Fifteen to Infinity*, 1983) also uses the glass/ window/mirror to chart a mid-Atlantic self-discovery. This time, a train journey allows the speaker to explore a much younger self reflected in the window and to reminisce upon the passing of time: 'Softened by the mirror of a tunnel, / my reflected face stared out, much younger.' She is warmed by the fact that her face – only half-seeming like her own – is softer and younger when gazed at from a distance, but she poignantly recognises the inevitability of aging: 'Suddenly, I learned I was not other.'[31] Fainlight returns to the theme of time passing in 'Passenger ' (*Fifteen to Infinity*, 1983) where she muses upon her childhood, with the longing to 'become again that watching dreaming girl / and this time live it out'.[32] The tunnel symbolises the point of juncture – much like the claustrophobic glass in the other poems – where the memories are engulfed and the adult self is left to consume her loss.

Fainlight expresses more of this reflective spirit in one of her most stylistically experimental poems 'The Boat ' (*Another Full Moon*, 1976) which captures the 'otherness' and female-centric nature of the journey experience. The language is highly evocative of disengagement from both reality and time. Typographically, the poem is more in the innovative style of Denise Levertov or Loy – the sentences are fractured and white space intersperses the text, resonant of a wave unravelling across the shore. The speaker watches another woman on the other side of the lake and the two become almost indistinguishable: 'Who is that person I see / . . . she looks like me'.[33] The narrative is strongly suggestive of disengagement, with 'drifting', 'slipping', 'float', 'dream' and 'empty' evoking a strangely ethereal sense of being fragmented, faltering or off course. The fractured form also reflects the desperate connection she longs to make with the other woman across the shore. The journey becomes a place of suspension where female affirmation is desperately wanted and yet elusive; as in other poems by Fainlight, it is also a place to reflect upon a self that is isolated or lost but arguably reclaimed in the writing of her.

Anne Rouse (1954–)

Rouse is an American-born poet who, having moved to England at the age of eighteen, has lived there longer than anywhere else. In all four collections of her poetry (*Sunset Grill*, 1993; *Timing*, 1997; *The School of Night*, 2004; and *The Divided*, 2008), she evokes the Virginian landscape of her childhood alongside the cityscapes of London. Her literary influences can be traced in both countries; when she began writing poetry she attached herself to Pound's Imagist dictums of condensation until she realised that 'poems occasionally failed to breathe, and had to be discarded'. It is in England, we sense, that she finds creative freedom; she also admits to a fascination with the country long before her arrival. This she attributes to 'children's books such as the Green Knowe stories and C. S. Lewis. Later, British pop music – especially the Beatles' "Penny Lane" – intrigued me. It seemed to be written in a secret language.' This secret language had such an impact upon Rouse that she even goes so far as to say that she sees London as her 'adopted imaginative home'.[34] Like Loy, only migrating the other way across the Atlantic, the act of expatriation provides Rouse with a creative outlet that would not have been possible in her homeland.

Unlike the other poets presented here, Rouse playfully observes England's fragile national emblems and takes delight in subverting the supposed gentility of English stereotypes. She offers a mischievous observation on the English football scene in 'England Nil' (*Sunset Grill*, 1993). Her speaker, an English football hooligan, tells of the foiled plan to cause trouble at a match with Germany. Adopting what appears to be a Cockney accent, her speaker issues a warning to the reader: 'You've been Englished but you won't forget it, never.'[35] Despite the mimicry, Rouse assures her readers that 'Rather than being a specific cultural critique, "England Nil" reflects a fascination with misdirected energies and excess.' Furthermore, she stresses her allegiance to her adopted country by claiming, 'Generally those early satires were written from the point of view of a participant in, and lover of, the culture.'[36] She teasingly and emboweringly pays homage to English poetic form by seizing the sonnet, while in 'Success' and 'Her Retirement' (again, *Sunset Grill*), she masters the tight villanelle. At the same time, words such as 'reckon', 'copped', 'parking lot' and 'shack' all belie her American heritage and frequently pepper her poems. The American vernacular might irk certain British critics and explain her struggle for acceptance. Sean O'Brien includes 'The Hen Night Club's Last Supper' in his influential *The Firebox* (1998), yet intimates that she is 'hard to place in any grouping'[37] and she was overlooked when the sequel to the New Generation poets (1994) was announced under the banner 'Next Generation' in 2004. However, editors of influential anthologies of women poets *have* recognised the unique and outspoken contributions by both Rouse and Salzman; they feature in *Making for Planet Alice: New Women Poets* (1997) and Linda France's *Sixty Women Poets* (1993).

For Rouse, standing both inside and outside becomes an exalted position from which to explore her surroundings. In 'The Passage' (*The School of Night*, 2004), the tiny space between two houses and the remnants that occupy that space symbolise liberation from the strangling codes of a cultural norm:

> In the passage between houses,
> a rucksack gaped in the dirt, revealing
> a milkpan, a toy kettle,
> and a greenish, flat bottle of olive oil.
>
> When I came up that narrow way again,
> the rucksack had gone.
> The cooking things lay absurd, under a wisteria.
> I took the olive oil home.
>
> The next time I climbed there,
> the kettle had been kicked down
> all 25 steps, and the milk pan

resembled a bopeep sunhat.
But today the passage undulates free
between the old-rose bricks,
the dark August leaves parting
for turrets, and captain's walks,

and a sliver of turquoise,
on which an immaculate sail
rides motionless, a small white yacht
whose invisible hull

winks, diamond, down the coast,
and what could it be signalling?
Never distress, the sea is too serene.
It must be the sun, its last late beam,
exiled, hailing, *goodbye*.[38]

As John Kerrigan states, 'you may be paradoxically less yourself in a room which mimics domestic space than in a room which doesn't'.[39] Rouse explains that each line of the poem represents another step of the passage.[40] The reader is disorientated as the steps are scattered with discarded domestic items that are literally out of place, and we follow the speaker making return visits in which she finds the items further removed and battered; the olive oil is taken, the kettle is kicked down the steps and the milk pan is misshapen. The idiom of the first three stanzas is terse, sharp and controlled, with end monosyllables, 'gone', 'home', down', accentuating finality. Then the imagination transforms the wreckage and emptiness to a condition of freedom, enchantment and serenity. Through sibilance and symbols of sunshine and sea the subject envisages the hope of endless possibilities. Avril Horner and Sue Zlosnik identify how women's constraints within the home engenders the strong desire to escape through writing about an alternative reality, where they can become someone else: 'We have a sense of space, envisaged in wide sweeps of land and unchartered tracts of sea . . . not just to give a sense of place but to suggest, sometimes with ambivalence, the possibilities for self that lie beyond society, outside patriarchy, and within the future.'[41]

Eva Salzman (1961–)

Like Rouse, Salzman's transatlantic passage saw her migrate from America to England. Apart from brief visits to New York, she has lived in Britain since 1985. Also like Rouse, Salzman expatriated with the expectation that a hospitable literary community awaited her:

I . . . held on to an idealised view of the European intellectual, considering England as part of Europe; hell, it never occurred to me that someone wouldn't *want* to be part of Europe! And I carried on my literary love affair with England. My first readings were eighteenth- and nineteenth-century novels, mainly English. I took my time joining modern times, living in a sort of (mainly) Victorian bubble.[42]

Along with other Anglo-American poets presented in this chapter, placing Salzman remains contentious. Her stylistic techniques are often an amalgamation of perceived British and American practices. She uses a rather loose villanelle in 'Power Games' and neat little quatrains in 'Promising' and 'Hatred' (all in *The English Earthquake*, 1992). In 'Helen's Sister' (*One Two II*) she works the heroic rhyming couplet for empowering humour in the face of being the 'ugly' sister: 'Once they know I'm beauty's twin / at the party door I'm in.'[43] At other times, Salzman is just as assured in free verse, and she has been likened to Plath on several occasions as well as Anne Sexton and Robert Lowell. David Herd of *The New Statesman* suggests that 'Her American voice swaggers sassily across the proprieties of English metre, pricking the bloat of monumentalism, and pointing up the slangy contingency of things.'[44] For Salzman, who is ordinarily quite content in her 'nowheresville', the problem lies with the incessant labelling that happens on British shores: 'I've always felt nationality to be something imposed on me. Maybe you also feel it when it's endangered. The English seem particularly deft at putting you in your place in this way.' She recognises that to have an overtly American voice in Britain often means sitting outside the mainstream poetry scene. When asked by Lidia Vianu if English poetry was a place she liked she replied:

English poetry is 'a place I like' . . . but I'm not sure it always likes me! Americans are recognised and even feted here, but usually after they're dead. During an Oxford event commemorating the Oxford Poets list, the Bronx poet, Michael Donaghy and I, both Oxford poets at that time, sat in the audience listening to English voices reading out absent or dead American writers. We weren't asked to read at all – were, in fact, the only current poets on the list who didn't read that night! That sort of thing makes you wonder.[45]

Clearly Salzman is disgruntled at the snubbing inflicted upon her by her Oxford contemporaries, yet there is also a sense that she can take these rebuffs as a positive reinforcement of her difference. By her own admission, she sees her voluntary 'exile' as creatively energising: 'feeling the "outsider" is the writer's habitual condition'.[46] Steve Clark and Mark Ford also point to this privileged liminality when they note how Anglo-American poets often 'avoid being contaminated by a "mainstream" they despise' by exulting in 'their very exclusion'.[47] Although bemoaning her plight, then,

Salzman seems to actively covet her position on the periphery, revelling in the reflected otherness her adoptive land yields.

To intensify these productive, verging on superior, feelings of in-betweenness, Salzman perceives a double censure in her homeland: 'being an outsider in England has made me an outsider back home too . . . I've become the foreigner in my own country, America being strange to me in precisely the way England used to be.' As if to enhance the simultaneous attachment and detachment of estrangement, she writes several poems, such as 'Brooklyn Bridge' (*One Two II: A Songbook*, 2002) and 'There is Nothing to See' (*The English Earthquake*, 1992), on her perceptions of New York as an observer. The sonnet 'Brooklyn Bridge' seeks to harmonise the impulses of belonging to and distancing from the cityscape of her childhood. When asked about the poem in a recent interview, she commented: 'The traffic hum of the Brooklyn Bridge was the background score of my childhood, and I wrote a sonnet about it, in order to re-possess what I felt to be mine.'[48] This notion of re-possession is what Lefebvre and Kristeva propose, in terms of a poem being a vehicle in which to heal the lesions experienced in the material conditions of lived experience. Paradoxically, it is the English sonnet form that Salzman uses to aggressively reclaim her home city, New York: 'This one's mine.' She renounces all the clichéd illusions (it is 'not a nail-less Bridge of Sighs', she claims, or a 'stage' where 'film crews shoot'), in favour of something more idiosyncratic: 'That dark harp was made for me to play.'[49] The harp in need of playing (exclusively by her) is an elegant symbol for appropriating non-verbal space for oneself.

As if to magnify the relationship between being outside and in, Salzman uses maternal metaphors to heighten her attachment to New York: 'I was harnessed by a yoke of fear, from birth.'[50] The play on the word 'yoke' implies the embryonic state of the unborn speaker who is maternally bound to a mother figure. This symbolic re-entry into life replicates the feelings that Salzman experiences when she returns to her native land; she concedes that her transatlantic crossings have often left her with a range of conflicting emotions when trying to make sense of her place in the world. Although pleased to be leaving New York for Britain in 1985, she admits that: 'After all these years, I've fallen back in love with my hometown – even appreciating the New York arrogance which is palliative to the stuffy Home Counties English stuff I was living with in Tunbridge Wells.'[51] As if to recreate the process of falling back in love, this poem echoes Kristeva as it becomes a place where the exhilaration of being reborn may be imaginatively realised.

Depicting the self-consciousness of the observer once more, Salzman's 'Ending up in Kent' (*The English Earthquake*, 1992) reflects her observations of rural England. In her pseudo-disdainful manner she paints a picture of the 'stuffy Home Counties English stuff' to which she earlier refers. The speaker opens the poem with the imperative, 'Postcard-picture me in a country of thatch', as if Salzman is writing to avid readers about the idealised fantasy of England that they would joyously anticipate. Implicitly inserting her American self into the stereotypical English scene, she joins her split cultural selves and carves a fictional space where both can co-exist. As an observer, much like Rouse, she inspects her surroundings with a keenly critical eye: 'I walk detergent streams, in search of trees. / Someone's put me in a story-book, but kills / every tree before my entrance', and 'I follow an ordnance survey map and find / frightening rows of straight and vacant pines', and finally, 'In warm weather / they sell sulphur from the wells for your pleasure.'[52] Salzman's toxic symbols position her as the detached cynic towards the environment she inhabits. Whilst she longs to be reborn as someone who belongs to America, she recognises that her departure from her own country warrants her as an observer on both fronts. Recognisably, her relationship with England causes her the greatest anxiety, yet it is through the poem that this discomfort is transposed into a semi-pleasurable act as she exults in the cathartic and empowering re-telling of her 'plight'.

Conclusion

Concerned as it is with the interrelationship between gender and non-colonised dual-nationality, this chapter illustrates how a mid-Atlantic imagination is most marked in the ways the poets variously shimmy between the role of observer and participant. Through the vehicle of the text, these writers find a contemplative space to reflect upon the frustrations and enchantments of voluntary migrancy. As a template, these permutations could just as easily refract through the voices of other Anglo-American poets, H.D. (1886–1961), Laura (Riding) Jackson (1901–91), Denise Levertov (1923–97), Sylvia Plath (1932–63) and Julie O'Callaghan (b. 1954).[53] With the prospect of more territories yet to uncover, the unruliness, occasional stridence and overwhelming insistence on female affirmation make this an energetic body of poetry that exults in the 'somewhere' of the imagination that the poem carves out of living in 'nowheresville'.

Notes

1 Interview with Eva Salzman conducted by Lidia Vianu, January 2003. Web source: http://lidiavianu.scriptmania.com/eva_salzman.htm (accessed June 2004).

2 In recent correspondence, Rouse mentions an important shift in the direction of her poetry:

My feeling is that we're in a critical stage in the West, and that poetry must not only confirm the need for an active reorientation (our fundamental selves vis-à-vis earth, the disadvantaged and the third world) but embody such a change. It needs to do this through joining with other art forms, finding new methods of dissemination, but most of all, by being an authentic, future-directed voice.

Correspondence between Anne Rouse and Melanie Petch, 22 May 2009

3 Keith Tuma, *Fishing by Obstinate Isles: Modern and Postmodern British Poetry and American Readers* (Evanston, IL: Northwestern University Press, 1998), p. 11.
4 Donald Davie's views are outlined by Andrew Duncan in 'The invisible museum', *Poetry Review* 92.2 (Spring 2002) (accessed online: www.poetrysociety.org.uk/review/pr92–2/duncan.htm.) In this article Duncan claims that the disgruntled reception that Tuma's anthology – Keith Tuma (ed.), *Anthology of Twentieth-Century British and Irish Poetry* (New York and Oxford: Oxford University Press, 2001) – has received in Britain is largely because reviewers 'still accept Davie's thesis – poetry which is expansive and exciting does not count as properly British'. Bearing this in mind, then, some of Tuma's choices, such as Mina Loy, John Rodker and Tom Raworth, tend to irk some critics who see this as an Americanised perspective on twentieth-century British poetry.
5 Henri Lefebvre, *The Production of Space*, trans. Donald Nicholson-Smith (1974; Oxford: Blackwell, 1991).
6 Julia Kristeva, 'Women's time', first published as 'Le temps des femmes' in 33/44: *Cahiers de recherche de sciences des textes et documents* (Winter 1979), 5–19. I refer to the version reprinted in Catherine Belsey and Jane Moore (eds.) *The Feminist Reader*, second edn (Basingstoke: Macmillan Press, 1997), pp. 201–16.
7 Lefebvre, *The Production of Space*, p. 39.
8 Kristeva, 'Women's time', pp. 212, 213.
9 Mina Loy, *Anglo-Mongrels and the Rose*, in Mina Loy, *The Last Lunar Baedeker*, ed. Roger Conover (Highlands, NC: Jargon Society, 1982), p. 123.
10 The general contours of Loy's life are outlined by Conover in 'Time-Table', *ibid.*, p. lxiii.
11 Loy, 'Notes on Childhood', *ibid.*, p. 314.
12 Virginia Kouidis, *Mina Loy: American Modernist Poet* (Baton Rouge and London: Louisiana State University Press, 1980), pp. 1–2.
13 Roger Conover, introduction to *The Lost Lunar Baedeker: Poems of Mina Loy*, ed. Conover (New York: Farrar, Straus, Giroux, 1996), p. xvii.
14 Mina Loy, 'America A Miracle', in *The Last Lunar Baedeker*, p. 227.
15 Loy, 'The Effectual Marriage', in *The Lost Lunar Baedeker*, pp. 36, 38.
16 Loy, 'Virgins Plus Curtains Minus Dots', *Ibid.*, p. 21.
17 Dana Gioia, 'Anne Stevenson poet–critic', in *The Way You Say the World: A Celebration for Anne Stevenson*, complied by John Lucas and Matt Simpson (Beeston: Shoestring Press, 2003), p. 33.
18 This was not Stevenson's first experience of expatriation; when she was six months old her American parents (residing in Cambridge, England, at the time) moved back to Harvard, where her father was an influential academic in philosophy. Stevenson's formative years were spent in America. She also made very brief return visits to America after 1954.

19 Gioia, 'Anne Stevenson Poet–Critic', p. 33.

20 Ruth Fainlight, interview conducted by Melanie Petch (April 2004).

21 Anne Stevenson, interview conducted by Cynthia Haven, *The Cortland Review* 14 (November 2000): www.cortlandreview.com/issue/14/stevenson14.htm (Accessed December 2004).

22 Anne Stevenson, 'The Fiction Makers', in *Poems: 1955–2005* (Tarset: Bloodaxe, 2005), p. 20.

23 Interview Stevenson/Haven.

24 Interview Fainlight/Petch.

25 Emily Grosholz, 'The Poetry of Anne Stevenson', in *The Way You Say The World*, p. 48.

26 Both Vermont and Powys are places which are poignant enough for Stevenson to detail in another of her earlier poems, entitled 'The Parson and the Romany: A Black Mountain Ballad to a Green Mountain Tune', in *Poems: 1955–2005*; the poem was composed in 1982 and clearly anticipates 'Green Mountain, Black Mountain'.

27 Anne Stevenson, 'Green Mountain, Black Mountain', in *Poems: 1955–2005*, p. 187.

28 Caren Kaplan, *Questions of Travel* (Durham, NC and London: Duke University Press, 1995), p. 142.

29 Kristeva, 'Women's time', p. 212.

30 Anne Stevenson, 'Travelling Behind Glass', in *Poems: 1955–2005*, pp. 50, 51.

31 Ruth Fainlight, 'The Journey', in *Selected Poems* (London: Sinclair-Stevenson, 1995), p. 185. Fainlight's new collection now supersedes all earlier versions of her work: Ruth Fainlight, *New & Collected Poems* (Tarset: Bloodaxe, 2010).

32 Fainlight, 'Passenger', in *Selected Poems*, p. 173.

33 Fainlight, 'The Boat', in *Selected Poems*, p. 49.

34 Anne Rouse, interview conducted by Melanie Petch (February 2006).

35 Anne Rouse, 'England Nil', in *Sunset Grill* (Newcastle upon Tyne: Bloodaxe, 1993), p. 27. The following collection replaces all earlier versions of her work: Anne Rouse, *The Upshot: New & Selected Poems* (Tarset: Bloodaxe, 2008).

36 Interview Rouse/Petch.

37 Sean O'Brien (ed.), *The Firebox* (London and Basingstoke: Picador, 1998), p. 421.

38 Anne Rouse, 'The Passage', in *The School of Night* (Tarset: Bloodaxe, 2004), p. 57.

39 John Kerrigan, 'Notes from the home front: contemporary British poetry', *Essays in Criticism*, 54.2 (2004), 111.

40 Interview Rouse/Petch.

41 Avril Horner and Sue Zlosnik, *Landscapes of Desire: Metaphors in Modern Women's Fiction* (London: Harvester Wheatsheaf, 1990), p. 7.

42 Interview with Eva Salzman conducted by Lidia Vianu (January 2003).

43 Eva Salzman, 'Helen's Sister', in *One Two II: A Songbook* (Brough: Wrecking Ball Press, 2002), p. 38. Salzman's most recent collection now supersedes all earlier versions of her work: Eva Salzman, *Double Crossing: New & Selected Poems* (Tarset: Bloodaxe, 2004).

44 A selection of reviews of Salzman's work can be found on the Writers and Artists website: www.writersartists.net/esalzman.htm

45 Interview Salzman/Vianu.

46 'Vianu and Salzman in Dialogue', *ICORN International Cities of Refuge Network* Web Source: www.icorn.org/articles.php?var=29#anchor61 (Accessed 31 May 2007).

47 Steve Clark and Mark Ford (eds.), *Something We Have That They Don't: British and American Poetic Relations since 1925* (Iowa City: University of Iowa Press, 2004), p. 12.

48 'Vianu and Salzman in Dialogue'.

49 Eva Salzman, 'Brooklyn Bridge', in *One Two II*, p. 51.

50 *Ibid*.

51 Interview Salzman/Vianu.

52 Eva Salzman, 'Ending up in Kent', in *The English Earthquake* (Newcastle upon Tyne: Bloodaxe Books, 1992), p. 12.

53 Neil Astley, who has published many of these poets adds, 'several other mid-Atlantic women poets come to mind also, not least Jane Duran, Carrie Etter and Jane Yeh' (email to Melanie Petch, September 24 2009).

7

CATRIONA CLUTTERBUCK

The Irish history wars and Irish women's poetry: Eiléan Ní Chuilleanáin and Eavan Boland

Introduction: the Irish history wars and women's voices

This chapter explores the idea of history as addressed in Irish women's poetry, illustrated by examples from the work of the current two most senior practitioners in the field, Eiléan Ní Chuilleanáin (b. 1942) and Eavan Boland (b. 1944). Eiléan Ní Chuilleanáin – poet, scholar, essayist, editor and translator – published her first main collection in 1972 and her seventh in 2009. Born in Cork, she is an Associate Professor in the School of English at Trinity College Dublin who specialises in Renaissance literature, literature and folklore, and literature and translation. Eavan Boland – poet, critic, teacher, essayist and editor – has published ten main collections of poetry since her first book in 1967. Born in Dublin, she is Professor in the Humanities and Director of the Creative Writing Programme at Stanford University.

Ní Chuilleanáin and Boland, in the famous words of the latter, 'began writing in a country where the word *woman* and the word *poet* were almost magnetically opposed'.[1] As foundational presences in the by now well-populated and recognised field of Irish women's poetry, their work continues to enable and challenge their peers, among whom are the poets Medbh McGuckian, Nuala Ní Dhomhnaill, Paula Meehan, Rita Ann Higgins, Moya Cannon, Mary O'Malley, Kerry Hardie, Vona Groarke, Sinéad Morrissey, Caitríona O'Reilly, Colette Bryce and Leontia Flynn. Through the work of reconnecting the identities of 'woman' and 'poet' over the course of the more than four decades to date of their coeval writing careers, Ní Chuilleanáin and Boland have realised, on behalf of Irish poetry, Boland's truism regarding the emblematic position of the woman poet today: that 'in the projects she chooses . . . are internalised some of the central stresses and truths of poetry at this moment [. . .regarding] the relation of the poem to the act of power'.[2] The 'act of power', that is the representation of the past, is a crucial arena for Irish women poets' projects of self-understanding as artists. Poems concerned with history pivotally focus the necessity for self-reflexive awareness by the writer of his or her processes in the acts of representation and witness: a defining aspect of the Irish literary tradition. To write or read poetry out of an awakened gender perspective is to have that awareness amplified. In codifying and democratising this self-reflexive consciousness, Eiléan Ní Chuilleanáin and Eavan Boland have produced a body of work which can justly be claimed as central to their art form's and their nation's renewal.

History here is understood, not in the sense of 'the matter of the past' but as 'the historian's mediation of that past in terms of retrieval, selection, evaluation, interpretation and narration'.[3] Accordingly, the following analysis focuses on what have become known as the 'history wars' that, directly or indirectly, have governed Irish studies in the past half-century. These wars are constituted by the stand-off between revisionism and counter-revisionism as approaches to history; the former is popularly associated with challenges to nationalist readings of the Irish story and the latter with their renewed defence.[4] Revisionists pertain to be realists, rejecting the value of accounts of the past that allow objects of historical knowledge to depend on the historian's activity of mind; counter-revisionists claim a visionary realism. This chapter will illustrate how the work of Ní Chuilleanáin and Boland diagnoses the malign effects of the history wars and offers resolution by re-aligning women's history and national history. Thus they exemplify how women's poetry conceptualises a newly generative model of relations between the antagonists in this debate.

Revisionism and counter-revisionism as approaches to Irish history both aim for the comprehensive representation of the past, but they differ in their respective emphases in fulfilling that purpose. Revisionism prioritises observable data over the act of interpretation, while counter-revisionism allows the larger direction of events to shape their recorded detail.[5] Revisionism first arose in the 1930s, finding full voice by the 1960s in response to then dominant traditionalist approaches to Ireland's history which relied on received wisdom and unquestioned assumptions about the country's remembered past. In particular, revisionists challenged 'the Irish version of providentialism', which held nationalism to be the self-evident medium and objective of the development of all Irish peoples – an approach which reached its apex at the time of the fiftieth anniversary of the 1916 Rising.[6] Revisionists set out specifically to deconstruct what Boland in her poem 'Love' proposes as a heroic history, one with 'the image blazing and the edges gilded', a history which encourages 'the epic question . . . // Will we ever live so intensely again?'[7] In terms of methodology, revisionism assumes that proper scholarship, founded on principles of reason-based interrogation, can produce accurate and authentic representations of the past. Thus it takes into account all possible pieces of evidence, however disparate, with the aim of presenting a complete picture. It focuses on the use of historical sources, such as overlooked records, to 'offer statements about the past which [are] both internally coherent and externally defensible'.[8]

From the mid-1970s, revisionism in turn began to come under sustained challenge from the alternative historiography – counter-revisionism – identified with postcolonial accounts of Irish politics and society, and with the fluidly interdisciplinary modes of cultural studies. Counter-revisionists critique revisionists' aspirations to value-free objectivity as naive and deceptive: naive because the ideal of 'faithfulness to what happened' risks 'produc[ing] a discourse without point and purpose, philosophically negligible, random in its accuracy and literal in its confusion'; deceptive, because the claims to authenticity and inclusiveness are usually deployed as a weapon against nationalism.[9] Counter-revisionism supports the idea that a 'positive dynamic of a developing national consciousness could be invoked as a useful concept of historical interpretation'.[10] Accordingly, it implies that the historian, in the act of speaking *from* the assembled record of bygone times, simultaneously and of necessity speaks *to* history, to its projected completion. Boland's poem 'The Muse Mother' explores a related claiming of wholeness, whereby a second-wave feminist desire to access the truths of motherhood correlates directly to the counter-revisionist desire to access the core of the past, from which centre, socio-political and cultural understanding can proceed outwards centrifugally. If Boland can 'only decline' the everyday mother she sees on the street 'to her roots', she tells us, this figure will teach her how to 'sing the past / in pure syllables'.[11]

From a revisionist perspective, however, Boland knows that to so 'decline' this woman also means to refuse her: in the poem, the living woman 'moves away' while the poet's mind 'stays fixed' in contemplation of the essential meaning of motherhood which this figure now represents for the poet.[12] In other words, this poet-speaker models the position of the historian who refuses to follow the messy lead of the actual material of history as it moves beyond that historian's terms of reference, drawing them towards what they fear may be a relativistic void of meaning. The dream of this wholeness is thus presented by Boland in its overdetermined meaning, simultaneously as radical and conservative: it is both a compelling and an unfulfillable promise, and a cautious yet a careless conception.

A measure of the investment of women in the debate above described, is the impassioned characterisation of their discipline, made in 1989 at the height of this conflict, by historians Maria Luddy and Cliona Murphy: 'And what is history in Ireland? A narrative account of the doings of men, largely carried out by men, written by men and taught by men.'[13] What this statement suggests is that hostilities between Irish historians have been conducted on the back of the silence of women. This silence is a condition of women's position in Irish culture as 'symbolically central and materially peripheral'.[14] It is well recognised that women fulfil this contradictory role in the course of territorial identity formation and contestation, wherein the female figure is deployed as symbolic medium variously of colonial and anti-colonial, traditionalist and modernising developments in the country's history, functioning always as 'a substance of [her] own / future form, both // fraction and refraction'.[15] Less obvious is the fact that women also fulfil this contradictory role in formal analyses of this history and in the often rancorous accompanying debates on that historiography.

The marginalisation of women as a function of conflicting ideas of Irish historical progress is both recognised and redressed in an Irish women's poetry alert to the poverty of the relationship of hostile difference – which plays out in practice as regressive co-dependence – that has too long defined these approaches. Diagnosing the ill effects of the dispute between revisionist 'truth tellers' and counter-revisionist 'sweet singers' (Boland, 'The Glass King'), their work promotes the need to recognise continuity between these two vocations as twin foundations of the only kind of historiography that can facilitate genuine self-knowledge.[16] In order to do this, they invest in the connective space between revisionism's concern with getting 'behind hindsight'[17] so as to speak clearly from history, and counter-revisionism's concern with acknowledging the necessity *of* hindsight so as to speak meaningfully to history.[18] In this space, history is understood as a 'passionate economy' of the whole truth which nevertheless *can* reveal the truth.[19] This paradox holds because in that new accommodation, the historian recognises that he or she also speaks *in* history: they 'chang[e] the story' of the source of their authority from one of a god's removal from human terms (whereby a 'total picture' of history is being claimed, whether through deductive or inductive means) to one where the god stays precisely *because* the historian's integral involvement with the present-centred terms of loss, limitation, need and desire is revealed (Eavan Boland, 'Formal Feeling').[20] Thus Irish women poets, in redressing the silence of women in Irish history as a discipline, conceptualise resolution of the oppositional terms of its defining conflict.

The (non)presence of the past in Irish women's poetry

It is well recognised that Irish literature is preoccupied with the presence of the past. A major focus of this interest is the paradox pertaining to the gap that exists between the historian who records the past and that past itself: that this gap is also a mediating plane, the window through which the historian peers at what has gone before. Irish women poets show that the quality of the historian's witness depends on him or her seeing the intervening glass, as much as seeing the light that comes through it. They do this in particular through seeking a medium for communicating the passage of time, which registers time as its own element too. These poets demonstrate, in other words, that the past can so complicate our understanding of it, that depth and cadence are recognised to be conditions as much integral to its access as to its realisable substance.

Eavan Boland 'sees the glass' through her career-long focus on the challenges and ethics of representation, as she seeks to bring a variety of forms of marginalised political experience – domestic reality, female bodily experience, the experience of exile abroad and at home, historical trauma (especially that of the famine) and the violence attendant on authoritative forms of such trauma's expression or elision – from outside to inside history. She shows that bringing these various forms of silenced realities into history is conditional upon two linked procedures: recognising the interconnections between these experiences, whereby in particular, territorial, gender and aesthetic conflict are revealed to influence each other, and interrogating the basis of claims to their proper witness, both by herself and others. For Boland, at the heart of this concern is the relationship between art and history as mutually informing flawed attempts to recover the real. Throughout her work, this poet's focus on aesthetics allows her to engage with political representation more generally. From her earliest poems she registers the disjunction between art and time, representation and reality, as giving rise to ethical questions around loss. She gradually recognises that it is art itself that can best annotate this loss as something that art produces in the act of setting itself against time. Later again, Boland comes to understand the radical implications of this understanding for Irish historiography.

The past towards which the work of Eiléan Ní Chuilleanáin is directed, is that associated with buried voices in culture.[21] These include the more personal close-range voices of women in religious life[22] and women touched by serious illness and death,[23] and the longer-range voices of Irish native experience at the period of the Renaissance and Counter-Reformation during which the power of the Gaelic order collapsed in Ireland,[24] along with the voices of women and men trapped in a post-independence conservative bourgeois Irish society immobilised by the unacknowledged trauma of a history of compromise with and resistance to colonialism.[25] Ní Chuilleanáin 'sees the glass' between herself and those worlds of secrecy and suffering, even as she witnesses the geography of their psyche whereby the unrepresentable in experience is brought to defy the limits which define it. She offers oblique perspectives on her material so as to unsettle its coherence, in particular by registering how the contiguous dimensions of time and place, through which that material finds its bearings, constantly readjust their relations. Her aesthetic is focused on the role of the expression of desire for wholeness, in offsetting the rigidifying presumption of that same wholeness as something achieved.[26] For Ní Chuilleanáin, a major form of that presumed wholeness is the phenomenon of essentialist claims to knowing the past. The danger of such claims in relation to Irish history is in their effect of sealing trauma consciousness as normal. In her poetry, however, the futility of these claims – once they are acknowledged in their full contexts as themselves having a history – makes them available to host more enabling ways of knowing. This involves the re-integration of the history of national, gendered and individual loss as part of an ongoing history. By such means, determinism and non-determinism, or, closed and open forms of meaning-making, can co-occupy the space of healing.

The work of Eavan Boland and Eiléan Ní Chuilleanáin is representative of Irish women's poetry more generally, as a body of art centrally invested in understanding the complexities involved in communicating historical reality. This complexity pertains to the fact that historical reality, which by definition is generated by change, is conveyed by necessity through forms – language, imagery, story, surviving records, statistics, preceding interpretations – that themselves are shot through with mutability. For example, in Eavan Boland's poem 'The Black-Lace Fan My Mother Gave Me', the fan is a fetishised substitute for the lost history of her parents' early relationship, but as such an unreliable marker of the past – 'darkly picked, stitched boldly, quickly' as it is – it becomes all the more resonant a symbol of such equivocally available, 'reticent' history. Its role is to tell the poet-historian that there is 'no way now to know what happened then – /. . . unless, of course, you improvise'[27] – unless he or she makes of history a purposeful fiction.[28] Thus, for these poets, history is constituted by the intimate relation between flux and stasis, not only in the material but also in the medium of historical enquiry.

Irish women's poetry engages with the double-edged task of history, by positing the possibility that the wish-fulfilling historian-witness can have genuine agency in their full awareness of the resistance of the real to their efforts: this is a poetry which endorses confidence in the act of representing the other which it also knows will always escape and undermine that same representation. The enclosed-order nun in Eiléan Ní Chuilleanáin's poem 'The Real Thing' knows this. She exposes a relic purporting to be a fragment of the most famous icon of culpable misrepresentation – the brazen serpent which in the Old Testament narrative externalises the Israelites' false witness and as such is reconstituted as the means to renewal of their relationship with God. 'She says [of the relic], this is the real thing', by which she calls us to understand that 'True stories wind and hang like this / Shuddering loop wreathed on a lapis lazuli / Frame.' In this poem as in Irish women's poetry more generally, it is the '*torn* end of the serpent' (my emphasis) – the point at which historical representation becomes visible as desire-filled construction – that 'Tilts the lace edge of the veil' of our understanding to become 'The real thing, the one free foot kicking / Under the white sheet of history'.[29]

Challenging the binary between revisionism and counter-revisionism, through exemplifying co-operative interaction between their key processes, is performed not only in women's poetry but in the practices of Irish feminism more generally. Clair Wills argues that 'feminist debates have rarely centred entirely on the analysis of representations and discourses, but have also sought to take into account the lives and experiences of women in Ireland, both past and present'.[30] This is supported by Gerardine Meaney, one of Wills' fellow editors on the massive project of compiling the fourth and fifth volumes of the *Field Day Anthology of Irish Writing: Irish Women's Writing and Tradition* (2003). Meaney's citation of Griselda Pollock's ideas in *Differencing the Canon* (1999), as model for this major recovery project, strongly suggests the kind of accommodation between revisionism and counter-revisionism which the present essay argues is advocated in the works of Irish women poets: 'To difference the canon, one must combine rereading the known with rendering visible the unknown': this involves theorisation brought to bear upon the empirical requirement, but also, crucially, the reverse: the empirical requirement brought to bear upon theory.[31]

Alternative relations between revisionism and counter-revisionism

Irish women's poetry calls for attention to the fact that all discourses speak *in* as well as from and to history, foregrounding this awareness as the key to 'balancing truth to the facts against the need for those facts to make sense'.[32] Without this awareness, in Boland's words describing the superannuated dolls who were oblivious witnesses to the revolutionary change generated by the 1916 Easter Rising, history can only operate as ideological tool, whereby the facts it should be true to become instead 'the hostages ignorance / takes from time and ornament from destiny. Both.' Whether through the terms of revisionist ignorance or counter-revisionist ornamentation (the main accusations thrown by the two sides in the Irish history wars), in such a case, historical representation fails its responsibility 'To be the present of the past'.[33] Irish women's poetry shows that to fulfil this responsibility involves sharing the ethical resources of both approaches to Irish history. Only when the relationship between these approaches remains in stand-off is their conflict malignant. When, instead, their inter-dependence is recognised through an understanding of the failure that ensues when each operates individually and in antagonistic relation with the other, the differences between these approaches can become generative.

The Irish history wars at the malignant stage signal themselves in the dependence of revisionist truth-seekers on the very terms of falsity that they have the responsibility to challenge in counter-revisionist 'sweet singing'. This co-dependence is suggested in Boland's poem 'Anorexic', collected the year before the 1981 hunger strikes in the Maze prison, and eerily prescient of that terrible episode in Irish history.[34] A connection was only much later made between this poem's direct theme of female self-starvation in service to the beauty myth and the context of militant nationalism that silently attends upon it.[35] This link arises through the association of the starvation motif in this poem with hunger strikes as a protest strategy practised by republican prisoners in the 1920s and 1980s, as well as with the political symbol of Cathleen Ní Houlihan as a figure reduced to hag-like emaciated status through lack of fulfilment of Irish national destiny, which hovers behind that strategy. Boland's poem on the eating disorder anorexia critically informs the larger historical political context, through the manner in which this text hinges on the irony that the 'pure' self of the anorexic who attacks her own 'witch' body cannot be divided from that same bodily self under attack, despite her effort to so self-cancel.

The political application of this motif can usefully be extended one step further, by reading the dilemma of the anorexic woman in the poem as a figure for a purist revisionism attacking what it sees as an entirely myth-based falsifying Irish historiography, understood only as a medium of corrupt ideology. Revisionism, read in this light, refuses to see the actual reality of an Irish history of desire for political coherence on national terms, of which this mythopoetic historiography – distorting of so many aspects of Irish life though it be – is a genuine expression. The anorexic's problem is that in seeking a perpetrator for the betrayal of self she experiences, she confuses the body itself for the distorted focus on the bodily purveyed in culture. In terms of Irish historiography, this translates as revisionism's rejection of important understandings of the Irish past embedded in the forms of nationalist cultural and political expression, through suspicion of the ideological freight attendant upon those forms. If the woman's self and her body cannot be divided because to do so is to identify, literally, with a paradigm which requires the female to be beyond history, then historiographical scepticism may equivalently need to come to terms with its 'witch'-like alter ego in a tradition of faith-based historical projection, so that history itself as a discipline is not threatened with eradication; if it is the case that woman cannot enter history without attending respectfully to her body, Irish history similarly cannot enter the past without attending respectfully to the forms in which that past has come down to us, however betraying they may seem. Such respectful attention is possible without it having to mean that Irish history is contained by and compliant to those same troublesome forms.

Irish women's poetry attends to the paradox that to show up the limitations of counter-revisionism is also to show up the limitations of revisionism. In so doing, it proposes that instead of either owning (in counter-revisionism) or disowning (in revisionism) the figures of myth that displace historical Irish subjects in the act of representing them, that the historian and/or poet own instead their use of myth. As fellow Irish poet Medbh McGuckian (b. 1950) puts it in 'Pulsus Paradoxus', 'Keeping magic out has itself the character / of magic': the revisionist's insistence on clear distinctions between history and myth will in the end facilitate rather than fend off the manipulation of Irish history by ideologues.[36] (This understanding is to be found not only among critics associated with the counter-revisionist position,[37] but among commentators on this debate sympathetic to revisionism.[38]) Equally, as Ciaran Brady argues, the critique of revisionist historiography as crudely empiricist and ingenuous in its claims to be value-free, takes insufficient account of revisionism's own understanding that objectivity is a serious aim informing historical practice, rather than a result of that practice that can finally be claimed.[39]

The cost of the stand-off between these options is explored by Eiléan Ní Chuilleanáin in the mid-seventies in 'Site of Ambush', a long poem on one of the originary occasions of this division, most likely a Civil War ambush such as that in which Michael Collins, leader of the Pro-Treaty side, was assassinated in 1923 – a decisive moment in the history of the Irish State.[40] Through her surreal replaying of the scene of this bloody event, Ní Chuilleanáin prises up its congealed meaning, using the knife of her oblique perspective to expose the damage still multiplying beneath. In this poem, charged nature imagery offers a microcosm of the psychological history of the divisiveness such occasions inaugurate in Irish culture: 'The clouds grew grey, the road grey as iron, / The hills dark, the trees deep'; the victims in the stream (of time?) 'Settled and lay quiet, nobody / To listen to them now. / They all looked the same face down there: / Water too thick and deep to see.' In this historical economy, 'time [is] at a stand. // And upright on horizons of storm the monumental crosses, / . . . flourish.' 'Waiting for the once-for-all wind', this economy predictably finds its focus through the archetypal figure of woman-as-Ireland, here a Joycean hag whose 'parcel of bread grows mouldy, / The milk in her jug sours fast under the sun'.[41] By her third collection, *The Rose Geranium* – published in 1981 at the height of the H-Block hunger strikes and at the start of a decade scarred by regressive and vitriolic debates on abortion and divorce legislation in Ireland – Ní Chuilleanáin is swamped by an overpowering sense of the suffocating, paralysing effect of the history wars on the whole culture, even as she seeks room to manoeuvre within these fixities. This is configured, for example, in the description of the pub interior in 'Cork' 3, where 'You face a window blank with dust / Half-inch spiderwebs / Rounding the squares of glass / And a view on either hand of mirrors / Shining at each other in the gloom', or of her native city as defined by 'Confraternity banners: / Cold wind and silence', in 'Cork' 8. This is a world in which 'The faces I meet are warped with meaning' ('Cork' 11),[42] where 'as always you are facing the past / Finding . . . // The names inscribed travelling / Into a winter of stone'.[43]

The degeneration of the potential of revisionism to offer a genuine alternative to mythopoetic historiography is both analysed and exemplified in Eavan Boland's 1975 engagement with the unrecognised collusion between civilised and atavistic responses to national crisis, in 'The War Horse', the title poem of her second volume.[44] This poem was collected in the same year as Seamus Heaney's poems on the same theme in *North*, especially 'Hercules and Antaeus' and 'Punishment' – work which similarly but more self-consciously risks replication of that which it critiques.[45] In 'The War Horse', Boland explores her fellow Dublin suburbanites' choice to subsume their awareness of the human cost of political idealism being enacted in the Northern Irish conflagration one hundred miles up the road, in favour of their undeclared fascination with this same 'fierce commitment'. This is represented in the poem through the metaphor of their simultaneous disengagement from and enthralment with a huge itinerant horse rambling destructively free among their gardens but who in the end causes little damage they deem worth caring about. The suburbanites here represent the position of a proto-revisionist deconstruction of militant nationalism that is simultaneously preoccupied with it as a form of sublimated tribal marking. However, the speaker's heavy irony in presenting this situation opens a Pandora's box – a Nietzschean void of moral responsibility – which she is ill prepared to close, as the irony itself seems to lead her to succumb to the very fascination with atavism that her work here presents others – those who 'use the subterfuge // Of curtains' – as subject to: the poem closes with an unselfconscious litany of nationalist shibboleths as she directs us to recognise that the minor damage of the smashed garden rose nevertheless 'recall[s] days // Of burned countryside, illicit braid: / A cause ruined before, a world betrayed'. Boland's much later commentary on the inadequacy of this poem pinpoints the source of that failure in the text's neglect of acknowledgement that the woman speaker observing the war horse, is herself, through her femininity, bound up with the idea of nation and of proper response to it that is the poem's main concern.[46] This refusal to see herself within the history of collusive relation between disowning and owning tribal identity that she as poet-speaker sets out to expose, by the end of the poem undermines the awareness Boland claims and leads her back to the role of spokesperson for, instead of explorer of, atavism: the position of uncritical Cathleen Ní Houlihan to which the symbolic Irish feminine traditionally has been reduced. The lack of awareness by the speaker of 'The War Horse' of the role she herself was playing in the drama of dissociated national identity she had set out to annotate, is a test case of the impulse to circular relation between the projects of demythologisation and remythologisation in Irish culture under larger discussion here.

We have seen that arguments which attack '[t]he teleological, nationalist story of Ireland as a tale of manifest destiny, leading ineluctably from bondage to freedom', themselves restrict the degree to which those elements of society marginalised by this same nationalist story, can be brought to visibility.[47] This is an irony arising not so much from the fact that the processes of revisionism are structurally similar to those of nationalism (in that they both focus on excavating authentic sources that can be directed towards altered understandings of Irish identity). It arises, rather, because in both discourses (viewed from a feminist perspective), woman is made present more as passive signifier of the agency of unnamed others than as a subject who is herself signified, herself counted as one of those others with agency.

Eiléan Ní Chuilleanáin's 1994-collected poem, 'Daniel Grose', can be read as annotating this fraught situation: the Irish nationalist tradition with its 'taste for ruins', is under assessment by a historian dramatised as a 'military draughtsman / . . . training his eye / On the upright of the tower' of that tradition. Ní Chuilleanáin, through the subtlety of her poem's deployment of verbs, refuses to allow us to clearly identify this historian's sympathies as either revisionist or counter-revisionist – he *could* be invested in deconstructing nationalism, 'Noting the doors that open on treetops' so as to diagnose that fantasy of authenticity and resistance to alternative histories often associated with the older political tradition, but equally he could be invested in validating this tradition through just those same characteristics: he '*catches* the light in the elder branches'; he '*captures*' how the scene 'keeps exactly / The dimensions of the first wounding', and it is unclear whether it is the older perspective or the newer one that is invested in '*Holding* in the same spasm the same long view' (my emphasis). The point is that in either case, the historian co-opts 'the human figure / He needs to show the scale / And all the time that's passed / And how different things are now'[48]– this figure, as Dillon Johnston notes,[49] being the highly traditional one of woman-as-nation: 'The old woman by the oak tree' who 'Can be pressed into service / To occupy the foreground'. Crucially, this draughtsman 'stands too far away / To hear what she is saying'. And what is that? In this poem published at the height of the history wars between revisionism and counter-revisionism, woman-as-nation calls down a plague on both their houses – a 'midwife's curse' upon 'the itch' of the 'trade' of representation in both directions. This is an itch occasioned by the collapse of difference between the accusative revisionist 'scholar's index finger' and the defensive, lamenting, instinctively proud counter-revisionist 'piper's hunch'.[50] Guinn Batten's vivid characterisation of this hag as 'A remainder, stuck in the opened gap between subject and object, male and female, colonist and coloniser', suggests her role as one who brings to birth self-recognition by these two historiographical approaches as each is called to see itself in the other.[51]

Women's history and national history

The two kinds of loss and silence in Irish history with which women's poetry is primarily concerned are that pertaining to women's lived reality and that relating to the broader question of Irish identity (this under the aegis of a range of possible socio-political dispensations). The relationship between these two concerns has moved from one of assumed convergence to one of presumed stand-off. In other words, it is now too generally understood that since territorial identity issues have blocked recognition of women's identity concerns, that women are thereby invested in denying the validity of a history focused on realisations of Irishness. But women's witness, as conveyed in Irish poetry, complicates this reading, suggesting instead that the interests of territorial and of gender politics cannot be so readily sustained in opposition. Irish women's poetry highlights the (suppressed) subject status of women in order to represent the loss and silence occasioned by the inadequate historicisation not only of Irish women as a group, but also of a variety of territorially identified groups, including the Anglo-Irish and

Ulster Unionists as well as the more obvious categories of the peasantry and Northern Nationalists. The Achill woman in the famous 1988 Boland poem of that title suggests this in the manner in which she speaks at one and the same time for the silence of women and the silence of victims of the Irish famine.[52] In other words, the female figure in Irish women's poetry still conveys what has been suffered in an Irish history of colonial race hatred and compromise, even though just this representative function, as traditionally assigned to her, has brought about the silencing of women's own voices in Irish history.

This usage does not, however, indicate a throwback to a naive endorsement of the patriarchal employment of the female symbol as static object. Crucially, Irish women's poetry presents that female voice representing territorial-political concerns, in its own terms, as one that addresses first the condition of her own situated womanhood. *Through* that womanhood, the condition of place and race-centred identity is explored. The Achill woman in Boland's poem 'pushed the hair out of her eyes with / her free hand and put the bucket [of servitude] down', in order to announce her own female presence at the centre-point of Irish political history – the foundation of the Irish Republic as codified in this poem through reference to the associated iconic time of year and the Yeatsian symbol of the living stream.[53] In the poem, 'An Easter moon rose' with the arrival of the Achill woman on the scene, suggesting history's call for the rise of the woman's voice in Irish culture, while the male sun temporarily declined: 'In the next-door field a stream was / a fluid sunset; and then, stars.' But this suggestion was not properly registered within the historical time under representation in this text (the early 1960s). As a result, the Achill woman does not herself speak in Boland's poem (as Gerardine Meaney has criticised).[54] However – unlike the many poems in the Irish tradition that use the female figure as a ventriloquist's dummy – here her absence of voice deliberately calls attention to itself. This is because the focus of this mid-career poem is Boland's own youthful yet still representative incapacity to register the politics of the Achill woman's gendered situation, and even less, of her own – how as a student, she was 'oblivious to // . . . the slow decline of the spring moon' of the female subject position in post-independence Irish culture, as well as to how this decline spoke to the larger Irish historical condition. It is in her foundational late 1980s essay now titled 'Outside history', at the beginning of the earlier pamphlet version of which this poem is inset, that Boland records the matter of what the Achill woman actually said on that early 1960s occasion: that she spoke about the sufferings and survivals of Irish people in the famine.[55] This woman's voice, in other words, is heard first (in the poem) in terms of its own absence and only then (in the prose) in terms of its presence. This order of presentation is important. It teaches us that unless absence is so registered as a historical condition of her present emergent voice, this subsequent speech, attributed to and rightly claimed by the Irish woman, will disable recognition of the difficult lived history of its own generation and reception. Through this disablement, Irish women's voices will continue to restrict communication of their own and others' historical truths.[56] Gerardine Meaney implicitly registers this warning as embedded in Boland's dual texts on the encounter between the Achill woman and her student poet-self, in this critic's focus on the contrasting problems of witness attaching to the prose and the poem versions. Arguing that 'The extent to which nationality, gender or indeed womanhood can have the same meaning for these two women is occluded in the pamphlet', Meaney points out that 'The inbetween is left open in the poem, allowing the differences between the women to remain and to define their relationship, allowing the gaps and silences . . . to question the terms of the poet's authority.'[57] Only through such questioning of the terms of the witness's authority by recognising the silence which underwrites it, Boland's work shows us, can that authority come into being.

Eiléan Ní Chuilleanáin, like Boland, recognises the danger that ensues when absence is ignored as a key aspect of present authoritative voice. In her poem, 'History', collected in 1989, the force of formally established Irish history – whether in the received or revised versions – asks women and men to 'Accept' as 'gift', the 'Ancestral flood' of their racial identity as one either under confirmation or dissolution, depending on with which side they are asked to identify in the Irish history wars. But this flood, by so 'Washing the living' so that living Irish men and women be either confirmed in or cleansed of their traditional race identification, also eliminates vital awareness of the past: it results in 'Shearing the bank of ghosts'. Ní Chuilleanáin, referring to these ghosts, writes next, 'These will not cauterise a wound', implying that, unlike the action of hegemonic history represented in the preceding race of text, ghosts do not foreclose upon the presence of a traumatic past. This past is represented here in terms of the alternative 'flood' of Irish women's 'menstrual stain'. Woman's mature sexual bodily life is the disavowed mark of an Ireland 'polluted' by the searing 'fire' of historical experience it still bears in the form of 'Ashes fat and bones / From the invaders' feast'. To register such traumatic experience requires rediscovering the 'lost art' of women's invisible writing; it requires registering the absent presence of their speech in 'The leaves of yellow metal / . . . floated to us on the stream' of time on which 'Our grandmothers wrote . . . / With reeds and vinegar' – the bitter means of sustenance offered Christ on the cross so that the gospel can be fulfilled. 'Our history', Ní Chuilleanáin writes – referring here both to women's and Ireland's history – is 'a mountain of salt', a block of sorrow gradually dissolving, 'A leaking stain under the evening cliff'. It is *through* not despite the association of this history with women's lived sexual lives, that it 'will be gone in time', even though 'Not in our time'.[58]

In order, then, to allow Irish people to wake from the nightmare to which the oppositional understanding of what constitutes their history has consigned them, women's poetry challenges the categorisation of women's history and national history as automatically at odds. The two aims of registering women's actual presence in history and exploring 'the hidden forces in Irish culture which find expression in these symbolic ideals and fantasies', must be brought to complement rather than contradict each other, albeit never without the acknowledgement and careful working through of tension that exists between them.[59] Eavan Boland powerfully configures this possibility in the essay 'Outside history', in the famous passage where she aligns the interests of women and nation through the urgency with which they share the aim of redressing distorted representation, notwithstanding the responsibility of nation in bringing about that misrepresentation of women in the first place: 'The truths of womanhood and the defeats of a nation? An improbable intersection? At first sight perhaps. Yet the idea of it opened doors in my mind which had hitherto been closed fast.'[60] The key to this intersection is the process of calling history to unmask the unreality of its own key tropes, while at the same time acknowledging the significance of their illusory coherence: that coherence is a function of the desire for resolution of historical loss, to which these images point. To this end, private history (especially of desire) is mobilised in Irish women's poetry, no longer in competition with, but as vital modifying constituent of, public history – a process that makes the meaning of that public history unrecognisable in its usual received terms.

Boland's poem 'The Achill Woman' again demonstrates this process. This poem famously sets the (unrecorded) testimony of the archetypal figure of the poor old woman regarding the suffering of local people in the famine against the 'grace' that 'language borrows from ambition' in the corrupt discourse of the Court poets of the Silver Age being studied by the student Boland at the time of her encounter with this woman on Achill. This art form colluded in the colonial enterprise that was to lead to the enormous levels of devastation suffered in the Irish famine of the mid nineteenth century, and calls to be read as such. That the old woman's witness would reveal the exclusions and power dynamics in the Court poetry is a clear position in this poem. Less obvious, however, is the fact that the Court poetry in turn reveals the literariness of the Achill woman's oral traditional testimony. The shaped forms of folklore narrative, like those of the Court poetry of the Silver Age, offer their fictions as a medium to access the reality of historical trauma, though in different ways in each case. Both the old woman and the student of the Court poems 'put[] down time' by engaging with each other through fictions of identity, ' "glass cloth[s]" ' that render the transparent wall that intervenes between the act of representation and the material of that representation, both invisible and sparklingly obvious.[61] Through the precision and attentiveness, then, with which the female image is recorded in the act of telling the story of the national desire for wholeness, that image is brought back to (its own) life, and with it returns the life of the nation.

In Ní Chuilleanáin's poem, 'Pygmalion's Image', when 'A green leaf of language comes twisting out of [the] mouth' of this image, it is because 'Not only her stone face, laid back staring in the ferns, / But everything the scoop of the valley contains begins to move.' Thus the constructed historical image – still in the shape of emblem but also in its own living shape – becomes 'a way of happening', its own webbed history becoming the vital means by which the historian can speak to other historical times, and they to it.[62] Therefore, in 'At the Glass Factory in Cavan Town', Boland challenges her own impulse to reject as culpable naivety, 'the safety // . . . assumed' by the living swans on the waterway nearby the place where glass swans – those mass-produced icons of Irish exile, otherworldly grace and the eternal hope of a history redeemed – were being blown into being. These real swans teach her how the living woman and nation can cope with the distortions of their history brought about by constructed versions of themselves: it is *because* the live swans 'took no care / not to splinter' that they could 'show[] no fear / they would end as / this [glass] one which is / uncut yet still might'. Sentient beings need to be open to the fractures of their own history if they are to offset the threat of being displaced by idealised images. Paradoxically, however, because those images are themselves bound towards fracture, they *are* truly capable of representing living organisms. Woman and nation alike must therefore learn the lesson 'that // the mirror [of such constructions] still holds / [their] actual flesh'.[63]

The paradox that it is exactly the foreclosed conceptual world generating the problem that can host the new life which may release its victims, is suggested in Ní Chuilleanáin's meditation on the possibility of gendered change in the 1981-collected sequence 'The Rose Geranium'. It is appropriate that this sequence comes from the volume of that same title which also marked (in the sequence 'Cork', also there collected), the low-point of her confidence in any such metamorphosis. It is '*In* my dream', she writes here, that 'I feel the shock of waking' (my emphasis).[64] In the thirteenth poem of this sequence, the revisionist-led 'bones' of Irish national identity, once they 'wake up' out of the Joycean nightmare of history, like their predecessor 'reach / Like tendrils for support' towards the female as supporting structure: 'lightly rising, they climb aloft on her shoulders. / . . . it is the same, / The pressure'. This convergence of the two historiographical approaches in their conjoined reliance on the passive feminine signals the redundancy attendant on each of them taken separately. However, taken together so as to be read in dialectical relation, these two modi operandi of Irish history reveal that they themselves can offer a feminine containing function, becoming the bearers of national desire:

> Empty as a diagram
> The laughable straight lines
> Even now hold secrets
> Of pleasure and fatigue. She sleeps,
> Her head in the dish of a pelvis:
> She knows how they stir beneath her.[65]

The 'straight lines' of nationalist and revisionist orthodoxy both, 'stir beneath' the woman on whose essentialist enfigurement they have too long relied, as they here become *her* supporting structure, in an important rebalancing of power relations.

A major insight offered in the work of Irish women poets, then, is that the failures of vision (to which women poets in their role as historians themselves are not immune) of both revisionism and counter-revisionism, is itself a historical stage in the process of resolution of the fraught relationship between these two approaches. This insight is crucial to Irish women poets' larger exploration of history's capacity for positive intervention, notwithstanding its falsifications: history as 'an aptitude', not only 'for injuring [the] earth' of given reality but also – simultaneously – for 'inferring it in curves and surfaces'.[66] A creative rather than destructive realisation of the history wars becomes possible, through the intensity of longing for meaningful change which that impacted conflict engenders: 'The precious dry rose-geranium smell / Comes down with spirals of sunlit dust / From the high sill.'[67] The overall pattern of these poems suggests that the act of attending in detail to the damage brought about by a patriarchal conception of Irish destiny (readable in this work as a function of the Irish history wars), allows the possibility of releasing the nation's future. This is directly proposed in the final section of Ní Chuilleanáin's 'Site of Ambush', through the figure of the child who has been threaded through this poem from the start as representative victim of the ambushing of that future by means of the determinism of these same politico-intellectual relations. This child, 'Soaked from her drowning' in this discourse, takes the imprint of a damaging patriarchal identity through those fixed relations. However, if historians choose instead to engage in a process of self-reflexive open attentiveness to each other's motives and methodologies, that delimiting identity can be recycled into nothingness, so as to allow this child at last to re-enter history. In such a process, historians must 'Lay fast hold of her / And [] not let go' even though '[Their] arms will be burnt / As she turns to flame'. It is through such cleansing immolation that the child's imposed phallic identity – 'A muscular snake / Spidery crawling' – can 'Becom[e] a bird / Then an empty space'. Its gradual dissolution here clears the way for 'The child exhausted / [to] Come[] back from her sleep'.[68] Thus history is reconstituted as a participatory improvisation of the real that offers itself as a patroller of the open yet still operative border between the representing self and the historical other.

Conclusion

Irish women's poetry not only suggests that a causal link exists between the silencing of women's lived reality and the trauma of national history, but that the silenced woman can speak most clearly for that trauma exactly in her own voice as woman. She can only do this, however, if her own identity is recognised as one in which is embedded her utterance as icon. Women's poetry thus maps but does not succumb to the cancellation of its own power of speech. It does this, recognising that the unspoken worlds of women's lives and contribution to public life have always been implicated – for good and for ill – in the unspeakable worlds of physical, cultural and spiritual evacuation and destitution that have marked Irish experience, on both sides of the border, before and after independence, and in all the main political and social groupings in this country. As Boland puts it in 'Beautiful Speech', 'it is too late // to shut the book of satin phrases, / to refuse to enter / an evening bitter with peat smoke, / . . . where // the dear vowels / *Irish Ireland ours* are / absorbed into autumn air'.[69] That such deterministic discourses are allowed their historical validity, we have argued here, by no means makes them unavailable for interrogation and change. Both interrogation and change are offered in the self-reflexive interwoven witness offered by Irish women to their own and the nation's history. This witness remains a continuing preoccupation of Irish women's poetry, both for its own sake and as an act of reclaiming the power and responsibility of the discipline of history in its potential to realise at last, as non-contradictory possibilities, both a living past and an open future.

Notes

1 Eavan Boland, 'Author's Preface', in *Object Lessons: The Life of the Woman and the Poet in Our Time* (Manchester: Carcanet, 1995), pp. ix–xvi; xi.

2 *Ibid.*, p. xv.

3 Gerald Fitzgibbon, 'Historical obsessions in recent Irish drama', in Geert Lernout (ed.), *The Crows Behind the Plough: History and Violence in Anglo-Irish Poetry and Drama*, Costerus New Series vol.79 (Amsterdam and Atlanta, GA: Rodopi, 1991), pp. 41–60; 49.

4 The term 'counter-revisionism' is used by Ciaran Brady in his important 1994 account of the development of historical revisionism in Ireland. Ciaran Brady, ' "Constructive and Instrumental": the dilemma of Ireland's first "New Historians" ', in Ciaran Brady (ed.), *Interpreting Irish History: The Debate on Historical Revisionism* (Dublin: Irish Academic Press, 1994), pp. 3–31; 14.

5 Gatherings of essays in which the debate between revisionism and counter-revisionism in Irish history is played out include Máirín Ní Dhonnchadha and Theo Dorgan (eds.), *Revising the Rising* (Derry: Field Day, 1991); Luke Gibbons (ed.), 'Challenging the canon: revisionism and cultural criticism', in Seamus Deane (ed.), *The Field Day Anthology of Irish Writing*, 5 vols. (Derry: Field Day Publications, 1991, and Cork: Cork University Press, 2002), vol. III (1991), pp. 561–680; *The Irish Review* 12 (1992); Brady (ed.), *Interpreting Irish History* (1994); Daltún Ó Ceallaigh (ed.), *Reconsiderations of Irish History and Culture* (Dublin: Léirmheas, 1994); and D.G. Boyce and A. O' Day (eds.), *The Making of Modern Irish History: Revisionism and the Revisionist Controversy* (London and New York: Routledge, 1996). Some summary accounts and assessments of this debate include: Edna Longley, 'Introduction: revising Irish literature', in *The Living Stream: Literature and Revisionism in Ireland* (Newcastle Upon Tyne: Bloodaxe Books, 1994), pp. 9–68; Willy Maley, 'Nationalism and revisionism: ambiviolences and dissensus', in Scott Brewster, Virginia Crossman *et al.* (eds.), *Ireland in Proximity: History, Gender, Space* (London and New York: Routledge, 1999), pp. 12–27; and Tony Canavan, 'The profession of history: the public and the past', in Ray Ryan (ed.), *Writing in the Irish Republic: Literature, Culture, Politics 1949–1999* (Houndsmills, Basingstoke: Macmillan, 2000), pp. 226–41.

6 Brady, 'The dilemma of Ireland's first "New Historians" ', p. 17.

7 Eavan Boland, *New Collected Poems* (Manchester: Carcanet Press, 2005), pp. 213–14; 214.

8 Brady, 'The dilemma of Ireland's first "New Historians" ', pp. 18–19.

9 Paul Hamilton, *Historicism*, The New Critical Idiom Series, second edn (London and New York: Routledge, 2003), p. 7.

10 Brady, 'The dilemma of Ireland's first "New Historians" ', p. 14.

11 Boland, *New Collected Poems*, pp. 102–3; 103.

12 *Ibid.*

13 Maria Luddy and Cliona Murphy, from *Women Surviving: Studies in Irish Women's History in the 19th and 20th Centuries* (1989), rept. in Deane (ed.), *The Field Day Anthology*, vol. v, *Irish Women's Writing and Traditions*, ed. Angela Bourke, Siobhan Kilfeather, Maria Luddy, *et al.*, pp. 1608–9; 1608. For an assessment of the conditions of mind underpinning this exclusion of women

in Irish history, see Mary Cullen, (ed.), 'History women and history men – the politics of women's history', in Ó Ceallaigh (ed.), *Reconsiderations of Irish History and Culture*, pp. 113–32.

14 Sabina Sharkey, 'Frontier issues: Irish women's texts and contexts', *Women: A Cultural Review* 4.2 (1993), 125–35; 130. See also Sabina Sharkey, *Ireland and the Iconography of Rape*, Irish Studies Centre Occasional Paper Series No. 5 (London: Polytechnic of North London, 1992), and C.L. Innes, *Woman and Nation in Irish Literature and Society 1880–1935* (Hemel Hempstead: Harvester Wheatsheaf, 1993).

15 Boland, from her poem 'At the Glass Factory in Cavan Town', in *New Collected Poems*, pp. 216–19; 219.

16 Boland, *New Collected Poems*, pp. 161–2; 162.

17 Roy Foster, as cited in Gearóid Ó Tuathaigh, 'Irish historical "revisionism": state of the art or ideological project?' in C. Brady (ed.), *Interpreting Irish History: The Debate on Historical Revisionism* (Dublin: Irish Academic Press, 1994), p. 311. See also Roy Foster, 'History and the Irish question', in *ibid.*, pp. 122–45.

18 This latter position is most directly associated with historian Brendan Bradshaw. See Brendan Bradshaw, 'Revising Irish history', in Ó Ceallaigh (ed.), *Reconsiderations of Irish History and Culture*, pp. 27–41, and Brendan Bradshaw, 'Nationalism and historical scholarship in modern Ireland', in Brady (ed.), *Interpreting Irish History*, pp. 191–216.

19 Boland, from her poem 'Watching Old Movies When They Were New', *New Collected Poems*, pp. 268–9; 268.

20 Boland, *New Collected Poems*, pp. 274–5; 275.

21 This summary account draws on the author's entry on Eiléan Ní Chuilleanáin in Brian Lalor (ed.), *The Encyclopaedia of Ireland* (Dublin: Gill and Macmillan, 2003), p. 783.

22 See Eiléan Ní Chuilleanáin, 'J'ai Mal a Nos Dents' and 'St Mary Magdalen Preaching at Marseilles', in *The Magdalen Sermon* (Loughcrew: The Gallery Press, 1981), pp. 29, 33; and Eiléan Ní Chuilleanáin, 'The Architectural Metaphor', 'The Real Thing', 'Saint Margaret of Cortona' and 'Man Watching a Woman', all from *The Brazen Serpent* (Loughcrew: The Gallery Press, 1994), pp. 14, 16, 24, 38.

23 See Ní Chuilleanáin, 'Fireman's Lift', 'La Corona', 'Passing Over in Silence', in *The Brazen Serpent*, pp. 10–11, 17, 23.

24 See, for example, Ní Chuilleanáin, 'Our Lady of Youghal', in *The Brazen Serpent*, p. 25.

25 See Eiléan Ní Chuilleanáin, 'Site of Ambush', in *Site of Ambush* (Dublin: The Gallery Press, 1975), pp. 22–8; Eiléan Ní Chuilleanáin, 'Cork' (a sequence), in *The Rose Geranium* (Dublin: The Gallery Press, 1981), pp. 10–22; and Eiléan Ní Chuilleanáin, 'Translation', in *The Girl Who Married the Reindeer* (Loughcrew: The Gallery Press, 2001), p. 25.

26 See also Catriona Clutterbuck, 'Good faith in religion and art: the later poetry of Eiléan Ní Chuillenáin', *Irish University Review* 37. 1 (2007), 131–56; 132.

27 Boland, *New Collected Poems*, p. 165.

28 See also Catriona Clutterbuck, 'Eavan Boland and the politics of authority in Irish poetry', *The Yearbook of English Studies* 35 (2005), 72–90; 81–2.

29 Ní Chuilleanáin, *The Brazen Serpent*, p. 16.

30 Clair Wills, Introduction to 'Feminism, culture and critique in English', *The Field Day Anthology*, vol. v (2003), 1578–87; 1579.

31 Gerardine Meaney, 'Engendering the postmodern canon? *The Field Day Anthology of Irish Writing, Volumes iv & v: Women's Writing and Traditions*', in Patricia Boyle Haberstroh and Christine St. Peters (eds.), *Opening the Field: Irish Women, Texts and Contexts*, (Cork: Cork University Press, 2007), pp. 15–30; 20.

32 Hamilton, *Historicism*, p. 8.

33 Boland, 'The Dolls Museum in Dublin', in *New Collected Poems*, pp. 208–9; 209.

34 Boland, *New Collected Poems*, pp. 75–6.

35 See Jacqueline Belanger, ' "The Laws of Metaphor": reading Eavan Boland's "Anorexic" in an Irish context', *Colby Library Quarterly* 36.3 (2000), 242–51.

36 Medbh McGuckian, *Shelmalier* (Loughcrew: The Gallery Press, 1998), p. 40.

37 See in particular, Richard Kearney, 'Myth and motherland', in *Ireland's Field Day* (Notre Dame, IN: University of Notre Dame Press, 1986), pp. 59–80.

38 For example, Ciaran Brady criticises T.W. Moody's 1977 statement on the difference between 'history', which 'is a matter of facing the facts of the Irish past, however painful some of them may be', and 'mythology', which 'is a way of refusing to face the historical facts', as one which 'provided the central focus of an unexpectedly rancorous debate that took place in the decade that followed'. T. W. Moody, 'Irish history and Irish mythology' (1977), in Brady (ed.), *Interpreting Irish History*, pp. 71–86; 86; Brady, 'The dilemma of Ireland's first "New Historians" ', p. 8.

39 Brady, 'The dilemma of Ireland's first "New Historians" ', pp. 16–19.

40 Ní Chuilleanáin, *Site of Ambush*, pp. 22–8.

41 *Ibid.*, pp. 22, 23, 24, 25.

42 Ní Chuilleanáin, *The Rose Geranium*, pp. 12, 17, 20.

43 Ní Chuilleanáin, from her poem 'Seamus Murphy, died 2nd October 1975', *ibid.*, p. 23.

44 Boland, *New Collected Poems*, pp. 39–40.

45 Seamus Heaney, *Opened Ground: Poems 1966–1996* (London: Faber and Faber, 1998), pp. 117–18, 129–130.

46 Boland, *Object Lessons*, pp. 175–9.

47 Jonathan Allison, 'Acts of memory: poetry and the Republic of Ireland since 1949', in Ryan (ed.), *Writing in the Irish Republic*, pp. 44–63; 55.

48 Ní Chuilleanáin, *The Brazen Serpent*, p. 34.

49 Dillon Johnston, ' "Our Bodies' Eyes and Writing Hands": secrecy and sensuality in Ní Chuilleanáin's baroque art', in Anthony Bradley and Maryann Gialanella Valiulis (eds.), *Gender and Sexuality in Modern Ireland* (Amherst: University of Massachusetts Press, 1997), pp. 187–211; 202.

50 Ní Chuilleanáin, *The Brazen Serpent*, p. 34.

51 Guinn Batten, 'Boland, McGuckian, Ní Chuilleanáin and the body of the nation', in Matthew Campbell (ed.), *The Cambridge Companion to Contemporary Irish Poetry* (Cambridge: Cambridge University Press, 2003), pp. 169–88; 186.

52 Boland, 'The Achill Woman', in *New Collected Poems*, pp. 176–7.

53 *Ibid.* Thanks to Catherine Kilcoyne of University College Dublin, who in discussing this poem, drew my attention to the link between the image of the bucket and the theme of servitude.

54 Boland, *New Collected Poems*, pp. 176–7; Gerardine Meaney, 'Myth, history and the politics of subjectivity: Eavan Boland and Irish women's writing', *Women: A Cultural Review* 4.2 (1993), 136–53; 140.

55 Eavan Boland, *A Kind of Scar: The Woman Poet in a National Tradition* (Dublin: Attic Press, 1989), pp. 5–6; Boland, 'Outside history', in *Object Lessons*, pp. 123–53; 123–5. Gerardine Meaney first drew attention to this important difference between the content of the poem and of Boland's prose comment on it. Meaney, 'Eavan Boland and Irish women's writing', pp. 140–1.

56 A foundational analysis of this issue as it pertains generally to Irish women's poetry (without reference to 'The Achill Woman') can be found in Anne Fogarty, ' "The Influence of Absences": Eavan Boland and the silenced history of Irish women's poetry', *Colby Quarterly* 35.4 (December 1999), 256–74.

57 Meaney, 'Eavan Boland and Irish women's writing', pp. 140, 141.

58 Ní Chuilleanáin, *The Magdalen Sermon*, p. 11.

59 Wills, Introduction to 'Feminism, culture and critique in English', p. 1582.

60 Boland, 'Outside history', in *Object Lessons*, p. 148.

61 Boland, *New Collected Poems*, pp. 176–7.

62 Ní Chuilleanáin, *The Magdalen Sermon*, p. 9.

63 Boland, *New Collected Poems*, pp. 216–19; 218, 219.

64 Ní Chuilleanáin, 'The Rose Geranium' 11, in *The Rose Geranium*, p. 37.

65 *Ibid.*, p. 39. This poem anticipates Moynagh Sullivan's analysis of how 'The understanding of multivalent Irishness . . . is enabled by the trope of Ireland as woman on which it can be draped.' Moynagh Sullivan, 'Feminism, postmodernism and the subjects of Irish and women's studies', in P. J. Mathews (ed.), *New Voices in Irish Criticism* (Dublin: Four Courts Press, 2000), pp. 243–51; 249.

66 Boland, 'Bright-Cut Irish Silver', in *New Collected Poems*, p. 173.

67 Ní Chuilleanáin, 'The Rose Geranium' 5, in *The Rose Geranium*, p. 31.

68 Ní Chuilleanáin, *Site of Ambush*, pp. 22–8; 27, 28.

69 Boland, *New Collected Poems*, pp. 211–12; 212.

8

LEE M. JENKINS

Interculturalism: Imtiaz Dharker, Patience Agbabi, Jackie Kay and contemporary Irish poets

'Interculturalism', like 'diaspora' and 'transnationalism', is a multivalent term, and one which has been contested for reifying differences *between* cultures while eliding differences *within* cultures. In this chapter, 'interculturalism' denotes a discursive space which accommodates differences *and* commonalities, allowing us to expand the paradigms through which we read women's poetry. The imperatives of our contemporary travelling culture, manifested in the transnational flow of people, information and finance, have impacted in significant ways upon the priorities of first- and second-wave feminism: the struggle for civil and social justice, the exploration of identity politics and the task of recovery. At the beginning of the 1990s, the woman writer could persuasively be defined by feminist theorists such as Susan Stanford Friedman as a 'Penelope [who] exercises her agency as a weaver/writer within and against' a patriarchal tradition.[1] Today's Penelope also works within the expanded contours of a world wide web and, whether by choice or through necessity, she demonstrates that migrancy and travel are not male prerogatives. In the lived experience, as in the poetics, of many women, 'home' is a condition of 'dwelling-in-displacement'.[2] Received notions of nation, place and female space are reconfigured in the global circuitry of diaspora, migration and the information superhighway.

Mapping women's diverse poetic geographies entails a remapping of the disciplinary parameters of the scholarship of women's poetry, and here Friedman is again an exemplary figure: as the 1990s drew to a close, she would embrace 'the spatial practices of third wave feminism'. Observing that 'national boundaries and personal borders become ever more permeable in the face of rapidly changing cultural terrains and global landscapes', she calls for 'the development of a multicultural, international, and transnational feminism'.[3] In doing so, Friedman reinflects in significant ways Homi Bhabha's argument that '[t]he move away from the singularities of "class" or "gender" as primary conceptual and organisational categories, has resulted in an awareness of the subject positions – of race, gender, generation, institutional location, geopolitical locale, sexual orientation – that inhabit any claim to identity in the modern world'.[4] Crucially, Friedman insists that 'moving *beyond* gender does not mean forgetting it, but rather returning to it in a newly spatialized way' that she defines as 'a *locational feminism*'.[5]

A locational feminism involves a politics of location of the kind for which Adrienne Rich had called in the mid-1980s. Motivated by her work with African American and Caribbean women writers and cultural critics, Rich urged women to explore the gendered and the ethnic locations of the female body, as well as the relationship of the body to the body politic or nation, insisting that we should exchange the homogenising category of 'woman' for the recognition and celebration of difference.[6] Caren Kaplan explains that '[a]s a practice of affiliation, a politics of location identifies the grounds for historically specific differences and similarities between women in diverse and asymmetrical relations, creating alternative histories, identities, and possibilities for alliances'.[7]

Where a transnational feminism surveys the 'grounds' for 'differences and similarities', postcolonial theory posits a 'third space' in which 'the negotiation of incommensurable differences creates a tension peculiar to borderline existences'.[8] Bhabha explains that it is '[t]he non-synchronous temporality of global and national cultures [which] opens up a cultural space – a third space'.[9] However, such 'homogenizing theories of diaspora' have proved problematic for those feminists who argue that 'location is still an important category that influences the specific manifestations of transnational formations'.[10] A case in point is Chicana poet Gloria Anzaldúa, for whom the US/Mexico border is a 'third country' rather than a third space[11] – her borderlands comprise, in Mary Louise Pratt's definition of the term, a 'contact' rather than a comfort zone ('contact zones' are 'social spaces where disparate cultures meet, clash, and grapple with each other, often in highly asymmetrical relations of domination and subordination').[12] Postcolonial theories of liminality suggest that 'it is the "inter" – the cutting edge of translation and negotiation, the *in-between* space – that carries the burden of the meaning of culture'.[13] For Anzaldúa, however, the border is a cutting edge at which 'the Third World grates against the first and bleeds'. Cultures and languages 'cross-pollinate and are revitalized' there – Anzaldúa's own poetry is a hybrid of English, Castilian Spanish, North Mexican dialect, Tex-Mex and 'a sprinkling of Nahuatl' – yet the border is nonetheless a wound, '*es una herida abierta*'.[14]

While she foregrounds the geophysical, economic and historical specificities of Chicana/o experience, Anzaldúa also suggests that '[t]he psychological borderlands, the sexual borderlands and the spiritual border-lands are not particular to the Southwest'.[15] A migratory feminism, a poetics in which displacement, relocation, cultural translation and untrans-latability are registered in formal and stylistic as well as in thematic terms, is a mobile paradigm, one in which border writing may be construed as 'world literature'.[16]

Texts such as Anzaldúa's *Borderlands/La Frontera* (1987) traverse and transgress generic and linguistic as well as geopolitical borders, thereby endorsing Jahan Ramazani's point that the 'most significant accomplish-ment' of postcolonial poets 'lies less in announcing their hybrid experience than in forging aesthetic forms that embody it'.[17] Nonetheless, a perceived link between nation and narration in postcolonial theory has contributed to the marginalisation of poetry as a postcolonial or post-national medium.[18] As 'a genre rich in paradox and multivalent symbols, irony and metaphor', poetry is, however, 'well-suited to mediating and registering the contradic-tions of split cultural experience'.[19] This chapter assesses the intercultural work of a selection of contemporary British and Irish women poets: Imtiaz Dharker (b. 1954), Patience Agbabi (b. 1965), Jackie Kay (b. 1961), Leanne O'Sullivan (b. 1983), Rita Ann Higgins (b. 1955), Mairéad Byrne (b. 1957) and Maggie O'Sullivan (b. 1951). In richly diverse ways, these women produce poetries which are invested less in a politics of identity than in the poetics of the borderland existence theorised by Anzaldúa and by Friedman as a condition of late twentieth- and early twenty-first century experience. This chapter therefore includes in its remit a number of post-twentieth-century poems, reading these in a continuum with the poetry of the 1990s: the year 2000, despite the millennium, does not represent for the poets discussed here the rupture that 1900 symbolised for W.B. Yeats.[20]

Diasporic space: Imtiaz Dharker

As a 'diasporic space', Britain is a proving ground for a politics and poetics of (dis)location.[21] Imtiaz Dharker is one of 'a heterogeneous community of women poets, many "British" more by association than nationality, [who] identify themselves with an often productively uncertain sense of "home"'.[22] Born in Lahore, Pakistan in 1954, Dharker grew up in Glasgow, defining herself as a Scottish Muslim Calvinist. An accomplished visual artist and a documentary film maker, she works across generic as well as national and ethnic borders. Her poetry is produced in and explores these borderlands, emphasising as Anzaldúa does that 'to make the mind bleed / into another country' may be productive and painful in equal meas-ure.[23] 'Borderlands', in the sequence of that title from her first collection,

Purdah (1989), are as likely to be psychological as geographical: Dharker's poems navigate what she calls 'the fine edge between / being trapped and being free'. Purdah – the practice of secluding women from public observation through the wearing of the veil and by the use of screens and walls within the home – has been both defended as 'an oppositional and revolutionary gesture' and decried as 'a coercive, institutional mandate'.[24] The female persona of 'Honour Killing', in Dharker's *I Speak for the Devil* (2001), removes the veil to speak on behalf of a woman shot by her family (she had demanded a divorce) in her lawyer's office in Lahore:

> I'm taking off this veil,
>   this black veil of a faith
>   that made me faithless
>   to myself,
>   that tied my mouth,
>   gave my god a devil's face,
>   and muffled my own voice.

'[O]ut here', she is 'making, crafting, / plotting at my new geography',[25] and in doing so she refuses what Chandra Talpade Mohanty critiques as the 'mode of defining women primarily in terms of their *object status*', as victims of religious, patriarchal, racial or economic oppression.[26]

For Dharker, the veil operates as 'a symbolic border', and a borderline is a 'Battle-line' in her poem of that title.[27] Rich has defined the body, for a woman, as 'the geography closest in': 'when the body becomes a territory', Dharker explains, the 'borderline' is 'of skin'. Her 2001 collection *I Speak for the Devil* explores that territory of the female body and the condition of 'travelling / between'; the poet's domain, in a further intensification of the borderlands condition, is 'the spaces *between* countries, cultures and religions', the interstices or 'cracks / that grow between borders'. The relationship between 'Here' and 'There' is negotiated on a linguistic borderline: 'my mouth spoke Punjabi / while my brain heard Scots', 'One language inside the house, / another out'. Dharker registers the 'daily displacement' where walking out of the front door 'means crossing over / to a foreign country'.[28] Her poetry is written on the interface between home and world, word and image, writing and the body.

As Clifford suggests, a location may be 'an itinerary rather than a bounded site', and, for Dharker, poetry is the 'waiting space' of the departure lounge, her medium 'stowaway words' and words which 'immigrate'. She explores the problematics, as well as the rich possibilities, of linguistic and cultural translation, such as the 'tripwire on the tongue' which exposes the 'alien'. 'I don't fit', she complains, 'like a clumsily-translated poem'. Testing the adequacy of her medium, she must 'scratch,

scratch' 'at this / growing scab of black on white'. At the same time, the poem itself is a potential site of reconciliation between self and other, the familiar and the foreign, the means of overcoming the 'stammer stutter' of subaltern speech.[29]

Dharker's 2006 collection *The Terrorist at My Table* examines the operation of language in a time of conflict and crisis, giving new life to the cliché that one person's 'terrorist' is another's 'freedom-fighter'. The mutual imbrication of visual image and text characteristic of her work is particularly powerful in the context of the abuse of prisoners in Iraq's notorious Abu Ghraib prison. The poet identifies with the victim of torture, his abjection at the hands of 'The woman // laughing for the camera, / pointing at my face'. Dharker urges us to '*see through the writing / look through the image*'. The data highway, the conductor of harrowing images like these, is configured in indigenous Asian terms in 'World Rickshaw Ride', the final sequence in the collection. Here, 'The real world is a road'. What Dharker calls 'The Driver's Domain' is the dynamic theorised by Maria Lugones as '"world"-travelling, a process of simultaneous displacement and placement that acknowledges multiple locations'.[30] In 'Halfway', Dharker comments that

> Halfway home or halfway gone,
> we have grown accustomed now
> to travelling on the faultline
>
> of daily miracles.

Faultlines, in Dharker's poetry, are a connective 'living tissue', they are 'notations on . . . skin'.[31]

Body language: Patience Agbabi

Patience Agbabi, poet and body artist, inscribes her poems on both paper and human skin. Born in London in 1965 to Nigerian parents, Agbabi was fostered at a young age in a white English family while maintaining close links with her birth parents. Her bi-cultural upbringing, she has said, has helped her move between cultures.[32] Agbabi moves with equal assurance between the establishment and the street, mixing cultural registers. During her 2005 residency at Eton College, bastion of the male English establishment, she orchestrated the first poetry slam there. In 1999–2000, she was in-house poet at Flamin' Eight, a London tattoo and piercing studio; Agbabi's work in this vein references her bi-culturality, invoking both West African practices of ritual scarification and the operation of the tattoo in Western culture as a 'metaphor of difference'.[33] Anthropodermic writing is a preoccupation both of Agbabi's 2000 collection *Transformatrix*, where 'Cruella De Ville' 'stitched hot, dark / ink into my taut flesh',[34] and of the *Blood Letters* sequence in her recent *Bloodshot Monochrome* (2008): her work-in-progress is titled *Body Language*. She both reflects and contributes to 'the emergence of tattooing, since the 1980s, as a new cultural, artistic and social form'.[35]

A member of female rap group Atomic Lip, Agbabi answered in the affirmative with her first collection, *R.A.W.* (1995), Jean 'Binta' Breeze's question, 'Can a dub poet be a woman?'[36] As poet and performance artist, Agbabi works a page/stage continuum: 'give me a page and I'll perform on it'. Her 'verbal acrobatics' feminise the masculine domains of rap and the Calibanisms or subversive wordplay of postcolonial poetics. In the work of Barbadian Kamau Brathwaite, for example, Caliban's appropriation of an Apple Mac ensures that 'prospero get curse / wid im own // curser'.[37] Agbabi styles herself as 'Eve on an Apple Mac' and her poetry as 'a rap attack': 'if you wanna know what rhyme it is', she explains, 'it's feminine'. Defining herself in the title poem of her second collection as a 'Transforma-trix', Agbabi also works within and against the formal poetic conventions of the sonnet and the dramatic monologue. Her *Seven Sisters* sequence explores the (trans)gendered topography of North London through the monologues of 'Ms De Meanour' and her six non-standard sister-speakers. Ufo Woman is one of Agbabi's *High-Flying Femmes*. Looked upon in London as an 'ALIEN', in Lagos,

> They call me Ufo Woman, oyinbo
> from the old days which translates as weirdo,
> white, outsider, other . . .

According to the 'intergalactic lingo' of this 'sci-fi' poem, the third space of cultural hybridity *is* 'space'.[38] 'Transformatrix' anticipates the experiments with the sonnet in Agbabi's next collection. She represents the poet as 'A pen poised over the blank page' waiting 'for madam's orders'. The dominatrix here is the sonnet form itself, as it 'trusses up / words, lines'. Carol Ann Duffy describes the sonnet as the 'little black dress' of poetry, sleek, smart, compact, classic.[39] The sonnet is a kinkier garment in Agbabi's hands: it is a 'corset' in which, as Jules Smith remarks, 'fetish sex and the act of writing come together'.[40] Agbabi's subject is the pleasurable pain of submitting to, fitting herself into, the strictures of her chosen form. Revising and queering its amatory conventions, Agbabi renovates the Petrarchan sonnet as a medium in which she can explore her (bi)sexuality and achieve the symbiosis that all her work attempts, between gender and genre, body and text.

'The London Eye', reprinted in 2008 in *Bloodshot Monochrome*, was written as a commission for *Earth Has Not Anything to Show More Fair*, an anthology published as a bicentennial celebration of William Wordsworth's 1802 sonnet 'Composed Upon Westminster Bridge'. Evoking the city not at dawn, as Wordsworth had done, but at the height of 'rush hour', Agbabi imagines a 'blind date' with him on the London Eye, and so playfully reintroduces the love conventions of the sonnet displaced in the male poet's paean to the city. The sonnet's origins lie, of course, in a male address to a female subject, but where Wordsworth's city is silent, Agbabi's speaker – she is London personified, the London 'I' – is 'shouting' to the poet as he stands upon Westminster Bridge, composing his poem. Agbabi nods in passing to the Italian origins of the sonnet, and to Wordsworth's choice of the Italian-ate form, looking as she does at London through her Gucci designer sun-glasses. Agbabi, however, who sees the city through her 'monochrome' shades, recasts Wordsworth's Italian or Petrarchan sonnet in the form of its English or Shakespearean variant, staging herself as the Dark Lady of her own poem. The 'SKIN .Beat™' Swatch she wears speaks to her ethnicity (the monologue 'Skins', in the same collection, asks 'You want to read my skin?'). Wordsworth and Agbabi enter their 'Cupid's capsule', their pod on the London Eye. It is 'a thought bubble / where I think, "Space age!", you think, "She was late" '. Agbabi is two hundred years late for her date with Wordsworth; yet, moving as it does in an anticlockwise direction, the London Eye takes her back to his 1802 poem (the digital display on her Swatch reads '18.02'). The capsule that the poets share, the venue for their 'date', is the sonnet itself. Agbabi's encounter with Wordsworth dramatises, with considerable poise, the 'intertextual temporality of cultural difference'.[41]

Agbabi engages with Wordsworth once again in the *Problem Pages* sequence of *Bloodshot Monochrome*. Assuming the role of literary agony aunt, she advises a number of sonneteers, among them Milton, whose 'When I consider how my light is spent' provides Agbabi with her structuring conceit (when the poet complains, in his octave, of losing his sight and so becoming useless to God and man, 'Patience' replies in the sestet, reassuring him that 'They also serve who only stand and wait'). In Agbabi's rewriting of his poem, 'Patience' advises Milton to 'Invest in a dictaphone that tran-scribes'. The advice she offers to Shakespeare, whose publishers are wary of his 'sonnet sequence, addressing a white man and black woman', recapitu-lates her own poetic credo: 'When will people stop categorising and embrace the page-stage, black-white, heterosexual-homosexual continuum'.[42]

Problem Pages itself contributes in significant measure to what Agbabi acknowledges as 'the long tradition of both political poetry and black poets

[Claude McKay, Gwendolyn Brooks] engaging with white forms'. The letters to Patience, and her replies, replicate in fourteen-line prose pieces the proposition-and-resolution dynamic of the Petrarchan sonnet. As Smith has argued, it is Agbabi's 'concern with form [which] makes her work different from contemporaries such as Jackie Kay'.[43]

To be black and Scottish: Jackie Kay

Born in Edinburgh in 1961 to a Scottish mother and a Nigerian father, Kay was adopted as a baby by a white Glaswegian couple. Her signature volume *The Adoption Papers* (1991) is written as a score for three voices (birth mother, child, adoptive mother), each rendered in its own typeface. Kay's poem-sequence is both a material inscription of difference and her poetic identity document. *The Adoption Papers* also prefigures the orality of Kay's oeuvre – 'A poem really begins for me with a voice', she has explained. Her writing draws on her love of black music: Bessie Smith, for instance, is celebrated in *Other Lovers* (1993), in a verse play and in Kay's novel *Trumpet* (1998). As Kay has remarked, 'blues and jazz would be a way of being black and being Scottish at the same time in words'. Kay recalls the advice given to her as a young writer by African American poet and essayist Audre Lorde: 'You're both. It's fine to be black and Scottish and you don't need to pick and choose.' Her poems draw, too, on the sonic possibilities of the Scots vernacular realised in poems 'written in Glaswegian' by Liz Lochead and Tom Leonard.[44]

Kay deploys the technique of code switching, moving between tongues, which is a feature of what Anzaldúa calls 'the language of the Borderlands'.[45] She appropriates the persona and idiom ('Crivvens!') of Scottish icon Maw Broon, a character from the long-running and much beloved black and white *Sunday Post* comic strip, *The Broons*. 'Old Tongue' recalls the linguistic cost of border crossing, of moving to England:

> I lost my Scottish accent.
> Words fell off my tongue:
> *eedyit, dreich, wabbit, crabbit*
>
> . . .
>
> . . . I wanted my old accent back,
> my old tongue. My dour soor Scottish tongue.
> Sing-songy. I wanted to *gie it laldie*.[46]

Kay is less than sanguine here about linguistic transplantation and the compensations of a grafted tongue. 'In my country' is her assertion of an identity that is as Scottish as it is black, that is, defiantly, 'both':

Where do you come from?
'Here,' I said, 'Here. These parts.'[47]

Kay's riposte echoes that of Joyce's Leopold Bloom who, refusing the identity of Wandering Jew, insists on his Irish birthright: 'What is your nation if I may ask, says the citizen. Ireland, says Bloom. I was born here. Ireland.'[48]

'Irish woman poet'? Leanne O'Sullivan, Rita Ann Higgins, Maggie O'Sullivan, Mairéad Byrne

Scotland and Ireland have both been defined as 'minority cultures' by Marilyn Reizbaum, who comments on 'the phenomenon of "double exclusion" suffered by women writing in marginalized cultures . . . where the struggle to assert a nationalist identity obscures or doubly marginalizes the assertion of gender (the woman's voice)'. She juxtaposes Scottish poet Liz Lochead's declaration (echoing Virginia Woolf) that 'my country was woman' with Irish poet Eavan Boland's insistence that 'as a woman I could not accept the nation formulated for me by Irish poetry and its traditions'.[49] As Colin Graham has argued, '[t]he recognition of the enforced silence of women and their simultaneous importance as a representational category integral to a dominant discourse is common to both Irish and post-colonial feminist thinking'.[50] Boland has stated that she 'began writing in a country where the word *woman* and the word *poet* were almost magnetically opposed', a mindset articulated by Seán O'Riordáin, 'Woman is not poet but poetry' ('Ní file ach filíocht í an bhean').[51] Boland, like Adrienne Rich, is a cartographer of women's silence: discussing representations of Ireland-as-woman in male-authored Irish poetry, she remarks that 'As the mute object of his eloquence her life could be at once addressed and silenced.'[52] Her 'Tirade for the Mimic Muse' deconstructs the relationship between gender and nation in Irish poetry that has silenced women's voices. Boland, who satirises the patriarchal invocation of the passive female muse, castigates the Irish Mimic Muse on behalf of 'The lives that famished for your look of love'.[53]

Patricia Coughlan has observed that 'most of the female poets emerging from the 1990s to date' in Ireland 'show a definite, if implicit, shift away from the proclaimed motives and thematic concerns of their predecessors and older contemporaries'. As Coughlan notes, this is 'part of a generational reaction to the concrete improvement of Irish women's conditions and status by the many legislative reforms and social changes since the 1970s, which seemed to culminate, in symbolic terms, in the 1990 election of

President Mary Robinson in the Republic'.[54] County Cork poet Leanne O'Sullivan's 2004 collection, *Waiting for My Clothes*, arguably recovers strategies of female troping rejected by Boland. Revisiting and revising Boland's 'Anorexic' (1980), O'Sullivan's 'Famine' invokes the self-starvation of young Irish women as a contemporary Great Hunger. O'Sullivan nonetheless resists translating profoundly subjective experience into broader configurations: 'Perfect Disorder' diagnoses what is a modern, if not a national, blight, 'a disease spreading across this island'.[55] Edna Longley has remarked that in an Irish nationalist context, anorexia is 'Cathleen ni Houlihan in a terminal condition'. It is, however, Maud Ellmann's definition of the woman with an eating disorder as 'the enigmatic icon of our times' that resonates in O'Sullivan's poems.[56] She presents us with a bulimic, rather than mimic, muse – the 'skinny saint' raving within her 'hungry church' starves the poet's younger, remembered self even as she sustains the poems. The poet's journal, her sourcebook for these searing lyrics, is her 'word made flesh'.[57] In *Waiting for My Clothes*, O'Sullivan is a hunger artist, writing poems on napkins: hers is a poetics of divestment, and of healing.

'Contemporary Irish women's poetry does not settle into distinct phases or schools in either ideological or geographical terms', as a juxtaposition of the work of Rita Ann Higgins and Mairéad Byrne demonstrates.[58] Born in 1955 in Galway, Higgins writes a demotic poetry the full register of which, its linguistic bravura and political passion, is disclosed in performance. In 'For Crying Out Loud', Higgins rejects 'airy fairy poems', insisting instead that 'my study / is the streets'. 'The Clemson Experience' critiques the academic expropriation of poetry, as delegates at an Irish Studies conference in South Carolina 'pick Heaney, poke Joyce' and 'O.D. on Yeats and queer theory, / Tiresias and Art O'Leary'. 'Donna Laura' deploys a heady mix of satire, sex and social commentary in Petrarch's lover's riposte to him:

> Petrarch you louser,
> I'm here plagued with the plague
> and you're off chasing
> scab free thighs.[59]

Higgins has little investment in the formal finesse which distinguishes Agbabi's gendered engagement with male-authored poetry. 'The Flute Girl's Dialogue' tells Plato and Socrates to stop 'acting the maggot'. 'Throw in the Vowels', the title poem of her 2005 *New and Selected Poems*, warns that Adonis, too, will be taken to verbal task 'If he does not gratify three nights in a row'.[60] Ailbhe Smyth has remarked that 'Women poets who write about sex . . . rarely get reviewed, or if and when they do, the sexy poems are politely not mentioned.' She discovers in Higgins a 'regenerative boldness' and 'delicious impropriety which subverts our understandings of the "proper" means and matter of poems'.[61]

Mairéad Byrne, born in Dublin in 1957 and resident in the United States since 1994, mocks those proprieties which assign Irish women to prescribed poetic categories:

> Editors of anthologies & special features on Irish poetry take note: I am available for inclusion in such publications in 3 guises: Irish Woman Poet, Innovative Irish Poet and, as the field is currently wide open, Ireland's First Concrete Poet. I can furnish a complete set of poems for each identity, in addition to sensitively selected yet pronounceable names: Minnie O'Donnell, Irish Woman Poet; Clare Macken, Innovative Irish Poet; and Bo Doyle-Hund, Ireland's First Concrete Poet . . . I am working on a fourth identity – 'A Remarkable Poet in Her Own Right.' The tentative title for this character is: 'Mairéad Byrne.'[62]

As Vona Groarke has insisted, 'the best of Irish women poets are not writing "Irish Women's Poetry." There is no convergence of subject-matter, no orthodoxy of theme or tone, no received notion of what is appropriate or what is beyond our reach.'[63] In contradistinction to Higgins and Leanne O'Sullivan, who, like Dharker and Kay, publish with Bloodaxe Books, Byrne opts for small press publication and non-standard formats, working without the sanction of what Harry Gilonis has termed the 'sanctifying grace' of 'mass-market poets/publications/presses/schools'.[64]

As editor of the 1996 anthology *Out of Everywhere: Linguistically Innovative Poetry by Women in North America & the UK*, Maggie O'Sullivan has assembled work by poets whose 'engagement in explorative, formally progressive language practices' has led to their exclusion from '"women's canons"'.[65] Her remarks alert us to faultlines *within* feminism, to practices of regulation, containment and exclusion in the scholarship of women's writing. Maggie O'Sullivan's own poetry – she was born in England in 1951 to Irish Catholic parents – is in several senses a 'land less writing'.[66] She defines her practice as 'deformance', a procedure exemplified in *red shifts* (2001): this 'bookwork' and 'scribble contusion' is an inter-media poetics of postlinearity comprised of 'text block' and 'cells of telling'.[67] Byrne's formal procedures are comparable – her recent *Talk Poetry* is made up of 'high bandwidth textblocks'.[68] Her work has affinities, too, with the practice of Catherine Walsh, described by Trevor Joyce as 'an Irish woman writer who sidesteps the ball and chain of conservative form with self-consciously "radical" thematics which has been represented for far too long as the only proper model for women poets in this country'.[69] Byrne's significant accomplishment, though, like that of Patience Agbabi, is that she refuses to choose between formal innovation and radical theme, thereby fusing Higgins' commitment to social justice with the linguistic innovations of Walsh and Maggie O'Sullivan. Her 2003 collection, *Nelson & the Huruburu Bird*, published by Randolph Healy's Wild Honey Press, includes a trio of poems dedicated *To the Travelling People of Ireland*. The first of these, playing on the title of Daniel Corkery's 1924 study of eighteenth-century Munster Irish-language poetry, is 'The Hidden Ireland', a phrase of iconic importance in Irish cultural history and nationalist tradition. Byrne, however, aligns herself and her own mobile poetics with another hidden Ireland, the submerged population of Ireland's travelling community. She shares the insider/outsider status of this 'indigenous nomadic or gypsy people' (the poet undertook a hundred-mile walk with travellers in the Southwest of Ireland in 1991).[70]

Alert to the varieties of Irish displacement, Byrne meditates on modern Ireland's exploitation of its history, one marked by forced emigration as well as internal exile, in 'A Typical Irish Cottage'. She deconstructs the myth of rural Ireland as the land of a hundred thousand welcomes ('céad mile fáilte', the slogan of Bord Fáilte, the Irish tourist board, is the title of the second poem in her sequence). The poverty and suffering of 'the freshly turfed out' has been whitewashed: 'the white of the wash is the whitest wash'. Byrne's note explains that the title of her poem is 'taken from the caption on a postcard, received from Ireland, bearing the image of a contemporary, whitewashed *bothán*' (hut).[71] As Ramazani has remarked, '[t]he postcolonial poem, like a postcard, risks miniaturizing, idealizing, and ultimately displacing the remembered native landscape'.[72] Byrne's poetry, though, works to other ends, exposing a 'native landscape' that, far from being idealised, is instead complicated, historicised and racialised. Her work-in-progress includes a multi-genre project on American former slave Frederick Douglass' 1845 visit to Ireland, and in 'For the Ear of the Auditor', Byrne reprises African American poet Langston Hughes' 'The Negro Speaks of Rivers':

> I wanted to be Langston Hughes
> to have written that poem about rivers
> but I have known footpaths
> I think I must know as much about sidewalks
> as anyone in this world –[73]

Byrne recasts Hughes' evocation of the transhistorical black experience of diaspora as the lived reality of the poet herself as transnational *flâneuse*.

Smyth argues that 'the great conspiracy of silence around the *fact* of Irish women's poetry has been broken'. She is, nonetheless, alert to an ongoing 'preoccupation with Irishness as the primary terrain of criticism [which] has disturbing repercussions for poetry, because *poems* which do not nourish these critical concerns are considered as not really Irish or not really poems'. Smyth's countervailing assertion is of the creative potential of 'poetic re-location' and emigration, 'the marked opportunities for poetic and political migration to a more welcomingly open terrain'.[74]

The publication in 2002 of volume v of the *Field Day Anthology of Irish Writing: Irish Women's Writing and Traditions* marked a significant and long overdue expansion of the Irish canon, albeit that formally innovative poetries would remain marginal to the national literary imaginary.[75] Now, Irish feminists are adopting an international and intercultural focus.[76] Interculturalism encourages us to recognise, but not to force, connections between British and Irish women of diverse postcolonial heritages – to respect difference, and explore the complex intersections between nation, gender, ethnicity and sexuality in which their poetries are produced. As Anzaldúa argues, if 'the Borderlands are physically present wherever two or more cultures edge each other', then 'more and more people today become border people'.[77]

Notes

I am grateful to Patricia Coughlan and Piaras Mac Éinrí for their creative and constructive criticisms of my terminology and topic.

1 Susan Stanford Friedman, *Penelope's Web: Gender, Modernity, H.D.'s Fiction* (New York: Cambridge University Press, 1990), p. 2.

2 James Clifford, *Routes: Travel and Translation in the Late Twentieth Century* (Cambridge, MA: Harvard University Press, 1997), p. 254.

3 Susan Stanford Friedman, *Mappings: Feminism and the Cultural Geographies of Encounter* (Princeton: Princeton University Press, 1998), pp. 3, 4.

4 Homi Bhabha, *The Location of Culture* (London: Routledge, 1994), p. 1.

5 Friedman, *Mappings*, p. 18.

6 See Adrienne Rich, 'Notes toward a politics of location', in her *Blood, Bread, and Poetry: The Location of the Poet* (London: Virago, 1984). For a lucid assessment of Rich's position and its implications, see Mary Eagleton, 'Adrienne Rich, location and the body', *Journal of Gender Studies* 9.3 (2000), 299–312.

7 Caren Kaplan, 'The politics of location as transnational feminist critical practice', in Inderpal Grewal and Caren Kaplan (eds.), *Scattered Hegemonies: Postmodernity and Transnational Feminist Practices* (Minneapolis: University of Minnesota Press, 1994), pp. 117–52; 139.

8 Bhabha, *The Location of Culture*, p. 218. For alternative theories of the 'third space', see Edward Soja, *Thirdspace* (Oxford: Blackwell, 1996) and David G. Gutíerrez, 'Migration, emergent ethnicity, and the "third space": the shifting

politics of nationalism in Greater Mexico', *Journal of American History* 86. 2 (1999), 481–517.

9 Bhabha, *The Location of Culture*, p. 218.

10 Grewal and Kaplan, 'Transnational feminist practices and questions of post-modernity', in Grewal and Kaplan (eds.), *Scattered Hegemonies*, pp. 1–33; 21, 16.

11 Gloria Anzaldúa, *Borderlands/La Frontera: The New Mestiza* (1987; San Francisco: Aunt Lute Books, 1999), p. 25. Smadar Lavie contrasts Anzaldúa's model of hybridity with Bhabha's in her 'Blow-ups in the borderzones: third world Israeli authors' groping for home', *New Formations* 18 (1992), 84–90.

12 Mary Louise Pratt, *Imperial Eyes: Travel Writing and Transculturation* (London: Routledge, 2002), p. 4.

13 Bhabha, *The Location of Culture*, p. 38.

14 Anzaldúa, *Borderlands*, pp. 25, 20, 24.

15 *Ibid.*, p. 19.

16 D. Emily Hicks, *Border Writing: The Multidimensional Text* (Minneapolis: University of Minnesota Press, 1991), p. xxiii.

17 Jahan Ramazani, *The Hybrid Muse: Postcolonial Poetry in English* (Chicago: University of Chicago Press, 2001), pp. 3–4, 179–80.

18 See Donald E. Pease, 'National narratives, postnational narration', *Modern Fiction Studies* 43.1 (1997), 1–23.

19 Ramazani, *The Hybrid Muse*, p. 6.

20 In his Introduction to *The Oxford Book of Modern Verse* (1936), Yeats remarked that 'in 1900 everybody got down off his stilts; henceforth nobody drank absinthe with his black coffee; nobody went mad; nobody committed suicide; nobody joined the Catholic church'. William H. O'Donnell (ed.), *The Collected Works of W.B. Yeats*, vol. v, *Late Essays* (New York: Charles Scribner's Sons, 1994), p. 185.

21 Clifford, *Routes*, p. 260.

22 Jane Dowson and Alice Entwistle, *A History of Twentieth-Century British Women's Poetry* (Cambridge: Cambridge University Press, 2005), p. 197.

23 Imtiaz Dharker, *Postcards from God* (Newcastle upon Tyne: Bloodaxe, 1997), p. 64.

24 *Ibid.*, p. 53; Chandra Talpade Mohanty, 'Under Western eyes: feminist scholarship and colonial discourses', in Patrick Williams and Laura Chrisman (eds.), *Colonial Discourse and Post-Colonial Theory: A Reader* (Harlow: Prentice Hall, 1993), pp. 196–220; 209. Purdah is discussed in a female Islamic perspective by Leila Ahmed in her *Women and Gender in Islam: Historical Roots of a Modern Debate* (New Haven: Yale University Press, 1992).

25 Imtiaz Dharker, *I Speak for the Devil* (Tarset: Bloodaxe, 2001), p. 13.

26 Mohanty, 'Under Western eyes', p. 201.

27 Deniz Kandiyoti, 'Identity and its discontents: women and the nation', in Williams and Chrisman (eds.), *Colonial Discourse and Post-Colonial Theory*, pp. 376–91; 383.

28 Rich, 'Notes toward a politics of location', p. 212; Dharker, *Postcards from God*, p. 55; Dharker, *I Speak for the Devil*, pp. 37, 39, 16, 19, 26.

29 Clifford, *Routes*, p. 11; Dharker, *I Speak for the Devil*, pp. 20, 27; *Postcards from God*, pp. 159, 157, 98.

30 Imtiaz Dharker, *The Terrorist at My Table* (Tarset: Bloodaxe, 2006), pp. 25, 40, 48, 125, 133; Maria Lugones, 'Playfulness, "world"-travelling, and loving perception', in D.S. Madison (ed.), *The Woman That I Am: The Literature and Culture of Contemporary Women of Color* (New York: St Martin's Press, 1994), pp. 626–38.

31 Dharker, *The Terrorist at My Table*, pp. 158, 14; *I Speak for the Devil*, p. 119.

32 Patience Agbabi, 'Crossing borders: from page to stage and back again'. Online document, www.crossingborders-africanwriting.org/writersonwriting/patience-agbabi/ n. p.

33 Margo DeMello, *Bodies of Inscription: A Cultural History of the Modern Tattoo* (Durham, NC: Duke University Press, 2000), p. 13.

34 Patience Agbabi, *Transformatrix* (Edinburgh: Canongate, 2000), p. 47.

35 DeMello, *Bodies of Inscription*, p. 2.

36 Jean 'Binta' Breeze, 'Can a dub poet be a woman' (1990), rept. in Alison Donnell and Sarah Lawson Welsh (eds.), *The Routledge Reader in Caribbean Literature* (London: Routledge, 1996), pp. 498–500.

37 Agbabi, *Transformatrix*, pp. 11, 9; Kamau Brathwaite, *X/Self* (Oxford: Oxford University Press, 1987), p. 85.

38 Agbabi, *Transformatrix*, pp. 10, 16; 'Ufo Woman' was made into a short film for Channel 4's *LitPop* series in 1998; see 'Shooting "Ufo Woman"' in Agbabi's *Bloodshot Monochrome* (Edinburgh: Canongate, 2008), p. 6.

39 Agbabi, *Transformatrix*, p. 78; Carol Ann Duffy (ed.), *Out of Fashion: An Anthology of Poems* (London: Faber, 2004), p. xii.

40 Agbabi, *Transformatrix*, p. 78; Jules Smith, 'Critical perspective', online document, www.contemporarywriters.com/authors/?p=auth163/ n. p.

41 Agbabi, *Bloodshot Monochrome*, pp. 9, 20, 9; Bhabha, *The Location of Culture*, p. 38.

42 John Carey and Alastair Fowler (eds.), *The Poems of John Milton* (London: Longman, 1968), p. 330; Agbabi, *Bloodshot Monochrome*, pp. 36, 34.

43 Agbabi, *Bloodshot Monochrome*, p. 45; Smith, 'Critical perspective', n. p.

44 Jackie Kay, 'Interview', *Poetry Archive*, online document, www.poetryarchive.org/poetryarchive/singleInterview.do?interviewId=6580/ n. p.

45 Anzaldúa, *Borderlands*, p. 20.

46 Jackie Kay, *Darling: New and Selected Poems* (Tarset: Bloodaxe, 2007), pp. 190–1.

47 *Ibid.*, p. 82.

48 James Joyce, *Ulysses*, ed. Jeri Johnson (Oxford: Oxford University Press, 1993), p. 317.

49 Marilyn Reizbaum, 'Canonical double cross: Scottish and Irish women's writing', in Karen R. Lawrence (ed.), *Decolonizing Tradition: New Views of Twentieth-Century 'British' Literary Canons* (Urbana: University of Illinois Press, 1992), pp. 165–90; 165–6.

50 Colin Graham, 'Subalternity and gender: problems of post-colonial Irishness', *Journal of Gender Studies* 5.3 (1996), 363–73; 366. C. L. Innes notes that '[t]hroughout the history of its colonization, Ireland has been represented by British imperialists as well as Irish nationalists and artists as female'. This is not, however, solely a nationalist and/or an imperialist trope, as the figure of the 'Sovereign Goddess' in pre-colonial Irish literature attests. *Woman and Nation in Irish Literature and Society* (Athens: University of Georgia Press, 1993), p. 2.

51 Quoted in Fionnuala Dillane, 'Changing the map: contemporary Irish women's poetry', *Verse* 16.2 (1999), 9–27; 9.

52 Eavan Boland, *Object Lessons: The Life of the Woman Poet and the Poet in Our Time* (1995; London: Vintage, 1996), p. xiv.

53 Eavan Boland, *Collected Poems* (Manchester: Carcanet, 1995), p. 55.

54 Patricia Coughlan, '"Chipped and Tilted Marys": two Irish poets and their contemporary contexts', in Britta Olinder and Werner Huber (eds.), *Place and Memory in the New Ireland* (Trier: WVT Wissenschaftlicher Verlag Trier, 2009), pp. 71–100: p. 77.

55 Leanne O'Sullivan, *Waiting for My Clothes* (Tarset: Bloodaxe, 2004), p. 12.

56 Edna Longley, *The Living Stream: Literature and Revisionism in Ireland* (Newcastle upon Tyne: Bloodaxe, 1994), p. 173; Maud Ellmann, *The Hunger Artists: Starving, Writing, and Imprisonment* (London: Virago, 1993), p. 2.

57 O'Sullivan, *Waiting for My Clothes*, pp. 18, 41, 64.

58 Dillane, 'Changing the map', p. 10.

59 Rita Ann Higgins, *Throw in the Vowels: New & Selected Poems* (Tarset: Bloodaxe, 2005), pp. 141, 142, 155, 110.

60 *Ibid.*, pp. 115, 206.

61 Ailbhe Smyth, '"Dodging Around the Grand Piano": sex, politics and contemporary Irish women's poetry', in Vicki Bertram (ed.), *Kicking Daffodils: Twentieth-Century Women Poets* (Edinburgh: Edinburgh University Press, 1997), pp. 57–83; pp. 64, 75.

62 Mairéad Byrne, *Talk Poetry* (Oxford, OH: Miami University Press, 2007), p. 73.

63 Vona Groarke, editorial, *Verse* 16.2 (1999), 708.

64 Harry Gilonis, 'Quasi-editorial', in Harry Gilonis (ed.), *For the Birds: Proceedings of the First Cork Conference on New and Experimental Poetry* (Sutton and Dublin: Mainstream Poetry and hardPressed poetry, 1998), p. 3.

65 Maggie O'Sullivan (ed.), *Out of Everywhere: Linguistically Innovative Poetry by Women in North America & the UK* (London: Reality Street Editions, 1996), pp. 9, 10.

66 Maggie O'Sullivan, *Palace of Reptiles* (Willowdale, Ontario: The Gig, 2003), p. 49.

67 Maggie O'Sullivan and Dell Olsen, 'Writing/conversation: an interview by mail, November–December 2003', HOW2 2.2 (Spring 2004) n. p.; Maggie O'Sullivan, *red shifts* (Buckfastleigh: Etruscan Books, 2001), n. p.; Lawrence Upton, review of *red shifts* (June 2001), online document, http://pages.britishlibrary.net/lawrence.upton/writing/redshifts.html, n. p.

68 Byrne, *Talk Poetry*, back cover.

69 Trevor Joyce, 'The point of innovation in poetry', in Harry Gilonis (ed.), *For the Birds*, pp. 18–26; 25.

70 Mairéad Byrne, *Nelson & the Huruburu Bird* (Bray: Wild Honey Press, 2003), p. 123.

71 *Ibid.*, p. 124.

72 Ramazani, *The Hybrid Muse*, p. 12.

73 Byrne, *Nelson & the Huruburu Bird*, p. 119.

74 Smyth, '"Dodging Around the Grand Piano" ', pp. 59, 60.

75 Angela Bourke *et al.* (eds.), *The Field Day Anthology of Irish Writing: Irish Women's Writing and Traditions*, vol. V (Cork: Cork University Press, 2002).

76 See Linda Connolly, *The Irish Women's Movement: From Revolution to Devolution* (London: Palgrave Macmillan, 2001); Claire Connolly (ed.), *Theorizing Ireland* (London: Palgrave Macmillan, 2002); and Breda Gray, *Women and the Irish Diaspora* (London: Routledge, 2003). Borbála Faragó provides an important supplement to this scholarship in her discussion of immigrant poets in Ireland, '"I am the Place in Which Things Happen": invisible immigrant women poets of Ireland', in Patricia Coughlan and Tina O'Toole (eds.), *Irish Literature: Feminist Perspectives* (Dublin: Carysfort Press, 2008), pp. 145–66.

77 Anzaldúa, *Borderlands*, p. 19.

9

ALICE ENTWISTLE

Post-pastoral perspectives
on landscape and culture

If ever it testified to the innocent charms of an unspoiled natural world, in the course of the twentieth century the literary 'pastoral' has become a dangerously prodigal signifier.[1] That said, most pastoral writing affirms the inescapably dialectical relation of urban and rural environments. For a growing number of critics like Terry Gifford, the 'post-pastoral' crucially reconfigures the 'closed circuit of pastoral and anti-pastoral', with its more holistic 'vision of an integrated natural world that includes the human'. As Gifford says: 'Now we have as much an interest in the welfare of Arden as in that of its exiled inhabitants, as much interest in their interaction with Arden as in what they take back from it, as much interest in how they represent their interaction with it as in how their representations of themselves as its inhabitants have changed.'[2] Keeping the culturally undecidable location of Arden firmly in mind, this chapter explores how the complexities of the post-pastoral play out in poetry by British and Irish women towards and beyond the end of the twentieth century. It focuses particularly on the way in which landscape enshrines the integration of the natural and the human; as John Kinsella notes, the pastoral has only ever been 'about landscape ... how land and the people within the land are marked – where signs of authenticity and belonging are imposed or laid'.[3] The poets treated here all insist, with the eco-critic Jonathan Bate, that 'every piece of land is itself a text with its own syntax and signifying potential'.[4] Invariably for them, significantly, 'landscape provides a way into the question of culture'.[5]

Women's interest in the link between nature and culture is understandable: as eco-feminists argue, the natural world has long been oppressively gendered. Drawing on Simone de Beauvoir, Alicia Ostriker explains, 'Identified with the Nature which men have sought to conquer, woman has remained trapped ... a physical, social and political inferior ... she becomes by extension a victim of culture.'[6] Similarly, women poets have found themselves confined by the traditions of literary pastoral to the ironically arid 'green pastures, and pleasant vallies, where they may wander with safety to themselves and delight to others', which one eighteenth-century reviewer urges on them.[7] As this chapter shows, today's poets respond by using the surreptitiously political medium of the post-pastoral to map, dilate and extend their own too easily simplified local and national landscapes.

'An unfolding map'

Critics have not been able to agree a precise definition of the literary post-pastoral, although many link it with the 'mature environmental aesthetics' envisaged by leading eco-critic Lawrence Buell.[8] Among those who share Gifford's particular sense of the genre's socio-political responsiveness, Matthew Jarvis locates the post-pastoral in the 'scarred garden' implicitly imagined by American critic Leo Marx.[9] The works I explore swap the cultivated privacy of the 'garden' for the more public, more porous space of the 'scarred' post-pastoral landscape.

First published in *Poetry Wales* in 1991, Anne Stevenson's 'Skills' studies a lone workman loading a cumbersome 'macadam-spreader' on to its carrier, 'the huge metal-plated tracks' advancing 'centimetre by centimetre forward' until the load is 'All of a piece and tightly wrapped'. Whereupon the scene abruptly shrinks:

> Imagine a plane ascending, him on the road,
> a special dinky-toy that takes apart,
> growing smaller, now still smaller, more compact,
> a crawling speck on an unfolding map.[10]

The poem seems to admonish the rapacious appetite of the human imagination while simultaneously vaunting the planet's capacity to ride out any impact caused by its human occupants. In both senses, the text converses with the tendencies Gifford ascribes to the literary 'post-pastoral', especially in its 'awe in attention to the natural world', its 'recognition of a creative-destructive universe equally in balance in a continuous momentum of ... growth and decay' and its 'recognition that our inner human nature can be understood in relation to external nature'. Most importantly, 'Skills' correlates and conflates its human and non-human worlds – like Gifford, reading 'nature as culture and culture as nature' – in the 'unfolding map' on which it comes to rest.[11]

Maps make equivocal signifiers. A mapped territory is empirically known; it registers the colonising processes – the surveying, evaluating, recording – behind the information it retails. Rightly, Ruth Padel argues 'Mapping is like road building, a way of exerting control.'[12] For Padel, maps inscribe not so much the cultivation as the irreversible acculturation of nature; as Stevenson herself says, 'It is practically impossible for human beings to observe a state of nature without in some measure – a track through the underbrush, a circle of rocks around a fire – changing it.'[13] On the other hand, always required to start and finish somewhere, a map can only fragment the territorial continuum which anchors and gives rise to the landscape it purports to represent: like any text what a map leaves out must affect its signifying activity. Their boundedness renders maps dependent on the out-of-sight, the unknown: their existence emphasises, as they attempt to traverse, the limitless and unbridgeable gap dividing the actual world from its aesthetic representation.[14]

Straddling and yoking its twin domains of nature and culture, as reliant on imagination as empiricism, the map 'Skills' points to remains, explicitly and subversively, unrealised. Suspended in the process of 'unfolding', it self-evidently undermines its own effort to fix, troubling the kinds of empirical assertions we expect it to provide. In this crucial closing image, therefore, Stevenson deliberately invokes the uncharted possibilities of the interrelation of human/non-human in the post-pastoral landscape on which her poem gazes. In doing so she echoes cultural geographer Doreen Massey's influential recognition of 'Multiplicity and space as co-constitutive', 'always under construction'; as both site and 'product of relations-between ... always in the process of being made ... a simultaneity of stories-so-far'.[15] Interestingly, though, the closing phrase of 'Skills' as it appears (almost a decade after the original) in *Granny Scarecrow* (2000) reads, more decisively, '*the* unfolding map'.[16] In this final manifestation, Stevenson's still richly mutable and equivocal image hints at the shifting cultural landscape of her own millennial 'Arden': the devolving United Kingdom.

The poems examined in this chapter find various reasons for, and ways of, making poetic space for the ever-unfolding 'relations-between' and 'stories-so-far' hosted by natural/cultural geopolitical landscapes of the (not always very Arden-like) 'British Isles' and Ireland. While not all are explicitly gendered, each discovers in the post-pastoral ways to address the partial, occluded and circumscribed patterns of women's cultural and literary history during and after the turn of the twentieth century.

Making space in the local

Much like Stevenson, Alice Oswald and (more occasionally) the Irish poet Moya Cannon seem wary of gendering the natural 'spaces' in which all three are keenly interested. The title poem of Oswald's first full-length collection, *The Thing in the Gap-Stone Stile* (1996), is vocalised by the eponymous voicebox-like 'thing' which seems to inhabit the liminal 'gap' of the equally liminal stile; a 'thing' which, in the event, comes to seem more like an absence, or space, just like the gap itself: 'My pose became the pass across two kingdoms, / before behind antiphonal, my cavity the chord.'[17] The space Oswald opens up in this fixed, anonymised 'pass' is as suggestive in its eloquence as its portal-like ambivalence. The spaces uncovered by other poets in other post-pastoral landscapes prove equally loquacious.

Cannon's 'West' echoes Oswald's 'The Thing in the Gap-Stone Stile' in emphasising the powerful interrelatedness of the natural landscape and the fractured, fracturing, cultural history it inscribes. The 'room-sized fields, / with their well made gaps', which 'open onto one another / in a great puzzle / of fragile wall and pasture / and more gaps', stage the silent inter-dependence of the non-human environs and the features of human construc-tion which contour and qualify them.[18] More explicitly than in Oswald's poem, the boundaries and the 'well-made gaps' which Cannon explores – both centralised as actual and metaphorical signifiers – combine in the 'stories-so-far' accommodated in this socially constructed, lacunae-filled landscape.

Partly in the still-'unfolding' stories it tells, 'West' illumines Cannon's interest in 'that most tangible of etymologies, the interface between language and landscape'. For her, in that 'interface' the landscape's inherently expres-sive potential is turned to specifically poetic use in the ancient signifying form of the place-name: 'it is the salient description which sticks, as if somehow the land has colluded in writing the poem of itself and the people who lived on it'. Cannon's words discover the landscape itself mapping – in the dual sense of creating and colonising – what Massey calls the 'relations between', of the spaces which inhere in it, by naming them.[19] Thus 'Scríob', the name of a Connemara village, both glosses and mines its multivalent title, Irish-Gaelic for 'scrape', 'scratch', 'notch', 'furrow':

> Start again from nothing and scrape
> since scraping is now part of us;
> the sheep's track, the plough's track
> are marked into the page,
> the pen's scrape cuts a path on the hill.[20]

This poem equates its own textual construction with the history of human cultivation (the 'scraping' and furrowing of the plough) which it disinters. Together, place and place-name, by testifying to the ancient 'scarring' interpenetration of culture and nature in the locale they share, expand the contemporaneous 'space' of their common context. The processes of this simultaneously self-excavating and self-extending text seem rooted in its determination to admit, in Neil Evernden's words, 'landscape not only as a collection of physical forms, but as the evidence of what has occurred there'.[21]

'Scríob's title-word recalls the Latinate-English 'scribe', itself trailing such verbal variants as 'inscribe', 'prescribe', 'proscribe'. Likewise some Gaelic uses of 'scríob' suggest encroachment upon a specified territory, recalling the regulating (inscribing/prescribing/proscribing) power of any 'pen's scrape'.[22] Thus the poem seems to concede the politically loaded fact that spaces usually depend for their existence upon borders and boundaries. In Ireland, of course, the differentiating effect of borders – actual, ideological and/or spiritual – has a violently divisive socio-cultural history. This may explain why in 'We Change the Map', the opening poem of A Furious Place (1996), Northern Irish poet Kerry Hardie disdains the freighted perspective of traditional cartography for the more arbitrary, minutely localised, 'mole's view. Paths and small roads and the next bend /... No overview, no sense of what lies where':

> I cannot hold whole countries in my mind,
> nor recognise their borders.
>
> These days I want to trace
> the shape of every townland in this valley;
> name families; count trees, walls, cattle, gable-ends,
> smoke-soft and tender in the near blue distance.[23]

Hardie's near-sighted tracing of the securing 'relations-between' human and natural affirms Evernden's astute understanding, borrowed from the cultural theorist John Dewey, of the 'individual as a component of, not something distinct from, the rest of the environment'.[24] Hardie's speaker's embeddedness in the text's socially constructed environs not only opens up the oxymoronic 'near blue distance' of this parochial, domesticated landscape; 'We Change the Map' also confirms the interest which Susan Stanford Friedman notices women taking in 'the geopolitics of identity within differing communal spaces of being and becoming'. [25] More explicitly than 'Scríob', the first person plural of Hardie's title finally acknowledges the political contexts shadowing the assimilation of any individual 'component' in his or her wider 'environment'. For, as Friedman argues, if identity connotes 'positionality, a location, a standpoint, a terrain', it also 'articulates ... the mapping of territories and boundaries, the dialectical terrains of inside/outside or center/margin'.[26]

The permissive but always potentially exclusive, because socially constructed, 'natural' landscapes examined by Hardie, Cannon, Oswald and Stevenson are worth comparing with the more explicitly gendered localities explored in the less 'mainstream' poetry of some of their peers. In their shared, linguistically self-conscious resistance to 'romanticism, sentimentality, nostalgia and the dualistic divide between rural and urban, cultivated and natural', the writers grouped by Harriet Tarlo as 'radical landscape' poets seem decidedly post-pastoral in outlook.[27] However, unlike their more mainstream peers, poets like Wendy Mulford and Frances Presley deploy the poetic text itself to interrogate the natural/cultural 'spaces' which landscape enshrines. Frequently for political reasons, such writers self-consciously exploit the signifying potential of poetic *form*: a poem's spatialised, concrete arrangement of words, phrases and lines on the page; its own textual terrain.

Angela Leighton reads in 'form' a constellation of contradictory-seeming ideas. For Coleridge, as she says, 'Form is not a body but an agent'; yet art historian Henri Focillon also persuades her that 'Form is realized in space and is shaped to be seen.' Above all, Leighton argues that as '"a capacity for", rather than an object of knowledge', form crucially 'shifts attention towards a kind of knowing which is an imaginative attitude rather than an accumulation of known things ... [It] does not close down into an achieved interpretation, but remains open to endless permutations of meaning.'[28] Mulford and Presley find in the visual, concrete, spatio-textual 'landscape' of a poem's form (which for Leighton 'looks two ways: to the thing it keeps in and the thing it keeps out') the 'capacity' to unsettle and ventilate the inclusive–exclusive interrelation of identity and locality which Friedman notes.[29]

Mulford's acclaimed *The East Anglia Sequence* (1998) is rooted in the poet's successive visits to the Norfolk village of Salthouse in the eighties and, a decade later, her status as 'blow-in', or incomer, in the Suffolk coastal town of Dunwich. Unsurprisingly, the work's preface invites us to read its conjoined sequences in the ambivalent terms of 'what the Buddhists call "nowhere country" ... a place I think at once peopled and empty ... retaining its profoundly resistant, unincorporated soul'.[30] Sequences are oddly 'unincorporated' poetic forms, preserving the economy of the lyric within their narrative-like but fractured, aporia-rich linearity.[31] This flexible, self-fragmenting form suits the permanent/transient processes of tidal invasion and retreat conditioning the impermanent environments, etched by loss, it orchestrates. Simultaneously, Mulford's generically and topographically liminal text makes formal as well as cultural-political space for the women's voices scattered through the 'stories-so-far' of its juxtaposed environments. Take Gabriel Piggott's indomitable mother, facing down her 'expropriate' landlord, from the moral and physical shelter of the church porch where she has installed her family,

listing her grievances viz.
    loss of eels
    loss of fish
    samphire
    grazing
    flags furzes
    whins from heath
    wildfowl plants marshland
    herbs
loss of food warmth shelter living[32]

Amid the performative ebb and flow of its restless, intelligent textuality, the spaces of *The East Anglia Sequence* suggest how and why such nameless but formidable women should have come to find themselves 'in exile of becoming'. Concluding the first section of 'Suffolk', halfway through the text's closing sequence, the last line of 'Inheritance' reprises Virginia Woolf's sage assertion that 'Women have no country'.[33] The statement resonates through Frances Presley's brilliantly literal mining of the gendered power relations sculpting and sculpted in the Somerset town of Minehead and its environs:

                          Mine
                is   mine
                    mine is the
myne   mynadd   meaning top of the hill
          from the Celt
she went back before the Celts
            to a time
          ...
             mined
further
           mind in search of
the quest for psyche
          tried once in the british library
east myne
    west myne
is just a circle on the hillside
          where farming interferes
with the Saxon theory
        which begins with my head
        myne heafden
            myne head
if it's my head how can it belong to the hill?[34]

Presley's spatially self-conscious study is much less whimsical than it might seem. The self-enclosing 'circle on the hillside' both invites and refuses the personal identification which the text (despite recognising a moment after the excerpted fragment that it 'makes no sense') seems compelled to try out. Under pressure, the apparently intimately possessive nominal conflation ('Mine'-'head') which should be so accommodating proves to exclude precisely the kinds of experience which actually constitute – for its speaker – 'myne head': its Celtic etymology points relentlessly back into its male-centred rural-industrial history. On the other hand, the poem decisively re-inscribes the subject's cultural autonomy ('myne heafden / myne head') on to the local topography it reifies. As this imaginatively map-like text rehearses, it opens up and begins to repair the gendered processes constructing, and reconstructed in, Minehead.

In and beyond the landscape(s) of nation

'Arden', the semi-imaginary forest that frames the satirical-pastoral plot of Shakespeare's *As You Like It*, makes a usefully undecidable topos for the contemporaneous post-pastoral. The name of an 'ancient wooded area in Warwickshire' long-vanished by Shakespeare's day, Arden not only affirms the damaging effect of acculturation on the natural environment; its name belongs to one of 'the very few English families whose ancestry could be traced to before the Norman conquest'.[35] Firstly, this essentially Anglo-centric trope introduces the question of nationality into the post-pastoral, post-devolution landscapes of what some critics call the 'Atlantic archipelago'.[36] Yet as Kevin Mills notes, Shakespeare's carefully named Arcadian-cum-Edenic forest also retains 'multiple possibilities of poetic usage: it is Arden in Warwickshire [but] Ardennes in France and even the Garden of Eden'.[37] In fact, as Robert Pogue Harrison warns at the start of his monumental *Forests*, 'the forest is uncircumscribable'.[38]

The remainder of this chapter finds British and Irish women probing the 'communal spaces of being and becoming' enshrined in and beyond the scarred landscapes of nation. As Ian Davidson argues, 'a place is identified through its relationship to other places and, as a consequence, is unstable. It will shift under different pressures, change from different perspectives and respond to different contexts.'[39] With political devolution 'unfolding' across the UK, Ric Caddell and Peter Quartermain foresee how terms 'like "British", "English", or "Irish" [will] begin to transcend ethnic origin or significance'.[40] In the process, gender-concerns gradually give way to growing interest in the cultural implications of 'relative and non-essential notion[s] of identity' in twenty-first century post-pastoral landscapes.[41]

Contemporary women poets' remapping of the often-gendered landscape(s) of nation can be retraced to Gillian Clarke's explicitly feminist 'Letter from a Far Country' (1982). Clarke's lyrics have from the first, as Katie Gramich notes, probed the legacy of Wales' gendered cultural history 'through an exploration of the Welsh landscape'.[42] Like 'Letter', Clarke's early poems expose the apparently unrecognised degree to which Wales' female-centred cultural history is embedded in, and imbues, the country's national terrain. Based in West Wales, 'Letter' seems to speak universally when it instructs, early on,

> First see a landscape. Hill country,
> essentially feminine,
> the sea not far off. Bryn Isaf
> down there in the crook of the hill
> under Calfaria's single eye.
> My grandmother might have lived there.
> Any farm. Any chapel.
> Father and minister, on guard,
> close the white gates to hold her.[43]

This much-quoted fragment has typically been understood as a moment of historical and political reclamation: a female-centred retrieval of Wales' landscape from the patriarchal grip of church and family. However, as Jarvis notes, the lines also register the predicament of the female inhabitants of this terrain, compromised as much as sheltered by the surveillance of the 'single eye' and 'crook of the hill'.[44]

The Scottish poet Kathleen Jamie is among the many women whose work converses with Clarke's powerful example. As Louisa Gairn argues, most poems in *Mr and Mrs Scotland Are Dead* (2002) – written during or about Jamie's travels in the remote estranging landscapes of the Asian sub-continent – affirm that for this poet 'coming home meant seeing afresh', not least Scotland's reluctance to concede women's part in its wider cultural and aesthetic history.[45] In the 'wedge / of rubber gateau' of the platform sole washed up on 'the dry sand of Cramond' ('A Shoe'), and in the mischievously arrowhead-like 'sherp / chert tongues' of the grannies chorusing through the feisty dialect poem 'Arraheids', Jamie boldly rewrites female experience into Scotland's exclusive-seeming landscape.[46]

The gendered cultural history Jamie indexes is reversed in 'Meadowsweet', rescuing the wronged, archetypal figure of the ancient (Gaelic) woman poet from her ritualistic burial, face downwards, in the very substance – the physical and natural ecology – of the Scottish landscape. The poem itself brings about the rebirthing of this redoubtable presence, from the very ground itself, into forceful articulacy: 'mouth young, and full again / of dirt, and spit, and poetry'.[47] The promise comes good in 'The Well at the Broch of Gurness', delicately rewriting the nameless girl it imagines descending 'to the sunken well ... left hand / on the roof's cool rock' into the palimpsestic landscape ('her homestead's lintels tilt / through mown turf') in which it submerges us:

> But we can follow her, descend
> below the bright grasses, the beat of surf
>
> step by hewn step, crouching
> till our eyes adjust – before we seek
> the same replenishing water ... [48]

Plainly, for Jamie, this landscape represents a text in which, as in Clarke's rural Wales, women's experiences have been profoundly hidden. At Gurness, in recompense, womanhood is uncovered as a kind of cultural stratum laid down, literally, in the land itself.

Partly thanks to its fabled female progenitors – whether 'Cathleen Ní Houlihan or Dark Rosaleen' – Ireland has treated women, especially poets, less hospitably than Wales and Scotland.[49] The disturbingly 'available and availed-of image' of the mythopoetic 'aisling', 'the dazzling idealised woman who is Ireland', perhaps connects with the paralysed femininity celebrated, as Seamus Heaney spots, in early Irish nature poetry: 'the curve of the hill is the curve of a loved one's beauty, its contour the contour of a woman with child'.[50] This creative-maternal paradigm is debunked – only half-humorously – in the ghastly presence menacing the daughter in Nuala Ní Dhomhnaill's 'Hag':[51] 'O Mam, I'm scared stiff, / I thought I saw the mountains heaving / like a giantess, with her breast swaying, / about to loom over and gobble me up.'[52]

Apparently picking up where Clarke's 'Letter' leaves off, Eavan Boland's magnificent long poem 'Anna Liffey' rehomes both Ireland's female imaginary and the woman poet in particular, in a manifestly post-pastoral landscape, its natural and human worlds held in permeable, fertile, equilibrium:

> The river took its name from the land.
> The land took its name from a woman.
>   *
>
>   . . .
>
>   *
> There, in the hills above my house,
> The river Liffey rises, is a source.
> It rises in rush and ling heather and
> Black peat and bracken and strengthens

> To claim the city it narrated.
> Swans. Steep falls. Small towns.
> The smudged air and bridges of Dublin.[53]

'Anna Liffey' seems to confirm Boland's conviction that Ireland's histori-cally feminised topography leaves her female poets, specifically, subver-sively empowered: 'the Irish woman poet['s] ... relation to the poetic tradition is defined by the fact that she was once a passive and controlled image within it; her disruption of that control in turn redefines the connec-tion between the Irish poem and the national tradition'.[54]

'Anna Liffey' suggests that Boland finds in the natural/cultural spaces of the post-pastoral a way of redressing the cultural positioning she has herself, as Irish woman poet, experienced. However, the more experimental approach of a poet like Catherine Walsh confirms that for some poets the axis linking literary and 'national tradition' in Ireland is itself exclusive. A writer who has spent time in Europe and America, Walsh's demanding, formally supple oeuvre persistently interrogates the socio-aesthetic contexts of her native Ireland. John Goodby notes how the 'personal sense of dislocation, of being in transit, not belonging' which imbues collections like *Pitch* and especially *idir eatortha* – translated as 'between worlds' – is compounded in the expressive provisionalities of Walsh's laconically pro-jective idiom.[55] Take the flimsy-seeming, self-puncturing textual fabric of 'A Wait', seemingly unable to assuage or provide shelter from the discom-forts it ascribes to 'place':

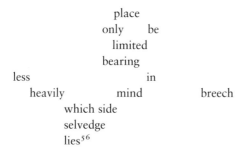

Both marking out and eroding the textual margins which might contain it (a 'selvedge' – punning on both 'salvage' and 'selvage' – marks the outer edge of a bolt of woven fabric), 'A Wait' suggests Walsh's sense of alienation from a literary status quo she disdains as culturally monolithic: 'You need to be incorporated into the tradition to be an Irish writer and you exist as an Irish writer on those terms or you might as well not exist.'[57] If 'pitch' suggests an impermanent site – occupied by a tent – it also signifies an argument, a (competitive, often commercial) proposal or position and, of course, a throw: Walsh seems to 'pitch' her singular idiom simultaneously into and out of the confines of Ireland's aesthetic and cultural landscape.

Historically, Wales has proved significantly more hospitable to its women poets than either Scotland or Ireland.[58] In its more permissive cultural-aesthetic landscape, gender and nationality are less insistent concerns for writers like Yorkshire-born Christine Evans, reclaiming the littoral landscapes of the remote North-West coastline, and the Irish citizen Anne Cluysenaar, Belgian by birth, domiciled in Monmouthshire. The opening text of Cluysenaar's sequence *Timeslips*, 'Landfall' savours the post-pastoral spatiousness of environs it constructs, equivocally, as bridge, slipway and insecurely fastened vessel: 'It must be / pastures anchored to hills that hold / the land unlaunched still / on this well-oiled causeway.' The text concludes by gently mocking efforts to 'map' such elusive dynamism:

> We like to imagine it, latecomers
> with language-maps so detailed
> and so different that, each moment,
> the places we named have again
> refused to become just home.[59]

Cluysenaar's words pre-empt Friedman, pointing out how 'Identity depends upon a point of reference; as that point moves … so do the contours of identity, particularly as they relate to the structures of power.'[60] Friedman's point is itself endorsed by Jamie; long-irked by Scotland's socio-historical disenfranchisement, political devolution radically altered Jamie's imaginary, let alone her socio-cultural landscape: 'I woke up … and discovered that half my poems were obsolete … historical documents which could be read differently after[wards].'[61] As Gairn suggests, devolution profoundly affected Jamie's sense of her national landscape. In interview she remarks, 'So much of what we would relate to in this country is because … the relics of the past are in the land, literally in the landscape.' 'The Reliquary', a draft published in the same interview, explains:

> The land we inhabit opens and reveals
> event before event: the stain
> of ancient settlements,
> plague pits where we'd lay
> our fibre-optic cables;
>
> but it yields also moment
> into moment: witness
> these brittle August bluebells
> casting seed, like tiny hearts
> in caskets, tossed onto battleground.[62]

In this text, the historical resources layered in landscape ('event before event') must 'yield' – open – to the post-pastoral future (succeeding 'moment / into moment') troped in the reach of the seeding bluebells: 'I was also thinking about how the natural order works ... replenishing and reinventing itself every moment, every instant, and casting seed into the future the whole time.'[63] If Jamie's new battleground seems more ecological than political, the 'hearts / in caskets' imply that it remains marked by its conflicted past (the bluebell is Scotland's national flower).[64]

Jamie's short lyric compares interestingly with Mulford's semi-autobiographical sequence 'Alltud' (2007), its title Welsh for 'exile'. Having left her childhood home in Usk for Cambridge in the seventies, Mulford has lived in East Anglia all her writing life but continues to identify with Wales. Her equivocal sense of connection with her homeland nuances the ever more historical and provisional-seeming landscapes explored by 'Alltud'. Sifting the centuries of 'relations-between' charging Wales' proudly 'resist-ant, unincorporated' environs, 'Alltud' concentrates on the undetermined spaces in which the known – navigated, mapped – world dissipates into the unremembered or unimagined: the territory lying beyond the horizon, beyond memory and myth. In this poem, trails peter out, history speaks through ruination, and dissolution – liberatingly – prevails:

> My phases are lost, Pre-Boreal – Boreal – Atlantic
> pre-history wiped in fenny mud
>   ...
>   No trace
> of my provenance remains.
>
> If you search for me you may find a brief label
> Name – species attributed – date caught

In its erasing of such 'provenance', 'Alltud' maps out a kind of territorial exile which seems a condition less of cultural refusal than of permission; a state – space perhaps – of Ardenic possibility. The final ten-line section, 'Ellennith', opens by avowing: 'in emptiness / is my source'. Like most of the sequence, this valedictory lyric eschews end-punctuation in ushering us towards where 'the barque waits that will bear you / to the edge'.[65]

Zoë Skoulding problematises the ethno-cultural zoning of landscape for more political reasons, not least in insisting, as Ian Gregson notes, that 'places can only be understood in relation to each other'.[66] 'Preselis with Brussels Street Map' manoeuvres between upland West Wales and cosmopolitan Brussels:

> Up Europalaan under blue
>   reach of sky   bare feet in spongy moss

> I need a map to tell me where I'm
> not   along the avenue de Stalingrad
>   squeal of a meadow pipit
> skimming
>   over rue de l'Empereur
> tread softly on the streets   the sheep trails
>   between bird call and bleat echo
> a street folds across two languages   here and there [67]

Mapping the sensual immediacies of Welsh rurality on to Europe's multilingual civic centre, with its Flemish/French nomenclature, this poem finds textual, aesthetic and political reasons for figuring 'multiplicity and space as co-constitutive'. Elsewhere, poems like 'Llanddwyn Beach with Directions for Copenhagen' and 'Žižkov' show how the 'multiple becomings' of contemporaneity proliferate in our increasingly virtual environment, since 'experience decreasingly takes place in the places in which the body is located'.[68]

As M. Gatens and G. Lloyd predict, in such culturally undetermined spaces Skoulding maps out 'new sites of [socio-cultural] responsibility'.[69] She explains, 'Even while you're in one location, you're simultaneously linked to many others. For me, this ... gets beyond there being an essential Wales and who it belongs to and who's allowed to write about it.'[70] The representation of what she calls the 'much-written about' landscape of Wales is crucial to this Bradford-born, Bangor-based writer. Recently appointed editor of *Poetry Wales*, Skoulding might seem entitled to make few cultural claims on the place where she lives and works, yet

> Wales is where my writing took shape; I write in English in a bilingual country, and I know that this context makes me see English as a provisional circumstance rather than something to be taken for granted: my national identity as a writer is therefore a set of negotiations rather than a fixed point within clearly defined national boundaries. Complex relationships between languages and cultures define Wales as much as Cymraeg itself does, and they define Europe too.[71]

Likewise, Jamie's latest collection, *The Tree House* (2004) opens with 'The Wishing Tree', impassively imagining a resolutely anti-essentialist landscape: 'I draw into my slow wood / fleur de lys, the enthroned Britannia. // Behind me, the land reaches towards the Atlantic.'[72] In different ways, both visions echo and are echoed in Boland's 'Home', reaching across time-zones, amid the exotic artificial twilight created by migrating monarch butterflies in southern California, towards Dublin's coastal, rural landscape:

> If I could not say the word *home*.
> If I could not breathe the Irish night
> air and influence of rain coming from the east,

I could at least be sure –
far below them and unmoved by movement –
of one house with its window, making

an oblong of wheat out of light.[73]

Assimilating as it spans its human/non-human, local/remote, atemporal 'spaces of being and becoming', 'Home' projects a suggestively intercontinental, socially responsive twenty-first century 'Arden'. Contrived 'out of light', its enigmatic, beacon-like closing image adumbrates the accommodating, acculturated, post-pastoral landscape troped in Stevenson's 'unfolding map'. It affirms Kinsella, declaring: 'some of the most interesting and challenging pastoral poetry being written in English today is by women'.[74]

Notes

My thanks to Matthew Jarvis, Kym Martindale and Jane Dowson for their patient support in the making of this chapter.

1 Terry Gifford, *Pastoral* (London: Routledge, 1999), p. 147.

2 *Ibid.*, p. 148.

3 John Kinsella, *Disclosed Poetics: Beyond Landscape and Lyricism* (Manchester: Manchester University Press, 2007), p. 4.

4 Jonathan Bate, *The Song of the Earth* (London: Picador, 2001), p. 65.

5 Wendy Joy Darby, *Landscape and Identity: Geographies of Nation and Class in England* (Oxford and New York: Berg Publishers, 2000), p. 9.

6 Alicia Suskin Ostriker, *Stealing the Language: The Emergence of Women's Poetry in America* (London: The Women's Press, 1987), p. 94.

7 Roger Lonsdale (ed.), *Eighteenth Century Women Poets* (Oxford: Oxford University Press, 1989), p. xxxiv.

8 Lawrence Buell, *The Environmental Imagination* (Cambridge MA: Harvard University Press, 1995), p. 32; quoted in Gifford, *Pastoral*, p. 148. See also Janet Wilson, 'The pastoral in the works of Fleur Adcock', in David James and Philip Tew (eds.), *New Versions of Pastoral: Post-Romantic, Modern and Contemporary Responses to the Tradition* (Cranbury, NJ: Associated University Presses, 2009), pp. 174–94; 186.

9 Matthew Jarvis, *Welsh Environments in Contemporary Poetry* (Cardiff: University of Wales Press, 2008), pp. 91–2.

10 Anne Stevenson, 'Skills', *Poetry Wales* 27.1 (1991), 23.

11 Gifford, *Pastoral*, pp. 152, 153, 156, 162.

12 Ruth Padel, *The Poem and the Journey* (London: Chatto & Windus, 2007), p. 264.

13 Anne Stevenson, 'Poetry and place', in Hans-Werner Ludwig and Lothar Fietz (eds.), *Poetry in the British Isles: Non-Metropolitan Perspectives* (Cardiff: University of Wales Press, 1995), pp. 199–211; 200.

14 This difficult terrain is theorised by Gilles Deleuze and Felix Guattari in *A Thousand Plateaus* (London: Athlone, 1988) but is more suggestively and

comprehensively explored in Christian Jacob's magisterial cultural historical survey *The Sovereign Map: Theoretical Approaches in Cartography throughout History* (Chicago: University of Chicago Press, 2006).

15 Doreen Massey, *For Space* (London: Sage Publications, 2005), p. 9.

16 Anne Stevenson, *Granny Scarecrow* (Tarset: Bloodaxe, 2000), p. 30. (My emphases.) The poem has subsequently been collected in *Poems 1995–2005* (Tarset: Bloodaxe, 2005).

17 Alice Oswald, *The Thing in the Gap-Stone Stile* (London: Faber, 1996), p. 32.

18 Moya Cannon, *Oar* (Galway: Salmon Publishing, 1990), p. 10.

19 Moya Cannon, 'The poetry of what happens', in Patricia Boyle Habestroh (ed.), *My Self, My Muse: Irish Women Poets Reflect on Life and Art* (Syracuse, NY: Syracuse University Press, 2001), p. 128.

20 Moya Cannon, *Carrying the Songs* (Manchester: Carcanet Press, 2007), p. 101.

21 Neil Evernden, 'Beyond ecology: self, place and the pathetic fallacy', in Cheryll Glotfelty and Harold Fromm (eds.), *The Eco-Criticism Reader: Landmarks in Literary Ecology* (Athens: University of Georgia Press, 1996), pp. 92–104; 99.

22 I am grateful to Patricia Coughlan and Claire Connolly for their help in glossing this text. See also Christine Cusick, ' "Our language was tidal": Moya Cannon's poetics of place', *New Hibernia Review* 9.1 (2005), 59–76.

23 Kerry Hardie, 'We Change the Map', in *A Furious Place* (Oldcastle: The Gallery Press, 1996), p. 13.

24 Evernden, 'Beyond ecology', p. 99.

25 Susan Stanford Friedman, *Mappings: Feminism and the Cultural Geographies of Encounter* (Princeton: Princeton University Press, 1998), p. 5.

26 *Ibid.*, p. 19.

27 'Women and ecopoetics: an introduction in context', HOW2 'Special Issue on Women and Ecopoetics' 3.2 (Autumn 2002). www.asu.edu/pipercwcenter/how2-journal/vol_3_no_2/ecopoetics/introstatements/tarlo_intro.html (last visited 20 April 2009). See also Tarlo's 'Radical landscapes: experiment and environment in contemporary poetry', *Jacket* 32 (2007), 1–13. http://jacketmagazine.com/32/p-tarlo.shtml

28 Angela Leighton, *On Form: Poetry, Aestheticism, and the Legacy of the Written Word* (Oxford: Oxford University Press: 2007), pp. 7, 17.

29 *Ibid.*, p. 16.

30 Wendy Mulford, 'Preface', *The East Anglia Sequence: Salthouse, Norfolk 1984 – Dunwich, Suffolk 1994* (Cambridge: Paul Green/Spectacular Diseases, 1998), p. ii.

31 See M. L. Rosenthal and Sally M. Gall, *The Modern Poetic Sequence: The Genius of Modern Poetry* (Oxford: Oxford University Press, 1983). See also Alice Entwistle, ' "A Kind of Authentic Lie": authenticity and the lyric sequence in Gwyneth Lewis' English-language poetry', *Life-Writing* 6.1 (2009), 27–43.

32 Mulford, *The East Anglia Sequence*, p. 14.

33 *Ibid.*

34 Frances Presley, 'Minehead', in *Paravane: New and Selected Poems 1996–2003* (Cambridge: Salt, 2004), pp. 52–3.

35 Charles Boyce (ed.), *Encyclopaedia of Shakespeare* (New York and Oxford: Roundtable Press, 1990), p. 32; Kevin Mills, *The Prodigal Sign: A Parable of Criticism* (Eastbourne: Sussex Academic Press, 2009), p. 85.

36 For example, Glenda Norquay and Gerry Smyth (eds.), *Across the Margins: Cultural Identity and Change in the Atlantic Archipelago* (Manchester: Manchester University Press, 2002).

37 Mills, *The Prodigal Sign*, p. 88.

38 Robert Pogue Harrison, *Forests: The Shadow of Civilisation* (Chicago: University of Chicago Press, 1992), p. x.

39 Ian Davidson, *Ideas of Space in Contemporary Poetry* (London: Palgrave, 2007), p. 89.

40 Ric Caddell and Peter Quartermain (eds.), *Other: British and Irish Poetry since 1970* (New England: Wesleyan University Press, 1999), pp. xvii, xix–xx.

41 Davidson, *Ideas of Space*, p. 89.

42 Katie Gramich, *Twentieth-Century Women's Writing in Wales: Land, Gender, Belonging* (Cardiff: University of Wales Press, 2007), pp. 147, 148.

43 Gillian Clarke, 'Letter from a Far Country', in *Collected Poems* (Manchester: Carcanet Press, 1997), pp. 45–56; 46.

44 Matthew Jarvis, 'Energies of commitment: poetry and politics in the 1980s', *Poetry Wales* 44.4 (2009), 11–16; 11.

45 Louisa Gairn, 'Clearing space: Kathleen Jamie and ecology', in Berthold Schoene (ed.), *The Edinburgh Companion to Contemporary Scottish Literature* (Edinburgh: Edinburgh University Press, 2007), pp. 237–8; 'Kathleen Jamie', in Clare Brown and Don Paterson (eds.), *Don't Ask Me What I Mean: Poets in Their Own Words* (London: Picador, 2003), p. 125.

46 Kathleen Jamie, *Mr and Mrs Scotland Are Dead: Poems 1980–1994* (Tarset: Bloodaxe, 2002), pp. 115, 137.

47 Kathleen Jamie, *Jizzen* (London: Picador, 1999), p. 49.

48 *Ibid.* p. 44.

49 Eavan Boland, 'The Irish woman poet: her place in Irish literature', in Habestroh (ed.), *My Self, My Muse*, p. 100.

50 Seamus Heaney, 'The sense of place', in *Preoccupations: Selected Prose 1968–1978* (London: Faber, 1980), p. 143.

51 See Peggy O'Brien (ed.), 'Preface', *The Wake Forest Book of Irish Women's Poetry 1967–2000* (Winston-Salem, NC: Wake Forest University Press, 1999), p. xxvii.

52 Nuala Ní Dhomhnaill, 'Hag', trans. John Montague, *ibid.*, pp. 152–3.

53 Eavan Boland, 'Anna Liffey', *ibid.*, pp. 31–6.

54 Boland, 'The Irish woman poet', p. 101.

55 John Goodby, *Irish Poetry since 1950: From Stillness into History* (Manchester: Manchester University Press, 2000), p. 308.

56 Catherine Walsh, 'A Wait', in *Pitch* (Durham: Pig Press, 1994), p. 43.

57 Goodby, *Irish Poetry*, p. 308.

58 Katie Gramich and Catherine Brennan (eds.), *Welsh Women's Poetry 1460–2001: An Anthology* (Dinas Powys, S. Glamorgan: Honno Classics, 2003), p. xvii.

59 Anne Cluysenaar, *Timeslips: New and Selected Poems* (Manchester: Carcanet, 1997), pp. 89–91.

60 Friedman, *Mappings*, p. 22.

61 Kathleen Jamie, 'Dream state', *Poetry Review* 94.4 (2004), 35.

62 'Kathleen Jamie interviewed by Lilias Fraser', *Scottish Studies Review* 2.1 (2001), 15–23; 18.

63 *Ibid.*, p. 19.
64 A shorter (eight-line) version of this draft subsequently appeared as 'Reliquary' in *The Tree House* (London: Picador, 2004), p. 37. Interestingly, Jamie herself links the image on which both versions conclude to a story about one of Scotland's most famous historical figures, Robert the Bruce: 'After Bruce's death his heart was removed, put in a casket and taken by Sir James Douglas on a crusade. There it was thrown into the heat of the battle. Something Bruce had requested, apparently.' (Email to Alice Entwistle, quoted with kind permission of the author, 15 September 2009.)
65 Wendy Mulford, 'Alltud', *Scintilla* 11 (2007), 153–61.
66 Ian Gregson, *The New Poetry in Wales* (Cardiff: University of Wales Press, 2007), pp. 137–8.
67 Zoë Skoulding, *Remains of a Future City* (Bridgend: Seren, 2008), p. 50.
68 Davidson, *Ideas of Space*, p. 163.
69 M. Gatens and G. Lloyd, *Collective Imaginings: Spinoza Past and Present* (London: Routledge, 1999), p. 80, quoted in Massey, *For Space*, p. 191.
70 Zoë Skoulding (interview), 'A city of words', *Planet* 166 (2004), 61.
71 Zoë Skoulding, 'Border lines', *Poetry Wales* 42.4 (2007), 40.
72 Kathleen Jamie, *The Tree House* (London: Picador, 2004), pp. 3–4.
73 Eavan Boland, 'Home', in *Wake Forest*, pp. 39–40; 40.
74 Kinsella, *Disclosed Poetics*, p. 4.

IO

LINDA A. KINNAHAN

Feminism's experimental 'work at the language-face'

> With what voices do women poets speak? In avant-garde, experimental or Language Poetry (to throw in three assorted and not particularly helpful labels), there is no unified lyric voice – its claims are exploded, its modes of expression done to death. In its place, we ... follow the text in all its provisionality, its multiple meanings, its erasures, silences, chora.[1]

> I do not want to make it cohere[2]

> voices all   well put down   then[3]

Women's voices vex literary histories of recent British poetry, whether cast as 'mainstream' or as 'postmodern', categories routinely invoked and questioned and invoked again, but nonetheless defined primarily in terms of male poets. Familiar narratives paint a picture of poetry retreating after World War II into an insular and provincial Englishness, a rejection of modernist experimentation that really begins before the war but finds its fullest popularity in the everyman poetry of the Movement. That an active continuation of modernist poetics persisted alongside the more dominant Movement – under the various labels of neo-modernism, postmodernism, innovative, experimental and/or alternative poetics – has remained relatively overlooked by critics, ignored by publishing powers and unsupported by arts funding through the later decades of the twentieth century. If the British experimental scene is a 'stretched and resolutely unnamed map of divergent factions, mostly held together by the poets themselves and a few critics',[4] what mappings exist focus, by and large, on men, too often ignoring not only the creative work of women but the political, theoretical and activist feminisms mediating their gender-aware constructs of the 'experimental'.

Influential accounts of mainstream *and* alternative poetries typically offer only glancing treatment of women poets and, moreover, customarily ignore trajectories of *feminist* thought, publication, activism or theory as important to conceptualising or historicising contemporary British poetry.[5] Broad surveys and critical histories most often bring up women's work and/or feminism as a side bar to the central narrative rather than as compelling forces within that narrative, or dismiss them altogether, as in Andrew Duncan's pithy conclusion, in surveying British poetry since the fifties, that he must 'report that feminism has played a relatively small role in the history of poetry'.[6]

Many poets begging to differ would actively interrogate the framing preconceptions brought to such a statement and the conditions of authority generating it. Indeed, such interrogations constitute one of the major impacts that feminism has had on poetry, unsettling notions of the poet, the text and the medium. While feminist poetry is most customarily associated with the preferred model of the Women's Movement – a lyric-based reporting of women's experience assuming a unified self, voiced through accessible language – a feminist poetics of radical language experimentation runs through the twentieth century to the present, tenaciously exploring how authority (and power) resides in the forms and operations of language, the contexts of linguistic systems and the production of meaning through these systems and operations.

Language innovation, women and feminism in the seventies

As the seventies drew to a close, a two-decade resurgence of formally experimental work brought a poetry of language innovation into tension with standard poetic practice in Britain. Groups particularly active in London and Cambridge took part in the British Poetry Revival, galvanised through readings, small press publications, festivals and, for a brief period, participation in national poetry venues, energised by the active presence of late Modernist poets like Basil Bunting and an interest in the 'new American poetry' of Black Mountain, Beat and New York Schools. Moreover, the infusion of continental, poststructuralist theory into British academic and intellectual circles activated a theory-informed set of questions about language, subjectivity and poetry for many poets. Concurrently, the cultural explosiveness of the Women's Movement compelled debates about women's position, power and identity.

Wendy Mulford's commitment to language innovation set her apart from communities of feminist poets who favoured expressive and accessible poetry. Also beginning to write in the sixties, Carlyle Reedy would retrospectively claim that the 'role of the poet' – an inherently 'social role' – was isolating for women.[7] Eric Mottram's history of the Revival lists a few women without actually discussing them, including Mulford, Denise Riley, Veronica Forrest-Thomson, Elaine Feinstein and Elaine Randell; Mulford adds Glenda George and Carlyle Reedy to this generation of experimentalists.[8] However, despite the presence of a few other women by the time she writes 'Notes on writing', Mulford expresses her 'sense of "otherness" relation to the 'neo-modernist tradition within which I see my work as located'; indeed, attuned to the dominance of men and of masculine experience underlying an 'experimental' poetics 'produced from a differently gendered place', she observes, 'I have, as it were, only a colonial relationship to such texts inhabiting a language and a culture which I'm not quite at ease in, which doesn't quite fit.'[9]

Mulford's unease was double-edged, responding to the primacy given male poets in experimental camps, and, concurrently, the resistance to experimental forms within feminist communities. An early case of constructing the 'experimental' around men is the early seventies anthology 23 *Modern British Poets*, published in America by the American poet John Matthias.[10] This anthology is not alone, as a spate of collections dedicated to avant-garde poets in the 1980s routinely include few women. The question of why women are so poorly represented raises a number of issues described recently as the 'troubled history of modern experimental women's writing':[11] for example, what discourses frame conceptions of the 'experimental' and who is doing the framing? How has the practice of earlier Modernisms been retained and reclaimed primarily through the work of men, ignoring British poets like Lynette Roberts, Sylvia Townsend Warner, Edith Sitwell or Mina Loy – or the cross-Atlantic activity of women modernists, like Gertrude Stein, H.D., Lorine Niedecker, Laura Riding or Marianne Moore?

Matthias' anthology followed by two years Michael Horovitz's *Children of Albion: Poetry of the 'Underground' in Britain* (1969), the first anthology to attempt a British counterpart to the American innovations signalled by Donald Allen's influential 1960 *The New American Poetry*. Horovitz's 'proto-Beat' scene included few women in its readings or audiences, and the anthology published only five women among sixty-three poets.[12] Horovitz includes Libby Houston, Frances Horovitz, Carlyle Reedy, Anna Lovell and Tina Morris; indeed, Houston would later remark that she felt herself 'an oddity . . . a woman; a poet'.[13] This marginalisation was further intensified in relation to popular formations of woman-centred poetics. Mulford's 'Notes' appeared in the same year as the first British anthology devoted to contemporary feminist poets, *One Foot On the Mountain: An Anthology of British Feminist Poetry 1969–1979*, edited by Lilian Mohin. Although Mohin notes that a 'community of feminist writers is evolving' around the ideas and practices she expresses in her introduction, the anthology's fifty-five women include no avant-garde representation or mention of experimental poetics.[14] Confronting such exclusion from mainstream formations of feminist expression, Mulford's essay insists that a feminist politics of the experimental *can* participate in the movement's goals: 'There will be, there must be, of course, many different ways of doing this', and *her way* is to 'work at the "language-face" '.[15]

Both Mulford and Mohin explicitly connect their ideas to the Women's Liberation Movement, speak to gender difference and share similar goals of cultural transformation at the ten-year mark for the movement each claims as transformative and vital. For Mohin, the 'imperative to make new definitions, identities, connections', is an expanding of – but not a radical questioning of – the categories of self, identity, and language.[16] For Mulford, however, the humanist frame for understanding those categories renders them suspect sites of investigation. Reading theories of Lacan, Derrida, Foucault, Kristeva, Irigaray, Althusser and others coincided with her 'involvement in the women's movement, and ... friendships with particular women':

> [t]hat was the time when the whole question of the 'construction' of the self started to form mistily on the skyline. Who was this 'I' speaking? What was speaking me? How far did the illusion of selfhood, that most intimate and precious possession, reach? How could the lie of culture be broken up if the lie of the self made by that culture remained intact? And how could the lie of capitalist society be broken if the lie of culture were not broken?[17]

Claiming a '[c]ontemporary experimental Marxist/Feminist writing', Mulford insists upon connections between material change and language structures, declaring that 'for the writer revolutionary practice necessitates revolutionary practice in the field of the signifier', a claim she admits sets her 'against the practice of most women' concerned with reporting women's experience in accessible, familiar language. In distinguishing work 'at the language-face' from an expressive reporting of women's experience, Mulford nonetheless seeks a coalition among feminist poets that would recognise her 'voice': 'I want to join my voice with the voices of other *women* struggling to destruct the lie of culture'.[18]

De-Authorising the 'I': Forrest-Thomson, Mulford and Riley

The work of individual women poets and their collective contributions to experimental poetry in contemporary Britain suggest a history that has yet to be told.[19] While beyond the scope of this essay, part of this history would include a fuller picture of earlier generations of experimental or Modernist writers, attending to a specifically British location for such work. Moving through the century, gaps persist into the contemporary period. What were women working in connection to the Modernist tradition doing in the sixties and seventies? Elaine Feinstein was reading the Black Moun poets by the late fifties, had published collections by 1970 and was one of the 'radical poets' involved with the Poetry Society in the early seventies. She was among the earliest British poets to read the 'new American poetry' of the fifties, especially the Black Mountain School, and her absorption of field composition and projective verse combines with a feminist consciousness of women's history and experience in her early work, while her letter to Charles Olson (1959) became the starting point of a section of his famous statement of poetics, the essay 'Projective verse'. Elaine Randell, whose work has remained largely out of print, had by the late sixties begun and edited the magazine *Amazing Grace*. Paula Claire was performing her visual text-based pieces as early as 1970, founded the International Poetry Archive in 1978 as a 'collection of sound and visual poetry' and in 1980 established ICPA Publications to publish the work of 'sound and visual poets'.[20] In 1972, Wendy Mulford began Street Editions as a press devoted to innovative poetries, and she had been writing poetry since 1968. Carlyle Reedy, part of the Beat-like 'underground' and anti-establishment poetry scene during the sixties, was developing experimental combinations of textual, visual and performance elements in the seventies and published a first book in 1979. Denise Riley, like Mulford, was part of the Cambridge group during these years, and her studies in philosophy and theory coincided with her development as a young poet. Another student at Cambridge, Veronica Forrest-Thomson, produced a body of poetry and poetic theory explicitly exploring contemporary theories of language, prior to her death in 1975.

Reading the 'experimental' through feminism alters the picture of experimental poetics, not merely through including women but through shifting the terms by which such poetry engages subjectivity and its constitution through language. Problematic for women has been the 'I-aversion' claimed by American and British poets alike, whose challenge to the Romantic inheritance of a self-expressive lyric voice has, in many instances, issued as an evacuation of the self. The influence of contemporary theory upon poets shifted – or at least inflected – discussions and poetry practices from the seventies onward, as Mulford's own references to a 'construction' or 'illusion' of 'self' indicate.[21] At this time, the phrase 'linguistically innovative poetry' appeared to signify a *creative* extension of the British Revival (in its 'increased indeterminacy and discontinuity, the use of techniques of disruption and creative linkage'), while enacting a simultaneous 'break' in the 'increased willingness of emerging poets to operate theoretically, in terms of poststructuralist and other theory, to even expound poetics more coherently ... in marked contrast to an earlier lack of such discourse'.[22] Remarkably, some of the earliest sustained articulations of this shift happened in the work of women, particularly in the poetic theorisation of

Veronica Forrest-Thomson, the cultural analysis of Denise Riley and the writings on women poets and feminism by Wendy Mulford, all working at the language-face.

Crafting a theory of poetic language through readings of experimental contemporaries like her teacher, J.H. Prynne, Veronica Forrest-Thomson pursued graduate studies at Cambridge in the sixties and seventies, participating in the Cambridge poetry community and its festivals. In 1971, her first book of poetry, *Language-Games*, was published, its title provocatively qualified in a 'Note' stating that 'questions of knowledge become questions of technique'.[23] Her doctoral thesis, 'Poetry as knowledge: the use of science by twentieth-century poets', was also completed in 1971 and published posthumously in 1978 as *Poetic Artifice*.[24] Rejecting a mimetic naturalisation of language, Forrest-Thomson asserts that 'the knowledge exhibited in a poem is *knowledge of certain forms of language and ways in which they can be brought together*'.[25] Alison Mark, in her valuable work to illuminate Forrest-Thomson's contribution to a 'line of [linguistically] investigative poets', claims that her 'early response to structuralist and poststructuralist thought establishes Forrest-Thomson as an important figure in both the development of critical theory and its articulation in poetic language'.[26] Forrest-Thomson's work explores how, in her words, poetic artifice can 'challenge our ordinary linguistic orderings of the world, make us question the way in which we make sense of things, and induce us to consider its alternative linguistic orders as a new way of viewing the world'. Naturalisation – for Mulford, the 'familiar poetics' of mimetic or referential language use – works differently to 'reduce the strangeness of poetic language and poetic organisation by making it intelligible'. Instead, a poetics of artifice 'must assimilate the already-known and subject it to a re-working which suspends and questions its categories, provides alternative orderings'.[27] Her theoretical writings and poems circulated within the Cambridge scene, as in a statement referencing Wittgenstein that accompanied a set of poems published in a 1969 issue of the Cambridge-based *Solstice* poetry magazine, exemplifying her 'process' of turning 'theoretical debate and abstract statement into a means of technical experiment in the actual medium of poetry, to explore new formal possibilities'. As an academic, she published prescient theoretical essays on poetics in various journals, discussing her theories of artifice, the work of William Empson and the poetry of the French *Tel Quel* group. In a 1979 review of *Poetic Artifice* in the avant-garde journal *Reality Studios*, Robert Sheppard proclaimed the book a 'theoretic for a poetry just beginning to be written'.[28]

Other poets recognised the crossover in her poetic work between philosophy and poetics. Denise Riley, studying at Cambridge during these years, remarks upon the 'tons of Wittgenstein' that she and others were reading: 'V's style in these earliest poems is very like Wittgenstein's voice in his half-tentative, half-assured self-notations ... Wittgenstein's is a catchy tone and Veronica perhaps caught it then.'[29] That sense of a 'half-assured' voice and the strategy of the 'self-notation' intriguingly suggest a displacement of the authoritative voice that may have appealed to Forrest-Thomson's sense of her position as a woman poet and intellectual, a position denied cultural authority. How does language shape that authority, that view of reality sustaining such authority and voice? How might a reordering of language interrupt such authority? One might turn with these questions to the poem 'Cordelia, or "A poem should not mean but be"'.[30]

This long poem, published in 1974 by Omens Press and included in *On the Periphery* (Street Editions, 1976), tellingly exemplifies to at least one critic a poetry inferior to her theory. Finding in this 'fairly characteristic' poem the 'conservatively discursive' approach that reminds one of the 'chatty, facetious intellectualism' he sees in her first book, Edward Larrissy castigates the poetry for lacking the 'scope, lucidity, and trenchancy of the theory'.[31] It is difficult not to read long-standing gendered associations into this equation, granting an authority to the masterful handling of (masculine) theory while bemoaning its dissolution by the 'chatty' (read: feminine) poetry. Larrissy admires Forrest-Thomson's critical/theoretical work that, Jane Dowson and Alice Entwistle comment, 'shows little interest in other women poets and hardly mentions gender', while he disdains a poem in which '[g]ender plays more part', especially in speaking to the poet's position, as in Alison Mark's assessment, it 'draws attention to, and attempts to elude the silencing of, the doubly marginalised female experimental poet'.[32]

By the time of this poem's composition, Forrest-Thomson had become interested in the 'Tel Quel group in Paris, in particular the semiotic theories of Julia Kristeva and the re-reading of Freud through linguistics by Jacques Lacan', publishing an article in *Language and Style* entitled 'Necessary artifice: form and theory in the poetry of Tel Quel' (1973).[33] The concepts of mirroring and of a psyche shaped in the language process, or of a textualised self and its relation to gender construction, provoke intriguing ties between the poem and ideas of the 'feminine' as disruptive of phallic law and a symbolic order, theorised by Kristeva and others. The poem's title immediately positions the text in relation to a literary daughter, creating the frame for encountering the statement of poetics 'A poem should not mean but be', taken from Archibald MacLeish. Throughout the poem, a female voice interrupts, parodies and references literary texts bespeaking male authority. The 'I', named as Veronica Forrest-Thomson, is pluralised and multiplied as an inconsistent discourse of self, making explicit claim to a voice of the poet and dispersing that claim through other textual constructions of voice. Much of the poem is conversational, repetitive and full of mimicry (of Eliot, MacLeish, Pound and other male figures), undercutting the authority of the tradition it references. With a jab towards Keats, for example, the speaker claims 'I get a kick out of larking up nightingales' but ponders the consequences of 'taking on' poetic fathers, explicitly here through veiled rewritings of Eliot and long literary traditions of the rape motif entering his poetry: 'March is the cruellest station / Taking on bullying men / And were you really afraid they would rape you?'. Such encounters with male tradition, through spliced chains of allusion and parody, question not only representations of women but gendered authority and voice. Other poems, such as 'The Lady of Shalott: Ode' and 'The Garden of Proserpine', 'argue with the canonical writings which frame them', an approach that surely appealed to Wendy Mulford in inviting publication through Street Editions and, subsequently, seeing the book into print after Forrest-Thomson's unexpected death in 1975.[34]

Mulford's own poetry at this time began exploring how signifying systems and practices shape gender in relation to power (masculine, capitalist), and how such practices construct poetic authority, a speaking self and poetic community. Mulford's early exploration of a specifically gendered 'I' imagines a provisional and multiple shifting 'self' that refuses lyrical authenticity (the singular, unique voice that accesses true experience) but also resists a complete elision or deconstruction of self. Gathering poems written since 1968, *Bravo to Girls and Heroes* appeared in 1977, its project announced in a hand-penned comment: '[T]hese poems indicate some of the problems facing a poet today... [and] they include some of the strategies I've used to confront those problems, or to attempt to "reclaim the language", for myself, as a [*woman*]'.[35] While adopting women's movement rhetoric, Mulford signals a different feminist emphasis on *strategies* of language, without jettisoning women's experience or an explicitly gendered voice. Corresponding to Forrest-Thomson's insistence in her 'Note' to *Language-Games* that 'questions of knowledge become questions of technique', Mulford's poems foreground women's experiences and knowledge, the 'I', as constructed – and reconstructed – through language. As though responding to Cixous' description of a woman speaking in 'The laugh of the Medusa', the speaking 'I' is halting, hesitant and fragmentary, disrupting smoothly logocentric linearity to assert 'voice'. Cumulative, paratactic and associative sequences pile up and careen down the page; throughout, an 'I' speaks but claims no clear position or view. Commingling with a myriad of sensual details, the 'I' becomes a matter of language and how it works rather than a stable entity with access to some 'truth'.[36]

A few years later, *Late Spring Next Year* gathers selections from chapbooks and volumes Mulford published in the early eighties, notably bringing theoretical considerations to bear upon the lyric voice, questioning the gendered ideologies of the traditional (romantic) lyric voice that positions 'woman' as passive, gazed upon, private or possessed. Rather than assuming an authentic self in control of an expressive language, this poetry, as she puts it, 'conducted an oscillating provisionality against traditional lyric voice', multiplying voice and fragmenting cohesive notions of subjectivity to examine the role of language in constructing cultural slots that keep women oppressed and silenced. Beginning also to read American experimental poets like Susan Howe, Rae Armantrout or Kathleen Fraser, she found their work 'stimulating, useful or necessary' in considering 'some related ideas about the questioning of the individual poetic voice'.[37] Inserting the body into discourse to disrupt this essentialising process, for example, a poem like 'how do you live' explores the female body's textualisation, understanding the body as an ideologically constructed discourse in a manner theorised by Cixous as *écriture feminine*, or writing the body. Originally printed in *The A.B.C. of Writing*, which Ken Edwards identifies as Mulford's 'most overtly theoretical text', the poem is dedicated to Cixous, 'who gave me the question'. Valuing the question and the process of questioning, the opening lines offer

> no clear answer, ambivalently.
> reciprocally.   in
> oscillation. lurching in surprise &
> wonder.   an
> after-affect of too much pricey
> delegation, herein described as daringly / close to
> disaster, danger's cousin. I said you can[38]

The poem is full of stops and starts, gaps, awkward and jagged rhythms, interruptions. The poem's 'I', introduced eight lines into the poem, continues in the poem to enter abruptly and lurchingly, just as the poem's radical enjambments, empty gaps, compressed phrases and feminine line-end stresses upset the sense of a coherent lyric voice. Visual interruptions of white space attend linguistic interruption, as collections of fragmented discourses collide and juxtapose. Feminised domesticity ('home', 'cradling cuddling care', 'home love'[39]) is yoked to images of sexual power and physical labour; at the same time, an economically laced diction riddles a language of expressive interiority, suggesting subjectivity as a site for intersections of public and private realms.

Like Mulford's work, Denise Riley's work of the seventies engages questions of female subjectivity, and her first book, *Marxism for Infants*, appeared in 1977 from Street Editions, written while pursuing an activist feminism accompanied by theories of language, gender and class. By the 1960s, she was reading de Beauvoir and Woolf and had joined the Abortion Law Reform Association. Into the 1970s, her feminist activism, participation in the anti-Vietnam War movement and involvement with the political Left were part of the 'changing Marxisms of 1970s Britain and their Althusserian critique of language'.[40] Labelling herself a socialist-feminist, she embarked upon a 'countereducation of reading Marx and Hegel, Engels, Althusser, Freud – among a great many other European socialists and theorists of society' – and entering debates that 'turned on different theories of the human subject', including feminist theories challenging the masculine humanist subject. Riley also drew from thinkers like Wittgenstein, citing as especially important his ideas about 'the intelligibility of words as depending on their positioning' and finding 'an immediate helpfulness about the idea of discursive formations', particularly that 'people understand their lives discursively'.[41] Her theoretical work, written concurrently with her poetry, brings decidedly feminist frameworks into relation with theories of discourse, language and subjectivity.[42] Her later poetry, especially *Mop Mop Georgette* (1993), reads as a cross-disciplinary encounter between lyric and theory, voice and discourse.

Marxism for Infants, collecting poems that began to appear earlier in the decade, imagines reconstituting the female 'I' outside of dominant, essentialised notions of 'woman' and explores how a female subject might view herself in the midst of such cultural images. Through insisting on links between the lived body, material conditions and language, these poems trouble what critics will later call the 'expressive' lyric 'I' and its claims to a transparent language of self-reportage. In 'Affections Must Not', economics serves as a material framework inscribing the experience of female 'love', as love's link to economics is figured through the description of the home and the conventional role of mother as 'straight out of colonial history, master and slave'. The poem's form torques punctuation and grammar, enclosing the 'I' in alternative textual configurations – such as the final line, 'I.neglect.the.house.' – that call attention to language as a material medium enacting what Carol Watts calls a 'drama of interpellation: the way in which language hails identity and brings it into social being, forming subjects "between love & / economics"'.[43]

Developing a 'potent early critique of romanticised projects in the female construction of identity' dominating feminist rhetoric, Riley speaks to that rhetoric in poems of this period. Rejecting the notion of a 'possibility of getting back to a feminine language, a "mother tongue"', Riley's poems present the female subject's struggle with systems of culture and language representing woman as Other. As articulated in 'A note on sex and the reclaiming of language', 'the necessary (feminist) task is e.g. to write "she" and for that to be a statement / of fact only and not a strong image / of everything which is not-you, which sees you'.[44] Rather than assuming an essentialised 'woman', the poem's engagement with discursive systems and various narratives of womanhood (mother, domestic, primitive savage) belies the authentic notion of feminine selfhood, the 'you' that culture 'sees' and reproduces through discourse.

Interventions

The poet Helen Kidd speaks of first encountering Mulford and Riley's work in the eighties, feeling 'that at last I had found other women who were exploring, stretching and questioning language. Yet these were also women who were not prepared to lose sight of the politics of gender and sexuality in the interests of pursuing the politics of the text.'[45] Despite evidence of a community, women's writing emerging in the 1980s and 1990s under the loose rubric of 'linguistically innovative poetry' continued to be systemically marginalised. During the eighties, a series of anthologies appeared, representing different facets of language innovation in the British Isles. Few women were included in these anthologies, prompting the question of why.[46] In 1990, Mulford cites the seemingly greater numbers of experimental women poets in North America, wondering why British women poets predominantly choose a 'familiar poetics' that does *not* problematise language; however, at the same time, she insists upon the significance of socio-historical conditions, claiming that a 'book [is] waiting to be written' about an aversion to formal experimentation that would attend to 'large questions of climate, island formation, history and settlement, as well as more immediate factors of the literary tradition'. That book would need to account for obstacles to the experimental community in general but with particular attention to the (in)visibility of women, the relative paucity of critical treatment, reviews and anthologised inclusions, and the long-standing erasure of earlier women Modernists who might constitute an enabling tradition for contemporary women. Significantly, at the turn of the twenty-first century, poet-critic Harriet Tarlo finds it necessary to introduce contemporary experimental women poets to a country where 'conservative tastes ... have dominated ... for several decades', burying the work of linguistically innovative women engaged in a 'self conscious attention to text' and the 'materiality of language' to enact a feminist 'scrutiny [of language] that is political in every sense'.[47]

Despite a proliferation of anthologies devoted to a 'new' British poetry in the eighties and early nineties, a need remained for a collection devoted to women's writing, placing it within an international context of innovative writing. Such an anthology appeared in 1996, seeking to intervene in the discourses and processes that, even by the mid-nineties, left women out of accounts of language innovation and of women's poetry. Edited by Maggie O'Sullivan and published by Mulford and Ken Edwards through Reality Street Editions, *Out of Everywhere: Linguistically Innovative Poetry by Women in North America and the UK* gathers thirty poets, nine from the UK. The title refers to a suggestion made to the American poet Rosemarie Waldrop: 'There's an extra difficulty being a woman poet and writing the kind of poetry you write: you are out of everywhere.'[48] While Robert Sheppard refers to the 'genuine paucity of [British] women writers' from which O'Sullivan could draw, this group nonetheless represents three generations of poets positioned in relation to cross-national connections. As Caroline Bergvall notes, the 'fundamental gesture' of the anthology 'highlighted the complexities of the relationship textual modes necessarily entertain with issues of identity and representational modes'; moreover, citing the reluctance to entertain these complexities in terms of gender in Britain, she argues that the anthology 'made it quite clear that if, as a rule, the conversation could not be had with any continuity in Britain (neither within experimental nor mainstream circuits), it could be and was being had elsewhere'.[49] British poets brought to the conversation include Bergvall, Paula Claire, Grace Lake, Geraldine Monk, Wendy Mulford, Maggie O'Sullivan, Carlyle Reedy, Denise Riley and Fiona Templeton. In their 'Postscript', Mulford and Edwards acknowledge that the 'range is smaller in the British Isles [than in the USA and Canada]', but nonetheless promisingly generative, noting that poets like Helen Kidd, Frances Presley, Elaine Randell, Hazel Smith and Catherine Walsh and 'younger writers coming up' could well be included. The current selection demonstrates the 'need for an anthology to showcase work by women who, broadly speaking, were working with language – disordering and deconstructive techniques, at the leading edge of new poetics', explicitly answering a string of male-dominated 'alternative' collections with a decidedly feminist agenda of language innovation, formal experimentation and cross-national affiliation outside of the standard focus on male poets and insisting on a conversation about gender.[50]

O'Sullivan's introduction elaborates upon this position, distancing the anthology's aesthetics from representational language use and habitual reading strategies. The poets' 'brave insistence and engagement in explorative, formally progressive language practices' are most often 'excluded from conventional, explicitly generically committed or thematic anthologies of women's poetry ... from "women's canons"'; moreover, these poets are not 'writing poems "about" something', but have 'committed themselves to excavating language in all its multiple voices and tongues, known and unknown'. They work in relation to the 'marginalised tradition of innovative writing practices' forged by 'pioneering poets' such as Stein, Loy, H.D. and Niedecker, and are 'expanding the horizons of this practice'.[51]

This expansiveness is clear even in the necessarily limited but diverse selections. Excerpts from Carlyle Reedy's 'The Slave Ship'aggressively splice discourses to unsettle historical narratives of the slave trade, and other poems play with grid-like constructions of word columns that defy linear reading strategies. Denise Riley's pieces pose theoretical questions about the embodied self through densely juxtaposed clusters crossing over multiple public and private discourses. Wendy Mulford's poems weave silences and white spaces amidst visually evocative and ekphrastic language. Fiona Templeton's genre-bending prose pieces move through a language self-reflexive about its operations and the ideological significations. Geraldine Monk's radical breakage of words into letters and phonemes, her embrace of a voice of stutter and hesitation, registers in page arrangements that emphasise graphic placement and white space. Of these poets, O'Sullivan highlights the impressive number also involved in magazine poetry press production.

Her own poetry linked to performance, O'Sullivan takes particular note of how 'inter- and multi-media work and performative directions' inform an 'engagement with larger poetic discourses and practices', all of which 'celebrates poetry as event'. The visual, aural and textual energy underlying much of the anthology's works is also distinctively manifest in a multi-generational cluster of three poets who identify as 'performance poets' and began publishing in different decades: Paula Claire (beginning in the seventies) Maureen O'Sullivan (beginning in the eighties) and Caroline Bergvall (beginning in the nineties). To suggest the range of textual experimentation occurring 'out of everywhere', these poets will be used as a kind of case study for thinking about reading strategies in the face of such unconventional poetry.[52]

Using the space of the page as a recording site for extra-textual performance, Paula Claire's selections involve a series of graphic line drawings, typographic arrangements and layerings of image and word. Each visual page represents a performance of the poem, which is described in a set of notes following the visual pages that record how the performance was structured, where it took place, what materials were involved and how the audience (in some instances) collaborated in the work. 'JETAKEOFF' recalls concrete poetry in its arrangement of letters and words diagonally slicing the page, with a wide base of words on the lower left corner transforming into a single column of letters reaching up to the right corner of the page, suggesting an extension (a 'flying') off the page. The 'base' begins with the word 'Moment' in the lower left corner; each subsequent line piles on top of this first one, as its letters transform and combine into words shoved together (as in the title), such as 'momentumomentous' or 'eneErgisengines' or 'ROARAOR'. The pressure of the lines mounting the page, as the words push in on each other, seems to compel the upward trajectory, finally, of the single letters shooting up the page, spaced out further and further as they reach the corner. The 'typewriter text', first performed in 1970, was designed 'as a large-scale permutational neon poem in red and blue, for an airport wall', and the visual dimensions amplified with sound, improvisation and audience participation in the performance she describes:

> The text is performed ... from the bottom upwards as far as the words in capital letters, accompanied by an increasingly loud hum from the audience. Then they shout out the words in capitals, making maximum noise in 'ROAR-AOR'. I then perform the diagonal line of text, my voice rising to its highest pitch, looking skywards with arm raised and finger pointing to the disappearing plane.

The collaborative involvement of the audience and the performative focus on the body's movements in relation to language suggest directions for feminist challenges to standard page-based poetry.[53] Other selections, ranging from 1974 to 1994, inscribe the 'handwritten performance page' as a space of tracings from nature that contain coded meaning, although not always to humans, such as 'BEE BIBLES'. With line drawings of 'split-open foxgloves, revealing the unique coded messages inside each one, privy only to the bees', this piece was performed 'using actual foxgloves' in a 1981 *Subvoice* reading series, an important London venue organised by Gilbert Adair for interdisciplinary and inter-arts innovations.[54]

Using the page as a field of energy and intervention, Maggie O'Sullivan's selections exemplify the 'range, risk and innovation' [that] begins with ... striking use of the page space. The short lines and multiple margins create a twisting sinewy figure; the capitalisations, differing sizes of font, slashes and dashes, and other punctuation symbols, seem to be used as much for visual effect as for organising meaning.'[55] A poet who performs her texts and pays exquisite attention to aural patterns, O'Sullivan speaks of 'using texts as source materials' and that the 'actual making, the constructing of a work continues into its performance'. Her work is often discussed in relation to the influence of shamanistic ideas and processes, especially *In the House of the Shaman* (1993), written in partial response to Joseph Beuys and concerned with the transformative quality of language O'Sullivan describes as 'an active physical presence in the world'.[56] O'Sullivan's attentions to sound or to '[a]ural patterns, inchoate sound in the ear' also 'make language visible' while 'refusing to bring sound into meaning'. Her work pushes the 'boundaries of language' and tests the 'borders of interpretation', rejecting mimesis, narrative and a unified voice while collaging 'silenced voices' (often from nature, including the body, animals, the earth) into the text. Enacting subjectivity as an 'interactive process', O'Sullivan's work explores the *'poetic "self"* as a composite of other voices and sounds, a permeable kinaesthetic state, a condition of awareness that merges with outer sounds and sights, a state that responds to the convergences and accidents of the unconscious as well as to the contingencies of the open field of conscious experience'.[57]

'Another Weather System', which opens *In the House of the Shaman*, moves words around on the page, using a language of physicality, body and animal being that she elsewhere describes as a 'drawing upon the earth and the other-than-human – voicing my body / bodying my voicings'.[58] Difficult to discuss in extracted form, the poem contains such language combinations as the following:

> Skull & Bone & comb
> breathe &
> river, the crow
> is in time
> thinned, stirred
> stabbing
> souther
> impings –
>
> all the greater multiplying — [59]

Within this long poem, the 'I' appears as an 'i', often woven into the poem through repetition and resembling a stutter that opens to others (such as animals). The 'i' serves as a place of entry and intersection, not only between subjectivities that include animal and earth, but also as intersection between different lexicons.

> Enthrone or Depose —
> inci /acci / incu/ —
> Bladders dirgey Aster imams.
>
> Be Bubbla   Beaks Broken
> Abrasions.   Arbitrations.   Absesses.   Arrow

licks
in fill
fear.

Twelve Blood Moon.   Day Lung.
        Whorledly   (i

                i
                and
                and i
                there
                and
                i

                i
                while
                i
                i
                hear[60]

The poem's performance takes place on the page and also in the physical spaces of O'Sullivan's multi-arts, bodily performances of poems. Importantly, for O'Sullivan, such work with language, voice and textuality has a 'political import' that is often overlooked in a contemporary understanding of political poetry as identity-based and plain-spoken. For 'anybody who's working in Britain who isn't working within the referential, transparent language axis', she claims, the result is being 'ostracised, invisible, shut out, unheard'; however, she continues, 'what all of us are doing in using radically imaginative language practices and procedures is very political and subversive', and she terms her work an 'eco-ethic politics of the earth'. Echoing Mulford's feminist call for a revolutionary work at the level of the signifier, Isobel Armstrong contends that '[t]o work at the level of phrase, syllable, morpheme and particle, rather than the sentence or clause' in O'Sullivan's poetry 'is to shatter the logos and radically remake it'.[61]

A shattering of the logos, for Caroline Bergvall, involves a retraversal of verbal, visual and media texts, producing what Marjorie Perloff has called 'hybrid work' of 'complex assemblages' that 'explore such areas of our conceptual approaches to female (and feminine) representation as well as the power structures within which these sexualities must function'. As a feminist poet-critic, Bergvall has contributed to debates about the feminist work of experimental poetry, helping bring such poets into view. Contributing a feature on experimental women poets to the online journal *HOW2* in 2001, 'Postings from Britain', for example, Bergvall insists in her biographical note upon the 'pertinence of poetic work as a mode of investigation which has a part to play in public discourses on art' and 'issues of representation'.[62] As a poet whose theorising has attempted to complicate easy divisions of the 'experimental' and the 'expressive' through exploring the specifically gendered assumptions about this divide, she takes issue with the foreclosure of the 'self' within prominent discourses about language innovation. She complains that 'issues of psycho-social identity as related to body configurations such as gendering or genderedness ... are only rarely explicitly acknowledged as viable methodological concerns in approaching the writing projects produced with the British experimental poetry scene'. These comments introduce a group of poets intervening in such a scene, creating text-based works that cross lines of visual, performance and page formats to comment upon formations of 'psycho-social identity as related to body configuration'. Recent works by O'Sullivan and Riley are joined by poets and artists from an emerging generation, including Tertia Longmere, Karlian van den Beukel, Shelby Matthews and Redell Olsen; moreover, the performative, visual dimensions difficult to capture in print form are available through the online technology, such as Bergvall's work that 'includes collaborations on performances and text-based installations'.[63]

Associated with the emergence of 'performance writing' in the mid-1990s as both 'an emergent field of practice' and 'an academic discipline', Bergvall helped initiate the Performance Writing degree programme at Dartington, an arts college in Devon, England.[64] Keith Tuma describes this theoretically informed practice as seeking 'to destabilize oppositions between the ephemerality of performance and the fixity of print', and he quotes Bergvall's interest in the 'manipulation of non-verbal signs such as the space of the page ... [and] typography' as elemental to this practice.[65] This manipulation is evident in Bergvall's 2001 *Goan Atom*, which foregrounds the singular mark of the letter and its circulation through multiple units of linguistic structure and meaning-making. Many pages contain single letters, or small groups of letters, sometimes in columns of different type size, sometimes sitting on the edge of the page, or placed so that the white space of the page surrounds them. The letters coalesce into syllables or word fragments, radically severed by enjambment:

> g
> GA
> g
> ging
> dis
> g
> orging[66]

Longer lines and phrases begin to appear, torqued by punning and phonemic breakage, while laden with pieces of found material and extra-literary reference. Reviewing this challenging text, Nicky Marsh has noted that '[s]uch lines resound with the interference suggested by the Kristevean pre-semiotic chora and, perhaps more interestingly, with the physical possibilities of textuality itself'. As a text that has existed in different versions, in both performance and print forms, *Goan Atom* addresses 'not only the mutability of the realised performance but also the centrality of the body, mouth and tongue to the articulation of language', questioning 'the false distinction between a text and voice-based poetics and the assumed silence of the printed page'.[67]

The formal, syntactical strategies of the text interact with its primary source, the Surrealist Hans Bellmer's collections of photographs and hand-tinted prints depicting dolls that have been broken apart and reassembled in unnatural, grotesque and eroticised arrangements.[68] Body parts are multiplied or missing, juxtaposed in violently aggressive ways and placed in suggestive settings – such as a bedroom, an empty stairwell, a forest. The manipulation of the female body through image re-production is reinforced in Bergvall's poem through other textual references, particularly the photographs of Cindy Sherman and the media treatment of the cloned sheep named Dolly. Acknowledging that Bellmer's 'take remained very misogynistic and even paedophilic', she nonetheless claims that 'the whole notion of the fixity or the stability of the body does become problematised' in his photographs from the thirties and forties; within her poem, in 'the same way the articulation or disarticulation of language ... becomes problematised', as breaking the body's 'fixity' undoes language stability.[69]

The partial version of the poem earlier anthologised rereads Bellmer's photographs in their formal qualities of artifice and violent severance, while questioning avant-garde representation of the female body. The opening lines introduce the doll image: 'Dolly / sgot a wides lit / down the lily / sgot avide slot / donne a lolly / to a head.'[70] The act of reassembly follows:

Pops
er
body partson
to the flo
ring the morning
it's never matt
ers what goes back
on w
here dolly

goodolly

in a

ny shape or form[71]

A later stanza proclaims in capital letters that 'ALL OF / DOLLY's / A FUNC', leaving off the end of the word.[72] The body of the word, the body of the female, the body of the reader, the body of the performer poet – all converge here in the question of function, suggestively within myriad contexts of systemic power and force: how does the image function? Or the text? Does the avant-garde image/text, in its radical nature, reiterate regressive gender ideologies? Arguing the text's 'adroit kinetic movement' as performing a feminist cultural critique, Marsh contends that 'Bergvall's attention to the simultaneity and conflicts between the processes of coming into language and coming into the body' carry important 'implications for the gendered and social political implications of representation'.[73] Indeed, Bergvall's own theorising about feminist experimental poetry early on insisted upon 'a rejection of the naturalizing concept of representation' and an exploration of language structures.[74] As a feminist, Bergvall claims to be motivated by questions of 'how you would use language to construct or de-structure assumptions about gender, about sexuality, about female gender. Where do you situate the use of language within that so that you don't fall into a kind of identity-based writing, or identity-based art, but so that the whole question of identity becomes questioned.'[75]

Bergvall's questions, posed at the turn of the twenty-first century, echo and build upon Mulford's early feminist interrogation of 'the self' as situated within and by language. Since Mulford's call for a greater community of women writing to 'destruct the lie of culture' through revolutionary work in the field of signification – of language and its operations and structures – a fuller picture of that community and its connections to a more internationalised community has developed. Moreover, conceptual frameworks for reading women's linguistic innovations have theorised intersections of feminism, theory and experimentation within a sequence of generations extending back to the Modernists and through several generations of contemporary British women poets. More of this work has come into published visibility. Different modalities of experimentation with the page, performance and sound have emerged at the same time that oppositions of the 'experimental' and 'expressive' have been productively complicated. Britain's postcolonial demographic shifts further complicate the 'revolution' taking place in the field of the signifier, as colonising structures of standard English undergo exposure, challenge and transfiguration in commingling and colliding with hybrid speech (the demotic, patois, creolised tongue) of the colonised. And a pattern of greater interaction with American poets, with both feminist and experimental inclinations, informs the practices and conversations of women poets on both sides of the Atlantic, aided by Internet technology and journals like *HOW2* or *Jacket*.[76]

Moreover, recent poetry undoes any easy category for the 'experimental'. Performance poetry provides a point of intersection, for example, between the works of a poet like Bergvall and Afro-Caribbean performance poets like Jean Binta Breeze;[77] the deconstruction of language structures and poetic conventions connects a poet like Carol Ann Duffy to impulses within the 'experimental';[78] questions of nationality and distinct national trad-itions of experimentation motivate considerations of an Irish poet like Catherine Walsh, whose airy pages and disjunctive word progressions pro-ceed within a grounded sense of landscape and place;[79] the postcolonial global movements and hybrid languages of Grace Nichols situate an 'experimental' or alternative poetics differently in terms of history, language and subjectivity.[80] Promise abounds for rich discussions across the 'language-face' of contemporary women's poetry.

Notes

1 Wendy Mulford, ' "Curved, Odd ... Irregular". A vision of contemporary poetry by women', *Women: A Cultural Review* 1.3 (Winter 1990), 261–71; 263.

2 Veronica Forrest-Thomson, 'Lemon and Rosemary', in Richard Caddel and Peter Quartermain (eds.), *Other: British and Irish Poetry Since 1970* (Hanover, NH and London: Wesleyan University Press, 1999), p. 81.

3 Catherine Walsh, from *A Wait*, in Caddel and Quartermain (eds.), *Other*, p. 262.

4 Caroline Bergvall, 'New writing feature: introduction to "Postings from Britain"', *HOW2* 1.5 (March 2001), n.p. WEB. All issues of *HOW2* are archived at the following URL: www.asu.edu/pipercwcenter/how2journal.

5 See Claire Buck, 'Poetry and the Women's Movement in postwar Britain', in James Acheson and Romana Huk (eds.), *Contemporary British Poetry: Essays in Theory and Criticism* (Albany, NY: SUNY Press, 1996), pp. 81–112.

6 Andrew Duncan, *The Failure of Conservatism in Modern British Poetry* (Cambridge: Salt Publishing, 2003), p. 151.

7 Carlyle Reedy, 'Working processes of a woman poet', in Denise Riley (ed.), *Poets on Writing: Britain 1970–1991* (London: Macmillan, 1992), pp. 260–71; 268.

8 Eric Mottram, 'The British poetry revival, 1960–1975', in Robert Hampson and Peter Barry (eds.), *New British Poetries: The Scope of the Possible* (Manchester and New York: Manchester University Press, 1993), pp. 15–50; Mulford, ' "Curved, Odd" ', p. 262.

9 Wendy Mulford, 'Notes on writing: a Marxist/feminist viewpoint', in Michelene Wandor (ed.), *On Gender and Writing* (London: Pandora Press, 1983), pp. 31–6; 33–4. First published in *Red Letters* 9 (1979). These quotations are taken from the

reprint essay. In 1978, Mulford's press merged with Ken Edwards' Reality Press to become Reality Street, continuing to publish experimental poetry.

10 John Matthias (ed.), 23 *Modern British Poets*, (Chicago: Swallow Press, 1971), pp. xiii–xiv.

11 Emily Critchley, 'A conference overview', *HOW2* 3.1 (Summer 2007), n.p. WEB. Selections from the 2006 Contemporary Women's Poetry Festival at Cambridge University, introduced by Critchley, can be found online.

12 Robert Sheppard, *The Poetry of Saying: British Poetry and its Discontents 1950–2000* (Liverpool: Liverpool University Press, 2005), p. 161.

13 Jane Dowson and Alice Entwistle, *A History of Twentieth-Century British Women's Poetry* (Cambridge: Cambridge University Press, 2005), p. 96.

14 Lilian Mohin, 'Introduction', in Lilian Mohin (ed.), *One Foot on the Mountain: An Anthology of British Feminist Poetry 1969–1979* (London: Onlywomen Press, 1979), pp. 1–7;5.

15 Mulford, 'Notes on writing', p. 33. By the 1990s, however, categories of 'experimental' and 'expressive' modes of feminist poetry often became opposed. For discussions of critical divides between 'experimental' and 'expressive' women's poetry, see Clair Wills, 'Contemporary women's poetry: experimentalism and the expressive voice', *Critical Quarterly* 36.3 (Autumn 1994), 34–52; Linda A. Kinnahan, *Lyric Interventions: Feminism, Experimental Poetry, and Contemporary Discourse* (Iowa City: University of Iowa Press, 2004); and Caroline Bergvall, 'No margins to this page: female experimental poetry and the legacy of Modernism', *Fragments* 5 (1993), 30–8.

16 Mohin, 'Introduction', p. 5.

17 Mulford, 'Notes on writing', p. 31.

18 *Ibid.*, pp. 33, 32, 33.

19 Since the early nineties, a handful of studies of contemporary poetry and language innovation have appeared, with varying degrees of attention to women poets. See Sarah Broom, *Contemporary British and Irish Poetry: An Introduction* (London: Palgrave Macmillan, 2006); Sheppard, *The Poetry of Saying* (2005); Keith Tuma, *Fishing by Obstinate Isles: Modern and Postmodern British Poetry and American Readers* (Evanston IL: Northwestern University Press, 1998); Acheson and Huk (eds.) *Contemporary British Poetry* (1996); and Hampson and Barry (eds.), *New British Poetries* (1993). Monographs and collections of essays on contemporary women poets have included useful attention to British experimental poets, although as yet there is no sustained study with this focus. See Vicki Bertram (ed.), *Kicking Daffodils: Twentieth-Century Women Poets* (Edinburgh: Edinburgh University Press, 1997); Alison Mark and Deryn Rees-Jones (eds.), *Contemporary Women's Poetry: Reading/Writing/Practice* (London: Macmillan, 2000); and Kinnahan, *Lyric Interventions* (2004). Also see the special issue of *Feminist Review* 62 (Summer 1999), on contemporary women poets, ed. Bertram. Online journals *HOW2* and *Jacket* are also useful sources for discussions. Salt Publishing has recently issued poetry books and companion volumes of essays on a number of linguistically innovative women poets. The inaugural issue of the *Journal of British and Irish Innovative Writing* was launched in Autumn, 2009.

20 Maggie O'Sullivan (ed.), *Out of Everywhere: Linguistically Innovative Poetry by Women in North America and the UK* (London and Suffolk: Reality

Street Editions, 1996). This quotation is from the biographical note on Claire, pp. 243–4.

21 See Sheppard, *The Poetry of Saying*, or Broom, *Contemporary British and Irish Poetry*, for accounts of this shift.

22 Sheppard, *The Poetry of Saying*, p. 142.

23 Quoted in Alison Mark, 'Veronica Forrest-Thomson: toward a linguistically investigative poetics', *Poetics Today* 20.4 (Winter 1999), 655–72; 659.

24 Veronica Forrest-Thomson, *Poetic Artifice: A Theory of Twentieth-Century Poetry* (Manchester: Manchester University Press, 1978).

25 *Ibid.*, p. 6 (emphasis added).

26 Mark, 'Veronica Forrest-Thomson', p. 655. See Alison Mark, 'Poetic relations and related poetics: Veronica Forrest-Thomson and Charles Bernstein', in Romana Huk (ed.), *Assembling Alternatives: Reading Postmodern Poetries Transnationally* (Middletown, CT: Wesleyan University Press, 2003).

27 Forrest-Thomson, *Poetic Artifice*, pp. xi, 53. This sequence of three quotations is also found on p. 144 in Robert Hampson, 'Producing the unknown: language and ideology in contemporary poetry', in Hampson and Barry (eds.), *New British Poetries*, pp. 134–55.

28 Mark, 'Veronica Forrest-Thomson', p. 658; Robert Sheppard, *Far Language: Poetics and Linguistically Innovative Poetry 1978–1997* (Devon: Stride Publications, 1997). Sheppard's review, 'Reading Prynne and others', originally appeared in *Reality Studios* 2.2 (August 1979), and is reprinted in this 1997 collection of his writings.

29 Mark, 'Veronica Forrest-Thomson', p. 657.

30 The poem is included in Veronica Forrest-Thomson, *Collected Poems and Translations*, ed. Anthony Barnett (London: Allardyce, Barnett, 1990), pp. 104–9. Quotations here are taken from Andrew Crozier and Tim Longville (eds.), *A Various Art* (London: Paladin Books, 1990), pp. 121–5.

31 Edward Larrissy, 'Poets of *A Various Art*: J. H. Prynne, Veronica Forrest-Thomson, Andrew Crozier', in Acheson and Huk (eds.), *Contemporary British Poetry*, pp. 63–80; 74.

32 Dowson and Entwistle (eds.), *A History*, pp. 158, 159; Mark, 'Poetic relations', p. 121.

33 Mark, *Veronica Forrest-Thomson*, p. 655.

34 Crozier and Longville (eds.), *A Various Art*, p. 123; Dowson and Entwistle, *A History*, p. 159.

35 See Wills, 'Contemporary women's poetry', and Kinnahan, *Lyric Interventions*, for more in-depth discussions of subjectivity; Wendy Mulford, *Bravo to Girls & Heroes* (Cambridge: Street Editions, 1977), n.p. Mulford actually pens the *symbol* for 'woman' rather than writing out the word.

36 Mulford's collaborative work with Denise Riley, *No Fee: A Line or Two for Free* (Cambridge: Street Editions, 1978), includes poems by both women but does not identify them by author. Creating a composition of blended voices, the collaborative structure insists upon an 'I' that is relational rather than autonomous.

37 Wendy Mulford, *Late Spring Next Year: Poems, 1979–1985* (Bristol: Loxwood Stoneleigh, 1987); Mulford, '"Curved, Odd"', pp. 261, 264.

38 Ken Edwards, 'Wendy Mulford', in Tracy Chevalier, *Contemporary Poets* (New York: St James, 1991), pp. 685–6; p. 686; Mulford, *Late Spring*, p. 54.

39 Mulford, *Late Spring*, p. 54.

40 Romana Huk, 'Feminist radicalism in (relatively) traditional forms: an American's investigations of British poetics', in Bertram (ed.), *Kicking Daffodils*, pp. 227–50; 240.

41 Denise Riley, 'A short history of some preoccupations', in Judith Butler and Joan W. Scott (eds.), *Feminists Theorize the Political* (New York: Routledge, 1992), pp. 121–9; 124, 127, 122.

42 Theoretical works include *War in the Nursery: Theories of the Child and Mother* (London: Virago, 1983); *'Am I That Name?' Feminism and the Category of 'Women' in History* (London: Macmillan, 1988); and *The Words of Selves: Identification, Solidarity, Irony* (Stanford, CA: Stanford University Press, 2000).

43 Denise Riley, *Dry Air* (London: Virago, 1985), p. 27; Carol Watts, 'Beyond interpellation? affect, embodiment and the poetics of Denise Riley', in Mark and Rees-Jones (eds.), *Contemporary Women's Poetry*, pp. 157–72; p. 166.

44 Huk, 'Feminist radicalism', p. 240; Romana Huk, 'Denise Riley in Conversation', *PN Review* (May–June 1995), 17–22; 21; Riley, *Dry Air*, p. 7.

45 Helen Kidd, 'The paper city: women, writing, and experience', in Hampson and Barry (eds.), *New British Poetries*, pp. 156–82; p. 171.

46 See Crozier and Longville (eds.), *A Various Art*, which includes Forrest-Thomson as the only woman representing a Cambridge collective; Gillian Allnutt, Fred D'Aguiar, Ken Edwards and Eric Mottram (eds.), *The New British Poetry* (London: Paladin, 1988), which includes six women out of forty-four identified as 'experimental'; Adrian Clarke and Robert Sheppard (eds.), *Floating Capital: New Poets From London* (Elmwood, CT: Potes and Poets Press, 1991), which asserts poetry's connection with theory and includes three women out of fourteen poets; Ian Sinclair (ed.), *Conductors of Chaos* (London: Macmillan, 1996), which includes five women out of thirty-six poets. Published in 1999, Caddel and Quartermain's *Other* expands 'alternative' to include Black British, Irish and 'other' poets, and includes nine women among its fifty-five poets.

47 Mulford, '"Curved, Odd"', pp. 261, 262; Harriet Tarlo, 'The challenge of contemporary experimental women poets', *Feminist Review* 62 (Summer 1999), 94–112.

48 Quoted in Sullivan (ed.), *Out of Everywhere*, p. 9. Waldrop's response to the suggestion was that she had 'more or less claimed this [out of everywhere] as the position of poetry.' The recorded talk appears in Charles Bernstein (ed.), *The Politics of Poetic Form* (New York: Roof, 1990).

49 Sheppard, *Poetry*, p. 162; Caroline Bergvall, 'New writing feature: introduction to "Postings from Britain"', *HOW2* 1.5 (March 2001), n.p. WEB.

50 Sullivan (ed.), *Out of Everywhere*, p. 252.

51 *Ibid.*, pp. 9–10, 10.

52 *Ibid.*, p. 10.

53 'JETAKEOFF' appears in Sullivan (ed.), *Out of Everywhere* on page 35, and the notes that describe the performance are on page 41.

54 Sullivan (ed.), *Out of Everywhere*, p. 37.

55 Scott Thurston, 'Maggie O'Sullivan: transformation and substance', *Poetry Salzburg Review* 6 (Summer 2004), 15–20; 15.

56 In Scott Thurston, '"Emerging States", interview with Maggie O'Sullivan', *Poetry Salzburg Review* 6 (Summer 2004), 3–15; 6, 10, 12.

57 Isobel Armstrong, 'Maggie O'Sullivan: the lyrical language of the parallel tradition', *Women* 15.1 (Spring 2004), 57–66; 59, 61.

58 Dell Olsen and Maggie O'Sullivan, 'Writing/conversation: an interview by mail, November–December 2003', *HOW2* 2.2 (2004), n.p. WEB.

59 Maggie O'Sullivan, *In the House of the Shaman* (London and Cambridge: Reality Street Editions, 1993), p. 12.

60 *Ibid.*, pp. 18–19.

61 Thurston, " 'Emerging States' ", p. 9; Olsen and O'Sullivan, 'Writing/conversation', n.p.; Armstrong, 'Maggie O'Sullivan', p. 59.

62 Marjorie Perloff, 'The oulipo factor: the procedural poetics of Christian Bok and Caroline Bergvall', *Textual Practice* 18.1 (2004), 23–45; 3; Caroline Bergvall, 'Postings from Britain', *HOW2* 1.5 (March 2001) n.p.

63 Bergvall, 'New Writing Feature', n. p.

64 Ric Allsopp, 'Performance writing', *PAJ: A Journal of Performance and Art* 21.1 (January 1999), 76–80, 76.

65 Keith Tuma, 'Carolyn Bergvall', in Keith Tuma (ed.), *Oxford Anthology of Twentieth-Century British and Irish Poetry* (Oxford and New York: Oxford University Press, 2001), pp. 911–12; p. 911.

66 Caroline Bergvall, *Goan Atom* (San Francisco: Krupskaya, 2001), p. 48.

67 Nicky Marsh, '*Goan Atom*', *HOW2* 2.2 (Spring 2004), n.p. WEB. See early print versions in *The Oxford Anthology of Twentieth-Century British Literature* (1998) and *Goan Atom: 1. Jets-poupee* (1999). Marsh notes earlier performances of the piece. See also Romana Huk, 'Introduction, Oxford Brooks Colloquium: the politics of presence: re-reading the writing subject in "live" and electronic performance, theatre and film poetry', *HOW2* 1.6 (Autumn 2001), n.p. WEB.

68 Bellmer's two collections are *Les Jeux de la poupée* (The games of the doll) (1949) and *Poupée: Variations sur le montage d'une mineure articulée* (Doll: variations on the montage of an articulated minor) (1934).

69 Carolyn Bergvall, 'Speaking in tongues: Caroline Bergvall in conversation with John Stammers', *Jacket* 22 (May 2003), n.p. WEB.

70 Carolyn Bergvall, 'Les Jets de la poupée', in Tuma (ed.), *Oxford Anthology of Twentieth-Century British and Irish Poetry*, pp. 912–19.

71 *Ibid.*, p. 913.

72 *Ibid.*

73 Marsh, '*Goan Atom*', n.p.

74 Carolyn Bergvall, 'No margins to this page: female experimental poetry and the legacy of modernism', *Fragments* 5 (1993), 30–8; 31.

75 Bergvall, 'Speaking in tongues', n.p.

76 Also, the recently introduced *Journal of British and Irish Innovative Poetry*, ed. Robert Sheppard and Scott Thurston, will contribute to such conversations.

77 See Huk's comments on performance poetry and experimentalism in Huk, 'Introduction, Oxford Brooks Colloquium', or Jean Binta Breeze, Patience Agbabi, Jillian Tipene, Ruth Harrison, Vicki Bertram, in Bertram (ed.), 'A round-table discussion on poetry in performance', *Feminist Review* 62 (Summer 1999), 24–54.

78 See Kinnahan, *Lyric Interventions*.

79 See Broom, *Contemporary British and Irish Poetry*.

80 See Romana Huk, 'In anOther's pocket: the address of the 'pocket epic' in postmodern black British poetry', *Yale Journal of Criticism* 13.1 (Spring 2000), 23–48.

11

BRIAN CARAHER

Carol Ann Duffy, Medbh McGuckian and ruptures in the lines of communication

Eight months before her announcement as Britain's first female Poet Laureate, Carol Ann Duffy's 'Mrs Schofield's GCSE' was first published on the front page of the *Guardian* for Saturday, 6 September 2008 amid considerable notoriety. Under the broad banner-headline, 'Poet's rhyming riposte leaves Mrs Schofield "gobsmacked"', Ester Addley reported on the attempt by Pat Schofield, an examiner in Leicestershire, to have the Academic Qualifications Authority (AQA) remove an anthology of poetry from its GCSE (General Certificate, Secondary Education) curriculum because one of its selections, Duffy's dramatic monologue 'Education for Leisure', 'supposedly glorified knife crime'.[1] Duffy's 'riposte' to the censorship advocated by Schofield comprises another dramatic monologue in the 'thrown voice' of an examiner who, in an opening octave, sets a sequence of tightly interlaced quotations from Shakespearean drama and questions about the import of literal and metaphorical 'knife crimes':

> *You must prepare your bosom for his knife,*
> said Portia to Antonio in which
> of Shakespeare's Comedies? Who killed his wife,
> insane with jealousy? And which Scots witch
> knew *Something wicked this way comes?* Who said
> *Is this a dagger which I see?* Which Tragedy?
> Whose blade was drawn which led to Tybalt's death?
> To whom did Caesar say *Et tu?* And why?[2]

Duffy's closing sestet, in a sonnet-like turn of thought, then raises questions about 'the state' and the power and authority of poetry to 'speak again' about the status of 'the human'. Perhaps Duffy's ventriloquised examiner waxes ironically bitter here:

> *Something is rotten in the state of Denmark* – do you
> know what this means? Explain how poetry

179

pursues the human like the smitten moon
above the weeping, laughing earth; how we
make prayers of it. *Nothing will come of nothing*:
speak again. Said by which King? You may begin.[3]

The pointed quotations from and barbed allusions to *The Merchant of Venice*, *Othello*, *Macbeth*, *Romeo and Juliet*, *Julius Caesar*, *Hamlet* and *King Lear* seize upon telling passages from seven texts often set for GCSE exams. Such canonical texts intimate connections among dramatic knife-crimes, unjust or excessive crimes of passion and unsettled or disturbed mentalities. One implication of this forceful sonnet – this front-page, broadsheet, poetic communication ventriloquised by a laureate-in-waiting – would be that 'knife crimes' once explored dramatically by Shakespeare may continue to be set for GCSE exams but that a contemporary poet concerned about 'something . . . rotten in the state' of contemporary Britain can issue no such troubling poetic communication.

Carol Ann Duffy often explores dramatised mentalities or 'thrown voices', as the title of the 1986 booklet *Thrown Voices* (Turret Books) – in which 'Education for Leisure' was first published – pitches her characteristic scene of poetic communication. Indeed, as Jane Dowson and Alice Entwistle have concisely formulated, 'Duffy's trademark is her ventriloquising through dramatic monologue and dialogic dramatisations of human interaction, frequently in the present tense.'[4] That is to say, her poetry 'pursues the human' by speaking again and again in the voices of a wide variety of characters – 'like the smitten moon / above the weeping, laughing earth' pursues the oddities and idiosyncracies of its beloved subjects below until it can shape 'prayers' of what it observes and what it overhears. The burden of communication in Duffy's 'Education for Leisure' falls upon the reader, the listener, the audience, hearing the projected voice of the person – a disaffected, unemployed young school-leaver of the Thatcher era – whom the poet casts upon a public proscenium to perform in his characteristic words and mental contours. The tone, voice and diction of the speaker in a dramatic monologue typically disclose the psychology and motives of his or her character at a significant moment or crisis, as enacted in the text of the poem.

When Mrs Pat Schofield reads Carol Ann Duffy as poorly as Duffy's dramatised school-leaver remembers Shakespeare, however, there is a disturbing breakdown in communication. Dramatic monologues do risk misinterpretation, especially when a reader perversely misconstructs the voice and character of the speaker and the communicative burden of the poet. As a sound reader probably should recognise, Duffy's violent school-leaver in 'Education for Leisure' skews the words and import of Shakespeare's Earl of Gloucester:

I squash a fly against the window with my thumb.
We did that at school. Shakespeare. It was in
another language and now the fly is in another language.[5] (lines 5–7)

The once influential Gloucester, blinded, meets his legitimate son Edgar
at the start of the fourth act of *King Lear* and knowingly, succinctly and
tragically encapsulates his own fate in the potent imagery of murdered
flies and idle young men: 'As flies to wanton boys are we to th'gods; /
They kill us for their sport' (*King Lear*, IV.1.36–7). Yet Duffy's speaker
seeks 'to play God' (line 3) and sport wantonly with a fly, a goldfish, a
cat, a budgie, a radio chatshow host and finally the anonymous human
on the street who is also cast as the reader of Duffy's poem: 'I touch your
arm' (line 20).[6] It's frightening and utterly chilling stuff. Duffy's nameless school-leaver has not been educated 'for leisure' but for insensitivity.
The tragic self-awareness of a Gloucester eloquently dramatised by
Shakespeare utterly eludes the wanton boy of the 1980s who can't hear
'another language' that should optimally be his own through education.
Life for him can only be rendered resentfully 'in another language' –
death, silence, violent extinction. Duffy employs all the pyrotechnics of
the dramatic monologue to throw the voice of the miseducated, and
often discarded and disadvantaged, 'wanton boy' of the 1980s upon
the public stage of poetic communication in order to catch the con-
science of our disjointed time – a time in which the social has been
sacrificed to selfish aggression, sadistic acquisitiveness and anti-social
self-assertion.

Is it a matter of social class, anxious contemporaneity or misjudged
political correctness that produces an errant, fractious and controversial
reaction to 'Education for Leisure' as that rendered by the examiner
Mrs Pat Schofield? Duffy's 'riposte' foregrounds ironies in the sharp juxtaposition of Shakespearean poetic practices and thus summons attention
once again to strong ruptures in the lines of communication with
'Education for Leisure'. With the latter poem Duffy brings the 'thrown
voice' of a murderous, anti-social wanton too close for contemporary
comfort. She finds a disturbingly powerful way to renew for a contemporary readership the cultural potency of a dramatist's ear for voices and
well-tuned Shakespearean metaphors.

The thirty, well-known, dramatic monologues of *The World's Wife*
can be cited here as corroboration for just this sort of social and cultural
critique aimed at a contemporary audience. In the unorthodox, blank-
verse sonnet entitled 'Anne Hathaway', for instance, Duffy voices the
widowed wife of the bard speaking in the borrowed linguistic livery of

her deceased spouse regarding his curious gift of the 'second best bed' to the mother of his children.

> Some nights, I dreamed he'd written me, the bed
> a page beneath his writer's hands. Romance
> and drama played by touch, by scent, by taste.
> In the other bed, the best, our guests dozed on,
> dribbling prose. My living laughing love –
> I hold him in the casket of my widow's head
> as he held me upon that next best bed.

The widow relives the passionate lovemaking that could well have been her desire in the 'spinning world'[7] of the 'second best bed' left deliberately by her husband as a memento of the 'drama played by touch, by scent, by taste', but otherwise invisible and unspoken in the prosaic language of Shakespeare's notorious will: 'Item I gyve unto my wief my second best bed . . .' At a stroke, Duffy revises the problematic sexual politics of Shakespeare's will by dramatising the voice and the character of an otherwise silent Anne Hathaway, allowing her for the moment to take the stage as an eloquent, equal and passionate companion of her uncharacteristically elliptical Will.

What seems at issue here are ruptures, revisions and reorientations in the lines of poetic communication. The occasional breakdown is a distinct risk, such as that exhibited in the furore over 'Education for Leisure', requiring a robust riposte on the part of the contemporary poet who wants to defend her claim to renewal of the fine art of dramatic ventriloquism – renewing even the metaphors, the poetic forms and the will-ful last line of Shakespeare. Carol Ann Duffy's 'thrown voices', however, do not provide a wholly unique, entirely unprecedented situation. Lurking beneath the pseudonymn 'Andrew Belis', Samuel Beckett published in *The Bookman* for August 1934 a strident and contentious defence of the poetic practice of 'Recent Irish Poetry', by which 'Belis' meant male poets such as the distinctively minor Irish Modernists Thomas MacGreevy, Brian Coffey, Denis Devlin, Lyle Donaghy, as well as the unnamed Beckett. Having learned, indeed been inculcated with, such poetic forms as the sonnet and prosodic techniques such as metre and rhyme, 'younger Irish poets', according to Belis/ Beckett, felt driven to perform a 'rupture of the lines of communication'.[8] Such testy challenges to poetic orthodoxy and calls to modernise the idiom of verse are themselves periodic and recurrent, at least since the 1790s. One lyric generation's bellowing or belligerent 'Belis' becomes a subsequent generation's 'lost leader' or even inculcated burden. However, Beckett's bellicose brief still makes a crucial point about the dynamics and pragmatics

of the lyric line in contemporary Anglophone poetry written by bot
and women. Contemporary poets work against as much as with the t
the line and the expectations of recurrent modern poetic forms. To rupture
learned lines of lyric communication is to renew the line, to learn to see and
sense the line and its perceptual and cognitive capabilities once again.

Beckett's 1934 manifesto might be briefly juxtaposed with the seventh
chapter, 'Rhythm and rhyme', of Louis MacNeice's 1938 study *Modern
Poetry: A Personal Essay*. There are some broad issues of agreement, yet
MacNeice's failure to sense the playful, disobedient rupturing of the blank-
verse, pentameter line in the opening phrase of Milton's *Paradise Lost*
inadvertently makes Beckett's point: 'Thus in Milton's line 'Of Mán's Fírst
Disobédience and the Frúit' I cannot find a fifth syllable worthy to be
matched against those which I have marked.'⁹ New poets rupture the
received lines of poetic communication in order to renew or to refashion
the line. Milton once wilfully and creatively sinned against the pentameter
line, but a later generation perhaps no longer hears or senses the original,
wanton sin and the significance of its lyric fruit. MacNeice's difficulty is not
unlike that of W. B. Yeats, when the latter uses the same opening line by
Milton as the exemplary index of his own inability to sense 'feeling' in the
blank verse metrics and 'passionate prose' of 'the Renaissance'.¹⁰ Poets and
readers are often circumscribed within what Richard Wilbur in *Mayflies*
(2004) calls 'our stiff geometries', our formal metrics and learned measures
of the line that would leave us tone-deaf 'in trackless woods'.¹¹

Carol Ann Duffy's 'Away and See' from her 1993 collection *Mean Time*
offers a contemporary touchstone for what Belis/Beckett praises in 'Recent
Irish Poetry' and MacNeice and Yeats perhaps cannot sense in their 1930s
scansion of the opening line of *Paradise Lost*. Duffy's distinctly *carpe diem*
poem about fleshly, transgressive love and 'new fruits' syncopates the
Anglophone or English alexandrine line, but in so doing produces a suggestive metapoetic lyric ('the flight / of syllables, wingspan stretching a noun')
which dances about the metronomic 'mean time' of the standard sequence
of quatrains.

> Away and see an ocean suck at a boiled sun
> and say to someone things that I'd blush even to dream.
> Slip off your dress in a high room over the harbour.
> Write to me soon.
>
> New fruits sing of the flipside of night in a market
> of language, light, a tune from the chapel nearby
> stopping you dead, the peach in your palm respiring.
> Taste it for me.

Away and see the things that words give a name to, the flight
of syllables, wingspan stretching a noun. Test words
wherever they live; listen and touch, smell, believe.
Spell them with love.[12]

Duffy's 'Away and See' works wonders with line, rhythm, time and key change. Twenty stresses or beats of routine pentameter quatrains are redistributed across a stanza that races with re-energising rhythm across three hexameter lines, only to round off with an emphatic dimeter injunction to action: 'write', 'taste', 'spell', 'ask', and 'away and see'. *Carpe diem* is written, spelled, enacted rhythmically at the turn of every one of the poem's five stanzas. The poem spells and sings at the level of theme, form, sound and rhythm all its 'new fruits'. It sings of new tastes, found on 'the flipside of night in a market / of language' that rings out, chimes rupturously and rapturously – 'Go on. G'on. Gon' (the penultimate line) – its new-found pleasures. The poem is Marvellian in its opening image and lyric genre; yet it renews the tropes of *carpe diem* at every turn in its hopeful, impassioned openness to 'the new, the vivid' rapping 'at the door' of the felt equivalent of an unending, always renewable, New Year's Day.

Skedaddle. Somebody chaps at the door at a year's end, hopeful.
Away and see who it is. Let in the new, the vivid,
horror and pity, passion, the stranger holding the future.
Ask him his name.[13]

'Away and See' needs to be sensed or heard against the lines of communication it strives to rupture, resound, restring and re-trope so disobediently, yet so fruitfully.[14] Duffy restrings the metrics of the quatrain and sins fruitfully against the pentameter line in 'Away and See'. Her poem delightfully finesses the passionate prose of unrhymed, long alexandrines and punchy, assertive dimeters with the ruptured baseline of the standard quatrain. Duffy's lyric 'mean time' plays lines and rhythms against the metronome of received tradition and expectation in order to destabilise 'our stiff geometries' and to retune the line, to sense the possibilities of line, rhythm, stanza and refashioned lyric form.

However, this scenario is an enduring as well as renewed tale of poetic communication. In rupture there is rapture. Beckettian 'rupture of the lines of communication' is not merely an act of modernising petulance directed against an old guard or an *ancien régime*; it encompasses humankind's originary poetic sin, an act of 'first disobedience' that helps us restring the lyre – each year, each generation, each contemporary epoch – so that new poetic fruits, however dangerous, might be seen, tasted, spelled and known, as if for the very first time.

Nothing's the same as anything else. Away and see
for yourself. Walk. Fly. Take a boat till land reappears,
altered forever, ringing its bells, alive. Go on. G'on. Gon.
Away and see.[15]

The melody of contemporary Anglophone poetry resists and must resist the metronome of the received line, pentameter or otherwise. This story of original poetic sin is not of necessity a gendered one, but the tale does all too often fall along gendered lines of poetic inheritance. Duffy's 'Away and See' permits the speaker to be constructed as female or as male, or indeed permits the reader to construct an imagination of the speaker along various lines in which gender is not a determined or fixed entity or social identity. However, the lines of poetic communication which Duffy so brilliantly ruptures are themselves often rendered or constructed as masculine, as part of a distinctively male lineage of poetic inheritance.

Perhaps to make clearer what is at stake here, look at Richard Murphy's 'Wellington Testimonial' – one of fifty Shakespearean sonnets which make up the capstone sequence to his *Collected Poems* (2000). 'Wellington Testimonial' comprises the fifth in a well-chiselled sequence on the folly of male ambition to set a sense of proud presence in stone within British and Irish landscapes. One could say that there's a phallic poetics, indeed a recurrent 'phallogocentrism', about the full sequence, *The Price of Stone*.[16] Such a claim may well undercut, however, the sequence's often deft critical and cultural politics. 'Wellington Testimonial' both asserts a certain mode of monumental male, Anglo-Irish presence in Dublin's Phoenix Park and then mocks, via the self-disclosing strategies of dramatic monologue, the hubris of maintaining monumentally 'a clean laconic style':

Properly dressed for an obsolete parade,
Devoid of mystery, no winding stair
Threading my unvermiculated head,
I've kept my feet, but lost my nosey flair.[17]

The sonnet marshals, as on a parade ground, fourteen strongly stressed lines of predominantly iambic pentameter. This lyric monument stands erect, solid on its own well-made, well-measured feet, pounding five beats to a line; but it's lost all 'nosey flair', through the monolithic maintenance of a marmoreal metronome: 'My sole point in this evergreen oak aisle / Is to maintain a clean laconic style.'[18] No late Yeatsian 'winding stair' troubles the stony insouciance of its 'unvermiculated head' with dialogic voices and experimental styles.[19] Is Murphy's 'clean laconic style' the measure of the contemporary masculine, Anglophone Irish and British poetic line? Yes, and No. Murphy's monument to masculine vanity has kept the pentameter line afoot but at the considerable price of obsolescence and mere phallocentric pride. Shakespearean sonnetry is a received traditional form, but it often stands in the contemporary landscape of British and Irish poetry like Wellington's obelisk in Phoenix Park, unless playfully ruptured like Duffy's 'Anne Hathaway' or brilliantly broken asunder like Paul Muldoon's 'The More a Man Has the More a Man Wants'.[20] The loss of one's 'nosey flair' registers not just as a gesture towards the changed socio-historical and national fortunes of parades that pass the Wellington obelisk in Dublin's Phoenix Park since 1922 but also to the felt rhythms of public performance and dramatic enactment. 'A clean laconic style' does 'obelize the victory of wit', as Murphy limns in the opening lines of 'Wellington Testimonial', into a rigid, rigorously maintained traditional form and traditional line. Murphy chisels both form and line lovingly, deftly, deviously, but not disobediently. A rather masculine lyric lineage is evoked, even as its limits are etched memorably in verbal stone.

Women poets, and male poets too, seem called to challenge the hegemony of such a poetic heritage not just in the interests of gender, gender difference, gender parity and matrilineal considerations but perhaps also in the interests of posterity, in asserting and naming, and in nurturing and fostering, other lineaments and lineations for the present and future of the lyric. I'll return to Duffy to discuss her dramatic monologue 'Warming Her Pearls' and her sonnet 'Prayer' in this context, but one finds the subtle detonations of Medbh McGuckian's poetic line answering keenly to the call to rupture the lines of received, traditional, poetic communication.

Much has been made of the difficulty of Medbh McGuckian's poetry, even her 'gnomic' or 'pointless' or 'postmodern' play.[21] Yet this perceived difficulty may owe as much to the received line, style and representational logic that McGuckian strives to resist, to rupture and to reorient. As Jane Dowson and Alice Entwistle have acutely summarised, 'battling with traditionalist Northern Irish culture, McGuckian's language confounds conventions of literary representation and interpretation'.[22] McGuckian's purported difficulty may not be idiosyncratic, elective or perverse, so much as a deliberate act of linguistic resistance to 'the lyric tradition's complacent presumption of a singular, coherent and representable voice'.[23] McGuckian resists the singular, often masculinist, even diffidently monumentalist construction of lyric voice one finds in Richard Murphy's 'Wellington Testimonial' or in the poetry of such notable Northern Irish writers as John Montague, Seamus Heaney, Michael Longley and Derek Mahon. McGuckian abjures 'the cohering disposition of the lyric "I"' and opts for a 'uniquely expressive obliquity' that deliberately engages 'metonymic slippages', 'self-deconstruction' and a polyvocality willing to cross-pollinate and harmonise a range of voices and evocations, both female and male.[24] As Ruth Padel notes, the surface 'shimmer' of McGuckian's 'electric metaphorical language . . . seems to some male readers provocatively "feminine" because it seems to work by association, by a gauzy, apparently inconsequential irrationality, rather than by logic'. However, 'under the shimmer, the thought is sharp, socially critical, impatiently intelligent'.[25] Justin Quinn has articulated this pointed, socially critical intelligence of McGuckian's poetic practice in a powerfully suggestive formulation: 'Readers of her work are shown an economy of desire – its slipstreams, eddies, debouchures – they never suspected of existing, or if they did could never have expressed. The poems are a continual conversation with a silent man in the midst of metamorphosing landscapes and house interiors.'[26] Women's voices speak in McGuckian's poetry, but her poems frequently construct scenes of engagement, conversation and intimate conflict between female and male investments in 'an economy of desire' that the poet labours to bring to the surface of discourse, despite the errancies and evasions incumbent upon masculinist preoccupations. Yes, the male perspective may often be 'silent', yet in McGuckian's poetry it is frequently mooted beyond any muteness, always elicited and solicited in her frequent employment of the second-person mode of address (as in, 'Well may you question . . .' or 'You call me aspen . . .' or 'And if you feel uncertain . . .').[27] Indeed, tracking the delicate, precise, highly charged and emotionally freighted conversation of friends, lovers and spouses – the 'nuanced ebb and flow in a relationship' – is, as Justin Quinn puts it, 'McGuckian's forte'.[28] Difficulty there is, but it is a figuratively rich and socially inflected mode of discursive difficulty.

This perspective on McGuckian's purported difficulty may also help comprehend her tactical uses of intertextuality, especially her substantial gleanings from a wide variety of texts in composing what has been called her 'montage-effect'.[29] For instance, Shane Murphy has well documented the sources for lines, phrases and images in McGuckian's poem 'Drawing Ballerinas' in passages from John Elderfield's *The Drawings of Henri Matisse*. Murphy underscores McGuckian's intertextual borrowings and montage-like palimpsest, as though the poet were putting into practice 'the rationale' of the painter Matisse to resist the pictorial presentation of war and to find an ease with drawing the feminine figures he chooses, rather than succumb to an 'obligation to respond to social strife'.[30] This interpretive construction may well be at least half correct. However, McGuckian does considerably more than construct an intertextual palimpsest of lines, phrases and images borrowed from readings in Matisse and his male interpreter. McGuckian ruptures lines of poetic communication concerning an influential, received and traditional mode of lyric communication about war and what constitutes 'war poetry'.

As McGuckian articulates in the title poem of her brilliant 2001 collection *Drawing Ballerinas*, 'the lines' desire is to warp to accommodate / a body, a lost and emptied memory of a lost / body'.[31] The poet ruptures received, largely masculinised lines of communication about war and the poetry of war in order to draw lines and craft figures that limn lost, fragile and tender forms of potent experience. As the quotation from Henri Matisse prominently displayed on the back cover of *Drawing Ballerinas* intimates, the artist's perspective is not so much pacifism or resistance to masculine trench warfare as a deliberate redefinition of what 'a front line' in the wars, in the culture wars, in the poetry wars and in the poetry of war can be: 'I may not be in the trenches, but I am in a front line of my own making.' McGuckian deftly appropriates this latter quotation from Matisse, dated 19 July 1916, and allows it to resonate with the anecdote mentioned in a note to her title poem: 'The painter, Matisse, when asked how he managed to survive the war artistically, replied that he spent the worst years "drawing ballerinas".'[32] The date of Matisse's statement about his 'front line' not only strongly echoes the month and days of the Battle of the Somme, but it also coincides with the date of publication of McGuckian's own volume, 19 July 2001, prominently displayed on the verso of the title page. With McGuckian, 'lines of communication' assume a subtly martial and masculine context which she seeks 'to warp to accommodate' a feminised subjectivity, another torn body of experience, a ruptured and rupturing otherness. The poem commemorates, but does not name or eulogise, 'Ann Frances Owens, schoolfellow and neighbour, who lost her life in the Abercorn Café explosion, 1972', as McGuckian's footnote to the text states.[33] The Abercorn Restaurant in central Belfast was torn apart by a bomb left in a shopping bag, one crowded day in March 1972, and the bodies of women diners were either ripped apart or left limbless in a scene of carnage characteristic of battlefields.

Thus, when McGuckian opens her poem 'Drawing Ballerinas' with the following five-line stanza, she fuses two actions and two scenes – namely, the drawing of a young woman as a ballerina and the making of a new sort of 'front line' in the annals of destruction:

> We are the focus of storms and scissor-steps.
> A young girl that dressed up as a woman
> and pulled her gown tight across her breast
> now pays men to dance with her, as we would tie
> the leaves to the trees and the trees to the forest.[34]

These are not difficult lines, but these lines draw a new perspective on the imagery of war and its toll on bodies and desires. Women, the 'we' of the poem, become in the 'front line' of McGuckian's poem, as well as in her poetic practice more broadly, 'the focus' of the storm and stress of violence, such as in the Abercorn atrocity; but 'we' are also at the same time remembered in the 'scissor-steps' and tightly drawn ballet 'gown' of a young ballerina. The 'now' of the remembered ballerina juxtaposes to her prepubescent body the body of a shattered woman, still wishing to dance, but 'now' needing to be repaired, reconstituted, re-membered, as we might try to remake a forest shattered by the 'storms' of warfare, restoring 'the leaves to the trees' and the uprooted 'trees to the forest'. And so the poem continues over its next eight stanzas, mixing the imagery of young and lost female bodies with the imagery of the violent destruction of bodies, typical of explosive warfare:

> The body turns in, restless, on itself,
> in a womb of sleep, an image of isolated sleep.
> It turns over, reveals opposing versions of itself,
> one arm broken abruptly at elbow and wrist,
> the other wrenched downwards by the force of the turning.

'Drawing Ballerinas' remembers lost bodies, stanza by stanza, but it does so in a lyrical manner that delineates simultaneously the contemporaneous moment of rupture and the re-membering of what has been lost or ruptured. Indeed, the third stanza of the poem powerfully suggests that the act of poetic lineation seeks to draw our contradictory desires and memories together in an act of commemoration that nevertheless witnesses violence, in the end, drawn across the face of a violated body, one that may well have been a ballerina in virginal youth:

> And the lines' desire is to warp to accommodate
> a body, a lost and emptied memory of a lost
> body, the virgin mind emptied from or of it,
> to discover the architecture of pressed-together
> thighs, or lips that half-belong to a face.

The alternating rhythm of anapestic and iambic feet dance across these lines. The poet strives to draw the figure and lost shape of her ballerina, including seeking 'to discover the architecture' of 'scissor-steps', 'of pressed-together / thighs', in the shape of scissored or enjambed lines. Yet, such evocations are shattered by the 'now' of 'lips that half-belong to a face', an image which itself draws in the 'front line' of destruction, of violence that ruptures the movement of dance, stanza by stanza.

Medbh McGuckian ruptures received lines of poetic communication in the poetry of war, a virtually exclusively masculinist tradition in modern lyric communication, in order to draw her ballerina differently, perhaps difficultly, but certainly not diffidently. There is vibrant, gendered, social critique rippling through the perfectly executed scissor-steps of McGuckian's lines and images, including her borrowed, intertextual voices and invocations. McGuckian challenges and revises the lyric form and poetic rhetoric of 'war poetry' and 'Troubles poetry' throughout many of the thirty-nine poems of *Drawing Ballerinas*.

Carol Ann Duffy challenges and revises the lyric form and poetic rhetoric of other modes of inherited poetic practice. This chapter concludes by looking at one of Duffy's early dramatic monologues, 'Warming Her Pearls', from the mid-1980s, as an exercise in reclaiming the transgressive qualities of lines of dramatic communication for the contemporary lyric of 'thrown voices' and of embodied social critique, as well as her reinvention of the sonnet as 'prayer' in the final poem from *Mean Time*.

'Warming Her Pearls' comprises the dramatic projection of a voice and a character rooted in a discussion Duffy once had with the woman to whom the poem is dedicated, Judith Radstone. According to Deirdre O'Day, Duffy's dramatic monologue 'was dedicated to [Radstone], inspired by a conversation with Judith about the practice of ladies' maids increasing the lustre of their mistresses' pearls by secreting them beneath their clothes to be warmed by their skin'.[35] This information is crucial to understanding the full context of the imaginative act undertaken. Through rather prosaic, declarative sentences and statements arranged in six stanzas of unrhymed quatrains, Duffy builds up the understated yet increasingly powerful speech of a maid, whose declarations of fact generate implications of hidden, secretive and scarcely controlled desire.

> Next to my own skin, her pearls. My mistress
> bids me wear them, warm them, until evening
> when I'll brush her hair. At six, I place them
> round her cool, white throat. All day I think of her,
>
> resting in the Yellow Room, contemplating silk
> or taffeta, which gown tonight? She fans herself
> whilst I work willingly, my slow heat entering
> each pearl. Slack on my neck, her rope.[36]

The 'rope' of pearls warms slowly round the neck of the maid, who works to prepare the pearls' sheen for her mistress, their owner. The choice of the word 'rope', though, also gestures towards the language not just of the maid, but of thievery and execution by hanging for anyone who might covet them mischievously or illegally. There are clear markers of social class throughout the poem; it is 'mistress' and serving maid; it is 'the Yellow Room' of the privileged aristocrat who can rest in extraordinary comfort and contemplate 'which gown [to wear] tonight', as opposed to 'my attic room', the remote and confined domestic space of the maid. The 'thrown voice' of this lyric monologue is that of servant, who though diligent in her work, covets the life of her mistress, but remains in her place.

Duffy, moreover, rather deftly insinuates another dimension of covetousness across social lines and barriers. As the poem progresses, there is also the intimation of illicit feelings and desires across not only social lines of class difference but also the cultural barriers of gender.

> She's beautiful. I dream about her
> in my attic bed; picture her dancing
> with tall men, puzzled by my faint, persistent scent
> beneath her French perfume, her milky stones.

Class difference subtly scents this stanza, with the puzzling aroma of the serving maid running underneath the surface glamour of the ballroom, for both mistress and her 'tall men' to sense. The maid certainly covets the life, yet perhaps also the attention and affections, of the mistress. 'In her looking-glass', as the fourth stanza of the poem even more suggestively articulates, 'my red lips part as though I want to speak'. Unspoken, hidden desires and feelings lurk in yet another object of the mistress's Yellow Room; the unequally shared mirror – as well as pearls – conceals what the maid can't broach in shared speech with her social better. Indeed, the last two stanzas of 'Warming Her Pearls' turns upon the maid's erotically charged imagination of her mistress returning home, undressing and 'slipping naked into bed, the way / she always does'. That last enjambment slides across a stanzaic break. Duffy orchestrates the secreted emotions of the maid in brilliant fashion, not only finding a prosaic measure in which to organise the loose pentameter rhythms of the servant's factual account of her work, but also to inspirit the monologue of the maid with a slowly emergent eroticism and desires which scarcely utter their names, other than through shared objects:

> And I lie here awake,
> knowing the pearls are cooling even now
> in the room where my mistress sleeps. All night
> I feel their absence and I burn.

The maid feels the absence of the pearls ('their absence'), not the imagined body of their owner; she can't or won't articulate a declarative desire for her mistress. The maid covets the mistress's mode of life as much as anything else in this dramatic monologue. However, an echo – a reverse, looking-glass echo – of Sappho's famous Fragment 38 runs as an undertone and a thematic undercurrent through the final three words of Duffy's poem: 'you burn me'.[37] The suppressed, carefully controlled heat of desire fuels the life, voice, character, dreams and diction of Duffy's imagined maid. 'Warming Her Pearls' knits transgressive social and erotic desires together in a lyric form which sins fruitfully against the *métier* of the dramatic monologue, especially if one compares it to Robert Browning's 'My Last Duchess' or even the once radically innovative 'The Love Song of J. Alfred Prufrock' by T. S. Eliot. Duffy recollects the aristocratic context of the former poem and subsumes the context of repressed desires of the latter monologue. 'Warming Her Pearls' works by finding a new line, a prosaic measure, a sapphistic sublimation, and a taught rope of images and objects through which to imagine the hidden life of a female servant.

Duffy's 'Prayer', the final poem of *Mean Time*, does for the sonnet what 'Warming Her Pearls' achieves for the dramatic monologue. 'Prayer' is a perfectly executed Shakespearean sonnet, replete with finely crafted pentameter lines, grouped in three quatrains and a concluding couplet of fulsome rhymes and with syntactic and sentential closure at the end of each of its four stanzaic moments. However, Duffy's 'Prayer' would not sit well in the monumental stone arch of Richard Murphy's sonnet sequence, *The Price of Stone*, with the keystone 'clean laconic style' of 'Wellington Testimonial'. 'Prayer' fuses lightly Shakespearean form with the minimal found notes of music and the unexpected sounds of forgiveness for transgressions, for trespassing against others, in happenstances outside the speechless sinner.

> Some days, although we cannot pray, a prayer
> utters itself. So, a woman will lift
> her head from the sieve of her hands and stare
> at the minims sung by a tree, a sudden gift.[38]

Hands held over the face in pain, in loss, in desolation seem shaped like a 'sieve' for tears to run through them. Yet the half-note sequence held for two beats – 'the minims' – made by the sound of birds in or breezes through a tree call 'a woman' to prayer and to 'a sudden gift' of consolation from outside the isolation of her wordless self. Indeed, the phrase 'at the minims sung' itself suggests rhythmically the very sense of 'minim' – half-notes held for two beats. Other prayerless sinners find sudden consolation in similar fashion: the 'faithless' deceiver and the no longer youthful 'man' of the second stanza, and 'the lodger' and the childless parent of the third stanza.[39] And then the concluding, sonorous couplet: 'Darkness outside. Inside, the radio's prayer – /Rockall. Malin. Dogger. Finisterre.'

The subtle modulation of strong trochaic rhythm to the sudden upturn of consoling iambs at the end of both lines of this concluding rhyme mimics the movement from pain to prayer, from solitary darkness to the 'sudden gift' of familiar words, sounds, rhythms and rituals in the shape of a new and contemporary rite of self-forgiveness. The shipping news and the weather forecast for the twinned islands of Ireland and Britain perhaps have never sounded so full of unexpected meaning, organised as the minimal but all so familiar notes of daily comfort from the ends of the earth ('Finisterre'). It's not 'The Lord's Prayer'; it's not 'The Our Father'. Yet it's the Shakespearean sonnet transgressed and trespassed, ruptured and remade from within the minims of its measures, so that it speaks anew to us now in the lineations and voices of the contemporary. Sinning fruitfully against the received or inherited line and received lyric form yields the measure of contemporary Anglophone poetry, especially that written by virtuoso British and Irish women poets such as Carol Ann Duffy and Medbh McGuckian.

Notes

1 Ester Addley, "Poet's rhyming riposte leaves Mrs Schofield 'gobsmacked'", The *Guardian*, Weekend Edition, 6 September 2008, pp. 1–2. (The Schofield case reminds me of a similar furore over Tony Harrison's 'V', a parodic rupture of Gray's 'Elegy in a Country Churchyard' that was made into a Channel 4 film. See Bloodaxe edition of the poem (1985) that includes press articles, photographs, letters, a defence by film director Richard Eyre, and Channel Four's phone call log. Ed.)
2 The *Guardian*, Saturday 6 September 2008.
3 *Ibid.*
4 Jane Dowson and Alice Entwistle, *A History of Twentieth-Century British Women's Poetry* (Cambridge: Cambridge University Press, 2005), p. 176. See also pages 214–19 of this text for a fuller exploration of Duffy's poetic ventriloquism in relation to Bakhtinian poetics.
5 Carol Ann Duffy, 'Education for Leisure', in *Female Standing Nude* (London: Anvil Press Poetry, 1985), p. 15.
6 Duffy, 'Education for Leisure', p. 15.
7 Carol Ann Duffy, 'Anne Hathaway', in *The World's Wife* (London: Picador, 1999), p. 30.
8 Samuel Beckett, 'Recent Irish poetry', in *Disjecta* (London: John Calder, 1983), p. 70. The essay originally appeared pseudonymously in the now-defunct Irish periodical *The Bookman*.
9 Louis MacNeice, *Modern Poetry: A Personal Essay* (London: Faber & Faber, 1938), p. 122.
10 William Butler Yeats, 'A general introduction for my work', in *Essays and Introductions* (London and New York: Macmillan, 1961), pp. 523–4. Yeats' introductory essay was initially written in 1937.
11 Richard Wilbur, 'In Trackless Woods', in *Mayflies* (Chipping Norton, Oxfordshire: The Waywiser Press, 2004).

12 Carol Ann Duffy, 'Away and See', in *Mean Time* (London: Anvil Press, 1993), p. 23.

13 *Ibid.*

14 It may be worth noting that 'Away and See' might also be argued as alluding to and also re-imagining the material possibilities of the metaphors at play in the eighth verse of Psalm 34: 'How good Yahweh is – only taste and see! Happy the man who takes shelter in him.'

15 Duffy, 'Away and See', p. 23.

16 Richard Murphy, *Collected Poems* (Loughcrew, Oldcastle, Co. Meath: Gallery Books, 2000), pp. 179–230. The notion of 'phallogocentrism' is derived from Jacques Derrida, *Of Grammatology*, trans. Gayatri Chakravorty Spivak (Baltimore and London: Johns Hopkins University Press, 1976), pp. 43, 101–268, and from Derrida, *Dissemination*, trans. Barbara Johnson (London: Athlone Press, 1981), pp. 63–171, 324–66.

17 Murphy, 'Wellington Testimonial', in *Collected Poems*, p. 185.

18 *Ibid.*

19 Of course, Yeats' late dialogic poems such as 'A Dialogue of Self and Soul', 'The Seven Sages' and 'Vacillation' as well as his sequence of twenty-five experimental Crazy Jane and Tom the Lunatic ballads are to be found in *The Winding Stair and Other Poems* (London: Macmillan, 1933).

20 Paul Muldoon, 'The More a Man Has the More a Man Wants', in *Quoof* (London: Faber and Faber, 1983), pp. 40–64. In this notorious concluding sequence to his fourth collection, Muldoon employs a series of forty-nine thoroughly destabilised, exploded sonnets to chart the interlacing narrative adventures of Gallogly and Beatrice across scenes evocative of the Northern Irish Troubles.

21 Michael Allen notes 'her gnomic tendency' in 'The Poetry of Medbh McGuckian', in Elmer Andrews (ed.), *Contemporary Irish Poetry: A Collection of Critical Essays* (Basingstoke: Macmillan, 1992), p. 287, and Thomas Docherty uses the 'pointless' play and semantic difficulty of McGuckian's early poetry as an opening gambit in his pursuit of 'a postmodern McGuckian', replete with 'a postmodern sublime' in 'Initiations, tempers, seductions: postmodern McGuckian', in Neal Corcoran (ed.), *The Chosen Ground: Essays on the Contemporary Poetry of Northern Ireland* (Bridgend: Seren Press, 1992), pp. 191–210.

22 Dowson and Entwistle, *A History of Twentieth-Century British Women's Poetry*, p. 178.

23 *Ibid.*, pp. 249–50.

24 *Ibid.*, pp. 250–1.

25 Ruth Padel, *52 Ways of Looking at a Poem* (London: Chatto & Windus, 2002), p. 95.

26 Justin Quinn, *The Cambridge Introduction to Modern Irish Poetry, 1800–2000* (Cambridge: Cambridge University Press, 2008), p. 167.

27 See, for example, the poem 'Aviary' in McGuckian's *Venus and the Rain*, second and rev. edn (Loughcrew: Gallery Books, 1994), p. 25.

28 Quinn, *Cambridge Introduction*, p. 169.

29 See, for instance, Shane Murphy, '"Roaming Root of Multiple Meanings": intertextual relations in Medbh McGuckian's poetry', *Metre* 5 (1998), 105, as well as Murphy's essay '"You Took Away My Biography": the poetry of

Medbh McGuckian', *Irish University Review: A Journal of Irish Studies* 28.1 (1998), 110–32.

30 Shane Murphy, 'Sonnets, centos and long lines: Muldoon, Paulin, McGuckian and Carson', in Matthew Campbell (ed.), *The Cambridge Companion to Contemporary Irish Poetry* (Cambridge: Cambridge University Press, 2003), pp. 200–1.

31 Medbh McGuckian, *Drawing Ballerinas* (Loughcrew: Gallery Books, 2001), p. 14.

32 *Ibid.*, p.15.

33 *Ibid.*

34 *Ibid.*, p. 14. All additional quotations from the poem will be from this page.

35 Radstone, born 23 August 1925, died 13 January 2001, aged 75, was a British political activist, bookseller and part-time organiser for the Poetry Society in London. See Deirdre O'Day's obituary, 'Judith Radstone: radical bibliophile devoted to the worlds of poetry and protest', The *Guardian*, 13 February 2001. www.guardian.co.uk/news/2001/feb/13/guardianobituaries.books

36 Carol Ann Duffy, 'Warming Her Pearls', in *Selling Manhattan* (London: Anvil Books, 1987), p. 58. All quotations will be from this text and page.

37 See Willis Barnstone, trans., *Greek Lyric Poetry* (New York: Schocken Books, 1972), p. 67. Barnstone supplies the title 'To Eros' for this otherwise evocative fragment. See also Anne Carson's very useful note on the difficulties of translating Sappho's Fragment 38, which she also renders 'you burn me', in *If Not, Winter: Fragments of Sappho*, trans. Anne Carson (New York: Alfred A Knopf, 2002), p. 365.

38 Carol Ann Duffy, 'Prayer', in *Mean Time* (London: Anvil Press, 1993), p. 52. All additional quotations will be from this text and page.

39 Ruth Padel, *52 Ways*, pp. 165–8, offers one of the most sensitive and probing readings of this poem I have come across. She also notes the same sequence of five marked persons in need of consolation for loss, however ambiguous or elliptical.

SELECTED READING

The notes to the chapters provide extensive references for the specialist areas they cover. The following list indicates the range of available poetry anthologies, theoretical and critical approaches. For more comprehensive bibliographies of primary works, anthologies and critical books, see Jane Dowson and Alice Entwistle, *A Cambridge History of Twentieth-Century British Poetry*, Cambridge: Cambridge University Press, 2005.

Poetry Anthologies

Adcock, Fleur (ed.), *The Faber Book of Twentieth Century Women's Poetry*, London: Faber, 1987.

Astley, Neil (ed.), *Bloodaxe Poetry Introduction 1 (Alexander, Alvi, Dharker, Kay)*, Tarset: Bloodaxe, 2006.

Caddel, Richard and Peter Quartermain (eds.), *Other: British and Irish Poetry since 1970*, Hanover, NH and London: Wesleyan University Press, 1999.

Chipasula, Stella and Frank (eds.), *The Heinemann Book of African Women's Poetry*, London: Heinemann, 1995.

Couzyn, Jeni (ed.), *The Bloodaxe Book of Contemporary Women Poets*, Newcastle upon Tyne: Bloodaxe Books, 1985.

De Souza, Eunice (ed.), *Nine Indian Women Poets: an Anthology*, Delhi and Oxford: Oxford University Press, 1997.

Dooley, Maura (ed.), *Making for Planet Alice: New Women Poets*, Newcastle upon Tyne: Bloodaxe Books, 1997.

Dowson, Jane (ed.), *Women's Poetry of the 1930s*, London: Routledge, 1996.

Duffy, Carol Ann (ed.), *I Wouldn't Thank You For A Valentine: an Anthology of Women's Poetry*, Harmondsworth: Penguin, 1992.

Elfyn, Menna and John Rowlands (eds.), *The Bloodaxe Book of Modern Welsh Poetry: 20th Century Welsh Language Poetry in Translation*, Tarset: Bloodaxe Books, 2003.

Etter, Carrie (ed.), *Infinite Difference: Other Poetries by UK Women Poets*, Exeter: Shearsman Books, 2010.

Fell, Alison, Stef Pixner, Tina Reid, Michèle Roberts and Ann Oosthuizen (eds.), *Licking The Bed Clean: Five Feminist Poets*, London: Teeth Imprints, 1978.

Forbes, Peter (ed.), *Scanning the Century: the Penguin Book of the Twentieth Century in Poetry*, Harmondsworth: Penguin, 1999.

France, Linda (ed.), *Sixty Women Poets*, Newcastle upon Tyne: Bloodaxe Books, 1993.

Kinsman, Judith (ed.), *Six Women Poets*, Oxford University Press, 1992.

Longley, Edna (ed.), *The Bloodaxe Book of 20th Century Poetry: from Britain and Ireland*. Tarset: Bloodaxe Books, 2000.

McCarthy, Karen (ed.), *Bittersweet: Contemporary Black Women's Poetry*, London: Women's Press, 1998.

Mohin, Lilian (ed.), *One Foot on the Mountain: An Anthology of British Feminist Poetry 1969–1979*, London: Onlywomen Press, 1979.

O'Brien, Peggy (ed.), *The Wake Forest Book of Irish Women's Poetry 1967–2000*, Winston-Salem, NC: Wake Forest University Press.

O'Sullivan, Maggie (ed.), *Out of Everywhere: Linguistically Innovative Poetry by Women in North America and the UK*, London and Suffolk: Reality Street Editions, 1996.

Powell, Anne (ed.), *Shadows of War: British Women's Poetry of the Second World War*, Stroud: Sutton Publishing, 1999.

Rees-Jones, Deryn (ed.), *Modern Women Poets*, Tarset: Bloodaxe Books, 2005.

Reilly, Catherine (ed.), *Chaos of the Night: Women's Poetry and Verse of the Second World War*, London: Virago, 1984.

Scars upon my Heart: Women's Poetry and Verse of the First World War, London: Virago, 1981.

Rumens, Carol (ed.), *Making for the Open: Post-feminist Poetry*, London: Chatto & Windus, 1987.

New Women Poets, Newcastle upon Tyne: Bloodaxe Books, 1993.

Penguin Modern Poets vol. II., *Carol Ann Duffy, Vicki Feaver, Eavan Boland*, Harmondsworth: Penguin, 1995.

Penguin Modern Poets vol. VIII, *Jackie Kay, Merle Collins, Grace Nichols*, Harmondsworth: Penguin, 1996.

The Poetry Quartets vol. II, *Fleur Adcock, Carol Ann Duffy, Selima Hill, Carol Rumens* (cassette), Newcastle Upon Tyne: British Council/Bloodaxe Books, 1998.

The Poetry Quartets vol. V, *Helen Dunmore, U.A. Fanthorpe, Elizabeth Jennings, Jo Shapcott* (cassette), Newcastle Upon Tyne: British Council/Bloodaxe Books, 1999.

Tuma, Keith (ed.), *The Oxford Anthology of Twentieth-Century British and Irish Poetry*, Oxford and New York: Oxford University Press, 2001.

Critical works

Acheson, James and Romana Huk (eds.), *Contemporary British Poetry: Essays in Theory and Criticism*, Albany, NY: SUNY Press, 1996.

Anzaldúa, Gloria, *Borderlands/La Frontera: The New Mestiza*, San Francisco: Aunt Lute Books, 1999.

Bernstein, Charles (ed.), *The Politics of Poetic Form*, New York: Roof, 1990.

Bertram, Vicki, *Gendering Poetry: Contemporary Women and Men Poets*, London: Rivers Oram Pandora Press, 2004.

Bertram, Vicki (ed.), *Kicking Daffodils: Twentieth-Century Women Poets*, Edinburgh: Edinburgh University Press, 1997.

Broom, Sarah, *Contemporary British and Irish Poetry: An Introduction*, London: Palgrave Macmillan, 2006.

Brown, Clare and Don Paterson, *Don't Ask Me What I Mean: Poets in Their Own Words*, London: Picador, 2003.

Campbell, Matthew (ed.), *The Cambridge Companion to Contemporary Irish Poetry*, Cambridge: Cambridge University Press, 2003.

Carroll, Clare and Patricia King (eds.), *Ireland and Postcolonial Theory*, Notre Dame, IL: University of Notre Dame Press, 2003.

Chevalier, Tracy (ed.), *Contemporary Poets*, New York: St James, 1991.

Childs, Peter, *The Twentieth Century in Poetry: a Critical Survey*, London: Routledge, 1999.

Christianson, Aileen and Alison Lumsden (eds.), *Contemporary Scottish Women Writers*, Edinburgh: Edinburgh University Press, 2000.

Cixous, Hélène and Catherine Clements, *The Newly Born Woman*, trans. Betsy Wing, *The Theory and History of Literature* vol. XXIV, Manchester: Manchester University Press, 1986.

Clark, Steve and Mark Ford (eds.), *Something We Have That They Don't: British and American Poetic Relations since 1925*, Iowa City: University of Iowa Press, 2004.

Clarke, Adrian and Robert Sheppard (eds.), *Floating Capital: New Poets from London*, Elmwood, CT: Poets and Poets Press, 1991.

Corcoran, Neil, *The Chosen Ground: Essays on Contemporary Poetry of Northern Ireland*, Bridgend: Seren, 1992.

Corcoran, Neil (ed.), *The Cambridge Companion to Twentieth-Century English Poetry*, Cambridge: Cambridge University Press, 2007.

Crawford, Robert, *Identifying Poets: Self and Territory in Twentieth-Century Poetry*, Edinburgh: Edinburgh University Press, 1993.

DeCaires Narain, Denise, *Contemporary Caribbean Women's Poetry*, London: Routledge, 2001.

Dowson, Jane, *Women, Modernism and British Poetry 1910–39: Resisting Femininity*, Aldershot: Ashgate, 2002.

Dowson, Jane and Alice Entwistle, *A History of Twentieth-Century British Women's Poetry*, Cambridge: Cambridge University Press, 2005.

Draper, R. P., *An Introduction to Twentieth-Century Poetry in English*, Basingstoke: Macmillan, 1999.

Duncan, Andrew, *The Failure of Conservatism in Modern British Poetry*, Cambridge: Salt Publishing, 2003.

Easthope, Anthony, *Contemporary Poetry Meets Modern Theory*, Hemel Hempstead: Harvester Wheatsheaf, 1991.

Poetry as Discourse, London and New York: Methuen, 1983.

Forrest-Thomson, Veronica, *Poetic Artifice: A Theory of Twentieth-Century Poetry*, Manchester: Manchester University Press, 1978.

Gill, Jo, *Women's Poetry*, Edinburgh: Edinburgh University Press, 2007.

Graham, Colin, *Deconstructing Ireland: Identity, Theory, Culture*, Edinburgh: Edinburgh University Press, 2001.

Gregson, Ian, *Contemporary Poetry and Postmodernism: Dialogue and Estrangement*, Basingstoke: Macmillan, 1996.

The Male Image: Representations of Masculinity in Postwar Poetry, Basingstoke: Palgrave Macmillan, 1999.

Grewal, Inderpal and Caren Kaplan (eds.), *Scattered Hegemonies: Postmodernity and Transnational Feminist Practices*, Minneapolis: University of Minnesota Press, 2004.

Haberstroh, Patricia (ed.), *Women Creating Women: Contemporary Irish Poets*, New York and Dublin: Syracuse University Press, 1996.

Hampson, Robert and Peter Barry (eds.), *New British Poetries: The Scope of the Possible*, Manchester and New York: Manchester University Press, 1993.

Herbert, W. N. and Matthew Hollis (eds.), *Strong Words: Modern Poets on Modern Poetry*, Tarset: Bloodaxe Books, 2000.

Innes, C. L., *A History of Black and Asian Writing in Britain, 1700–2000*, rev. edn, Cambridge: Cambridge University Press, 2002.

Jump, Harriet Devine (ed.), *Diverse Voices: Essays on Twentieth-Century Women Writers in English*, Brighton, Harvester Wheatsheaf, 1991.

Keller, Lynn and Cristanne Miller (eds.), *Feminist Measures: Soundings in Poetry and Theory*, Ann Arbor: University of Michigan Press, 1994.

Kinnahan, Linda A., *Lyric Interventions: Feminism, Experimental Poetry, and Contemporary Discourse*, Iowa City: University of Iowa Press, 2004.

Poetics of the Feminine: Authority and Literary Tradition in William Carlos Williams, Mina Loy, Denise Levertov and Kathleen Fraser, Cambridge: Cambridge University Press, 1994.

Kristeva, Julia, *Revolution in Poetic Language*, trans. Margaret Waller, New York: Columbia University Press, 1984.

Larissy, Edward, *Reading Twentieth Century Poetry: The Language of Gender and Objects*, Oxford: Blackwell, 1990.

Loizeaux, Elizabeth Bergmann, *Twentieth-Century Poetry and the Visual Arts*, Cambridge: Cambridge University Press, 2008.

Longley, Edna, *The Living Stream: Literature and Revisionism in Ireland*, Newcastle upon Tyne: Bloodaxe Books, 1994.

Mark, Alison and Deryn Rees-Jones (eds.), *Contemporary Women's Poetry: Reading/Writing/Practice*, London: Macmillan, 2000.

Matthias, John (ed.), *23 Modern British Poets*, Chicago: Swallow Press, 1971.

Michelis, Angelica and Antony Rowland, *The Poetry of Carol Ann Duffy: 'Choosing Tough Words'*, Manchester: Manchester University Press, 2003.

Montefiore, Jan, *Feminism and Poetry: Language, Experience, Identity in Women's Writing*, London: Pandora, 1987; 3rd edn, 2003.

Montefiore, Janet, *Arguments of Heart and Mind: Selected Essays 1977–2000*, Manchester: Manchester University Press, 2002.

Monteith, Moira (ed.), *Women's Writing: A Challenge to Theory*, Brighton: Harvester, 1986.

Morris, Pam (ed.), *The Bakhtin Reader: Selected Writings of Bakhtin, Medvedev, Voloshinov*, London: Edward Arnold, 1994.

Morrison, Blake and Andrew Motion (eds.), *The Penguin Book of Contemporary Poetry*, Harmondsworth: Penguin, 1982.

Orr, Peter (ed.), *The Poet Speaks*, London: Routledge and Kegan, 1966.

Padel, Ruth, *52 Ways of Looking at a Poem*, London: Chatto & Windus, 2001.

Parker, Andrew, Mary Russo, Doris Sommer and Patricia Yaeger (eds.), *Nationalisms and Sexualities*, New York: Routledge, 1992.

Quinn, Justin, *The Cambridge Introduction to Modern Irish Poetry, 1800–2000*, Cambridge: Cambridge University Press, 2008.

Rees-Jones, Deryn, *Consorting with Angels: Essays on Modern Women Poets*, Tarset: Bloodaxe Books, 2004.

Rich, Adrienne, *Blood, Bread and Poetry: Selected Prose 1979–1985*, London: Virago, 1987.

Riley, Denise (ed.), *Poets on Writing: Britain 1970–1991*, London: Macmillan, 1992.

Scott, Bonnie Kime (ed.), *The Gender of Modernism*, Indianapolis: Indiana University Press, 1990.

Severin, Laura, *Poetry off the Page: Twentieth-century British Women Poets in Performance*. Aldershot and Burlington: Ashgate, 2004.

Sheppard, Robert, *Far Language: Poetics and Linguistically Innovative Poetry 1978–1997*, Devon: Stride Publications, 1997.

  The Poetry of Saying: British Poetry and its Discontents 1950–2000, Liverpool: Liverpool University Press, 2005.

Somerville-Arjat, Gilean and Rebecca E. Wilson (eds.), *Sleeping with Monsters: Conversations with Scottish and Irish Women Poets*, Edinburgh: Polygon, 1991.

Tuma, Keith, *Fishing by Obstinate Isles: Modern and Postmodern British Poetry and American Readers*, Evanston, IL: Northwestern University Press, 1998.

Wandor, Michelene (ed.), *On Gender and Writing*, London: Pandora, 1983.

Warhol, Robyn. R. and Diane Price Herndl (eds.), *Feminisms: an Anthology of Literary Theory and Criticism*, Basingstoke: Macmillan, (revised) 1997.

Wills, Clair, 'Contemporary women's poetry: experimentalism and the expressive voice', *Critical Quarterly* 36.3 (Autumn 1994), 34–52.

  Improprieties: Politics and Sexuality in Northern Irish Poetry, Oxford: Clarendon Press, 1993.

Yuval-Davis, Nira, *Gender & Nation*, London: Sage, 1997.

Special magazine editions on women's poetry

Aquarius Women 19/20 (1992).

Feminist Review 62 (Summer 1999).

HOW2 'Special issue on women and ecopoetics' 3.2 (Autumn 2002).

Poetry Review 86.4 (Winter 1996/1997).

Poetry Wales 23.1 (1987).

INDEX

Cambridge Companions to . . .

AUTHORS

TOPICS